INDIAN ROOTS, IVY ADMITS

Praise for the book

'Distinguishing the extraordinary from the ordinary, Viral Doshi, US College admissions guru, and his co-author Mridula Maluste, have compiled an authoritative book of students' essays that masterfully showcase the effort that took students to the coveted Ivy League universities and Stanford. *Indian Roots, Ivy Admits* is a must for students from India and the Indian diaspora: thoughtfully selected, skilfully categorized and insightfully analyzed, these essays will inspire students for crafting the perfect application.'

—*Aarti & Neil Chandaria,* Parents, Singapore

'Most of us can appreciate the pressure that comes with higher education applications, but few can comprehend the tremendous effort, precision and rigor that goes into the overall admissions process. Fortuitously, experts like Viral and Mridula rise up and offer access with their combined wealth of knowledge and experience in successfully taking high-schoolers and undergrads through their further education applications process. I have immense respect for their expertise. And I would highly recommend that students aspiring to the Ivy League and other reputable colleges enjoy this wonderful collaborative journey on which these student authors and their advisors take us.'

—*N. Chandrasekaran,* Chairman, Tata Sons

'Essays in the college admissions process provide a window into the students' dreams, aspirations, and worldviews that set them apart from other candidates. *Indian Roots, Ivy Admits* is a very timely initiative that will enable Indian students to learn from peers, understand and implement best practices, and enhance their essays in order to attain their dream of attending an Ivy League. This could be truly game-changing!'

—*Ashish Dhawan*, Philanthropist and Founder of Ashoka University

'The essays I read in *Indian Roots, Ivy Admits* are akin to personal interviews with the student writers. We journey with them as they bare their souls – their dreams, challenges, problem-solving, reflections, shifts, life changes, and victories. These are penned with authenticity and skill. Congratulations to the students in this amazing compilation! And to those who are starting their application process – learn from the successes of these students. Find the gems in your own life that reflect your personal experiences. And following their lead, write your own, hard to put down, personal stories.'

—*Anant Goenka*, Executive Director,
The Indian Express Group

'*Indian Roots, Ivy Admits* reflects the authors' exceptional engagement with the students whom they advise. Their experience over the years in enabling high school students to effectively create their "voice" or "story" in an imaginative and innovative manner, is evident in this compilation. The essays are presented against the background of the recent challenges of increased competition along with the exponential rise in applications and the consequent drop in admission rates. The importance of authentic and effective essays to demonstrate a good "fit" has become even more urgent. This collection of essays is an excellent navigational resource for aspiring applicants to prestigious universities.'

—*Meera Isaacs*, Educationist; Ex Dean & CEO,
The Cathedral & John Connon School

'*Indian Roots, Ivy Admits* – Guided by the best, this is a must-read collection of essays by Indian students and will be an inspirational resource for anyone aspiring to study at the Ivy League universities, Stanford, and other top colleges. Counselors, this is a fantastic book to refer to and put on your reading list.'

—*Shivangi Panchal*, College Counselor & Executive Director (Administration), Ahmedabad International School

'Mridula and Viral have been the spiritual guides for countless students who have navigated the complex waters of the US college application process for more than a decade. I have seen them develop and hone their craft and skills with the selfless ambition to help these students achieve their individual dreams. As an early beneficiary of the US Ivy League and a very involved alumnus in that system today, I have come to realize how valuable their counsel is, and this book is a tribute to them and those students who have indeed fulfilled their dreams.'

—*Sanjay Patel*, Partner, Chairman International, Apollo Global Management; Member, Harvard Board of Overseers, 2013–2019; Member, Stanford GSB Advisory Council

'A selection of top essays that helped students secure seats in Ivy League colleges. The book includes detailed, extensive analyses of each piece by respected educational experts Viral Doshi and Mridula Maluste. What more could students aspiring to study overseas want to help them realize their academic dreams? This lovely collection is sure to interest not just students but any lover of the written word.'

—*Anand Raj*, Editor, *Friday Magazine & InsideOut*, *Gulf News*, Dubai

'*Indian Roots, Ivy Admits* is a much-needed resource for students seeking admission in the best American universities. It has a wide range of essays that shows the different ways in which students can project their personalities and talents to the admissions officer. India's most respected education counselor Viral Doshi and co-author Mridula Maluste have critically analyzed each essay – they take you through the students' minds, peeling each layer to reveal how they showcase their unique personalities. A must-read for students looking to go overseas.'

—*Jayant Mammen Mathew,* Executive Editor & Director, *Malayala Manorama*

'*Indian Roots, Ivy Admits* is an outstanding book that has emerged out of decades of inspiration, counseling and mentorship provided by Viral Doshi and Mridula Maluste to Indian students aspiring to pursue higher education at the world's leading universities. The book is a delight to read as it provides a kaleidoscopic view into the journeys of 101 amazing individuals who, through their hard work, determination and dedication, could pursue their dreams. The 101 essays delineated in 12 sections reflect their aspirations and motivations, and Viral and Mridula capture this in a compelling manner by their introduction and the thematic framework that provide context and contours to the book. As a Rhodes scholar myself and somebody who had the privilege to study at Oxford and Harvard, I believe this book is a must-read for any student who aspires to pursue their higher education in world-class universities abroad. It will not only engage and empower aspiring students, but also give them valuable perspectives in thinking, reflecting, analyzing and writing essays that will capture the imagination of the admissions committee in the leading universities of the world. This is a fantastic work that will serve as a beacon of hope and yearning in the pursuit of excellence.'

—*C. Raj Kumar,*
Founding Vice Chancellor, O.P. Jindal Global University

'What interests me deeply, as an author, is the human side of every individual, the personal stories of ongoing action, learning and self-actualization. Being able to present that journey, and getting readers interested is critical because it's what makes you stand out. *Indian Roots, Ivy Admits* is the golden key all parents and students need to open the door to the Ivy League universities, and Stanford.'

—*Richard Rothman*, Author, Thought Leader, and Former US Trade Commissioner to India, Italy and Indonesia

'A much-needed book! A compilation of essays by students who got into the most sought-after institutions of learning, is a treasure trove for the next generation of aspirants with the same goals! This is so much more than a compendium of essays for admission; it's a service to the vast diaspora of Indian students who will be able to frame their own unique learning experiences, inspired by relatable and distinctly Indian voices.'

—*Dr Indu Shahani*, Founding President and Chancellor, ATLAS SkillTech University, Ex-Sheriff of Mumbai and Ex-Member of the University Grants Commission

'This book is a treasure for young minds not just to understand what a winning essay reads like but more to acknowledge and accept that each one of us has our own "mantra" and universities like to celebrate that and see that stroke of color in our applications. I enjoyed the variety that this book has to offer to its readers – 101 strong essays or if I may say 101 sparkling jewels to build a conceptual understanding of why and how an effective essay should be weaved. A deep understanding of this will definitely make you feel empowered about the skills that are required for writing "your" unique story. Enjoy reading the "TREASURE".'

—*Dr Sonia Soni*, Head, Career Guidance Counselor, Aditya Birla World Academy

'Essay writing for US university applications requires honesty, imagination and clarity of thought. This collection of outstanding essays is a valuable resource for students, parents, and student counselors. It makes the often stressful process of choosing a topic, expressing oneself with precision and writing impactfully so much clearer while encouraging students to introspect and challenge themselves. I wish I'd had a resource like this when my children were applying!'

—*Priyanka Gandhi Vadra,* Parent, Congress Leader

'There are essays here from students from across Asia – from big cities like Dubai, Mumbai, Delhi, and Hong Kong, to smaller ones like Patna, Jalandhar and Dhanbad. Their personal statements are as diverse as their geographies, and where there might be an overlap in topics or types of experiences, the voices are completely unique. Being a parent first and an education consultant, I know how much anguish young students and their parents go through during the university application period. This book is the first of its kind.'

—*Sanjeev Verma,* Parent & Education Consultant, Dubai

2ND EDITION
REVISED AND EXPANDED

Indian Roots, Ivy Admits

101 ESSAYS that got Indian Students into the IVY LEAGUE and STANFORD

VIRAL DOSHI
MRIDULA MALUSTE

AMARYLLIS
An imprint of Manjul Publishing House

AMARYLLIS

An imprint of Manjul Publishing House Pvt. Ltd.
• C-16, Sector 3, Noida, Uttar Pradesh 201301, India
Website: www.manjulindia.com
Registered Office:
• 2nd Floor, Usha Preet Complex, 42 Malviya Nagar,
Bhopal 462 003 – India
Distribution Centres
Ahmedabad, Bengaluru, Chennai, Hyderabad,
Kochi, Kolkata, Mumbai, Noida, Pune

Indian Roots, Ivy Admits
101 Essays that got Indian Students into the IVY LEAGUE and STANFORD
by Viral Doshi and Mridula Maluste
2nd Edition – Revised and Expanded

First edition published in India in 2021
This revised and expanded edition published in India in 2023
Third impression 2026

ISBN 978-93-5543-337-4

Cover design by Bhavi Mehta
Portrait illustrations by Wasim Helal

Printed and bound in India by Repro India Ltd.

CONTENTS

3
THE VIRTUOSOS

4
REFLECTORS AND MUSERS

5
COMING OF AGE

6
THE LEADERS

7
THE MELDERS

8
THE HEAVY-LIFTERS

9
THE CHRONICLERS

10
THE EXPLORERS

11
MIRROR, MIRROR...

12
METAMORPHOSIS

INTRODUCTION

The connections between India and higher education overseas are longstanding and constantly shifting and evolving. As stories of foreign education—with its ideas of freedom and exploration—made their way to India, the numbers of applicants seeking education abroad multiplied. The Ivy League colleges and Stanford became increasingly attractive as dream destinations. With rising affluency, aspirations, opportunities, and the democratization of information fostered by the digital revolution, several thousand people of Indian descent began knocking on the doors of universities in North America, the UK, Canada, Europe, Australia, and even Russia and China! Yet, the eight Ivies, Stanford and some flagship universities continue to be the apex benchmark.

Accompanying the growth of this college-centric focus, colleges strove to look beyond academic parameters: spurring a process that encouraged students to create and present holistic student profiles worthy of admission into these coveted halls.

Enter the Common App essay with its thought-provoking prompts, through which students convey their unique personas, and what 'makes them tick'. These prompts—which also transit to the 'Universal Application'—draw out students' passions and concerns, ways of thinking and learning, decision-making and problem-solving skills, their ability to surmount failure, and deftness in navigating uncertainty.

'What will I bring to the university?', 'how will I shift the campus landscape?', 'how will I make a unique dent?' are prominent questions that students aim to encapsulate as they attempt the often daunting

Common App essay prompts. These are thought-provoking, soulful questions, that command students to deep dive and excavate from the deepest crevices of their minds, experiences and epiphanies—both profound and mundane—that shaped who they are.

So why this book? And that too, a revised, and expanded edition? And why now?

Many reasons!

The Common App essay is indeed like none other, and we were naturally thrilled at the news that *Indian Roots, Ivy Admits* (*IRIA*), through its four reprints in just one year, had quelled the application anxieties of many aspirants: successfully helping them peel back the layers of their personas, enabling them to ponder upon and introspect their unique personal accomplishments, and the qualities that set them apart.

The reception for the first edition of the book has been overwhelmingly positive and helped us understand more deeply the pressing need for a reliable resource that students could reference for writing their own successful Common App essays. We were delighted at the global reach that *IRIA* enjoyed and the responses we received from far-flung geographies: right from Bhatinda to Hong Kong, Chennai to Texas, North Carolina to Geneva, and to Toronto. The response reaffirmed the pressing need for more books of this caliber – books that would allow students and Ivy aspirants to better understand the nuances of the elaborate, sometimes quotidian Common Application essay.

In mentoring students through their application pathways, we've seen how the application journey can be hurdle-ridden. The essay section, particularly, can cause considerable anxiety. The first book germinated in response to our students' desire for a collection of essays that was rooted in their analogous experiences. Surprisingly, there was no one common resource from which they could read and understand how other Indians who successfully gained admission to top colleges had written their essays. This drove us to curate the first edition of *Indian Roots, Ivy Admits*.

During the months that the first edition was in circulation, and in observing and assisting the applications of aspirational students, we continued to be guided by our seasoned instincts that remain true in this new, expanded edition. Scouring through our resource bank, we knew instinctively which essays met the gold standard of admission to the Ivy League colleges and Stanford. In making these accessible, we hope to share our counselling experience with a wider audience. Overarchingly, we wish to portray to qualifying aspirants across India and the world, that every story is distinctive and compelling – that with focused effort and good writing, an education at a top university is entirely possible. Read between the lines as you peruse the commentaries, and you will find guidance and advise that you might marshal to write your essay.

We do believe we've removed the Common App from its black box of anxiety-inducing mystery, while emphasizing the diversity of applicant profiles, stories, and unique writing styles that have met the taxing standards of these hallmark universities. While reading, you will find a congregation of characters and chronicles: siblings fighting for their individual identities, a physics-loving thespian making a case for her passionate love for multidisciplinary studies, an accomplished cook exploring Computer Engineering, an eccentric birdwatcher making startling discoveries for his inventions, and a student who established a slew of writing workshops. There are other quiet, astute accounts of reflection and rumination from artists, biologists, mathematicians, chefs and musicians! Marvel at a Chemistry student who deems Benzene to be her spirit chemical!

While some essays directly address the students' academic fields of interest, most narratives often have little relevance to the students' eventual majors. Yet, they all work. Those showcased in these pages gained admission to more than one top university – highlighted, though, is the university they finally chose to attend.

We'd like to believe that in meeting the stringent standards of the Ivies, these Common Application essays showcase some of the best writing in the world. From offering different worldly perspectives, to destigmatizing, and even prioritizing the discussion of relevant, contemporary issues that often go overlooked, they hold wisdom for students, Ivy aspirants, writers, and avid readers alike. These essays wend their way into stories of resilience and wit. Of valor and tenacity. Here, you will find incredible stories of transformation, courage, and disruption, which we expect readers to enjoy as both slice-of-life short stories, as well as Common App essays. The guidance embedded in the commentaries will, we hope, imbue and assist your own writing.

As you read this new, augmented collection of 101 essays, you will find parts of yourself nestled in these pages. For clarity and ease of access and interaction, we divided the essays under twelve carefully selected themes, which formed chapters that draw from the writer's intention and broad subject matter. There are two new chapters included in this expanded edition.

Importantly, this is not a show-and-tell exposition about successful admission essays. The essays in this book are *illustrative* but not *instructive*, which is perhaps, best summarized by Gayatri Meswani's (p. 89) beautiful quotation of her wise *nanima*, 'These are their masterpieces; you need to find yours.'

We hope this updated edition helps you uncover your most authentic voice and helps you write your masterpiece.

Viral Doshi
Mridula Maluste

1

THE FAMILY CRUCIBLE

'If you cannot get rid of the family skeleton,
you may as well make it dance.'

—George Bernard Shaw

The sense of belonging and alienation, accord and conflict, love and betrayal that can be traced back to family is singular and pervasive. Families can bolster your spirit, carry you high, and bring you down! In this section, parents, siblings, identical twins, fraternal twins (some who have their own stories in later sections!) and more become sources of self-conception, even as the relationships explored provide an avenue for evolution and growth.

While hilarity or poignancy, even grave inner contemplation distinguish these narratives, they are marked by a unifying candor and sincerity that set them apart from other efforts in a popular genre for undergraduate college essays.

VISHAAL KUMAR

UPenn, Class of 2023

Major: Networked and Systems Engineering
School: Dubai International Academy, Dubai, UAE
Hometown: Dubai, UAE

OF SIBLINGS AND SAUCES

Entrenched wisdom posits that those from the same gene pool, treated equally, develop thus. Perhaps, but I, having shared space with a two-year older sibling since infancy, argue the premise. We fought continuously and were invariably separated by our long-suffering parents and lectured, albeit fruitlessly, on the proverbial bond between brothers.

Unsurprisingly, we grew apart. Realizing neither could tolerate the other in proximity and being anyway battle-fatigued, we sought détente and restricted communication to the ubiquitous 'that's my toast', and 'I was playing on the Xbox!'

Our relationship so proficiently analogized the mayonnaise jar we fought over every Friday night to dress our burgers, because of the unlikely amalgam of its constituents. Making this 'sauce for all seasons', though prima facie simple, like our relationship, necessitates detailing and much concentration. We begin by mixing the contraindicative ingredients egg yolk (52% H2O) and oil that, having different densities, will only emulsify if the oil is released in droplets into the yolk and both whisked continuously. There is no margin for error. My brother's ongoing initiatives to trouble ('whisk') me have likewise catalyzed my development as a social being. I learned to handle conflict—in committees, internships, and in academics. Interning at Al Habtoor Motors, I was considered a liability by the workers I helped but my initiatives to leverage my knowledge of Mathematics and Physics to address problems changed perceptions. I dismantled a car's engine, and after sustained deliberation, diagnosed issues, and proposed a solution. My technical insights and application led them to appreciate my engineering expertise.

My brother and I represent the oil and yolk respectively, disparate, but willfully bonded by our brotherhood, the container. We do try to 'emulsify' but even minor anomalies such as temperature play spoiler despite the indefatigable constants, our parents' ongoing attempts to broker harmony. Fights over ice-cream morphed into bigger squalls: I remember him trying to wrest my favorite book, *The Man Who Knew Infinity*, that celebrated a globally renowned mathematician's life. We battled vociferously and Mom sided with him; perhaps 'Fortune favors the "old!"' I now believe he just wanted to read it. And then there are existential divergences—well, arguments, on phenomena like 'Matter and Anti-matter—do they equally constitute the universe?' Unwilling to meet midway, we quote X and Y, flash proof and remain obdurate.

Would I that things had been different; yet, given this background, my experience of resolving conflicting issues paid off over time. As Student Council member, I now recognize diverse opinions as exemplified by my selecting the hoodie for our graduating batch. Understanding its import, I chose an imposing design after much deliberation. Predictably, there was much dissent, 'Why that?' or 'Try green'. I resignedly changed the purple font to peppermint; surprisingly, it looked good! Similarly, I tweaked and changed for my brother. Difficult, but like the samurai's fine sword, I went through flame and forge, and emerged transformed.

Today, I realize those fights, paradoxically, brought us closer, and know, like the yolk and oil, we too can 'emulsify'. He is now at university, and our unraveled brotherly bonds are slowly being rewoven. We have evolved, learned from error and value our brotherhood. Conversations now include, 'Have that toast' and 'Wanna play the Xbox?' The jar too is growing, making room for further attempts at emulsification. I know, we will someday seek new horizons, perhaps swim in the Adriatic, climb Kilimanjaro, or visit Cern to fuel our common passion for Physics. Against all odds, we now complement each other like condiments in mayonnaise. He, fiery mustard, tempered by me, the sweet-edged balsamic.

This I know: We have been layered and united by difference; my brother will ever have my back, as I will his. Like yolk and oil, our relationship has emulsified into a mayonnaise, piquant, mellow and mature. Buddhists believe, 'You cause me to be, and I cause you to be.' How true.

OUR THOUGHTS ON VISHAAL'S ESSAY

Vishaal warms up readers with his title 'Of Siblings and Sauces'—a literary device clubbing two words to achieve 'musical' alliteration with the syllable sounds, as well as, signaling two dissimilar concepts to achieve contrast—often for humorous (and luminous) effect.

The sibling rivalry that existed between him and his older brother, which disproved 'entrenched wisdom' on the proverbial bond between brothers pervades Vishaal's essay. He uses 'the jar of mayonnaise we fought over every Friday night to dress our burgers...' as an analogy for their relationship. Why? Because 'of the unlikely amalgam of its constituents,' ruminates Vishaal.

And unlikely they are. Vishaal scientifically likens 'mixing the contraindicative ingredients... having different densities...' through a certain detailed and focused process, to his brother's concentrated efforts 'to trouble ("whisk") me.' He attributes his conflict-resolution abilities—'in committees, internships, or academics'—to his brother's 'ongoing initiatives [which] catalyzed my development as a social being.' In doing so, he establishes two things: First—that, on the positive side, the filial adversity had helped him acquire and refine these skills. Second—that he had been able to put them to good use in many areas of his life, and finally also, in dealing with his familial adversity. Here the timbre of his words is passionate, a reflection of the intensity of experience he underwent: 'Similarly, I tweaked and changed for my brother.... I went through flame and forge, and emerged transformed.'

Continuing to describe their 'brotherly' relationship, Vishaal also reveals his interests—through the scientific explanations of the mayonnaise metaphor; his 'favorite book', about a 'mathematician's life', the 'existential... arguments, on phenomena like "Matter and Anti-matter—do they equally constitute the universe?"'

Maturity helps Vishaal see in hindsight that his brother 'just wanted to read' that book. His rumination: 'Our unraveled brotherly bonds are slowly being rewoven. We've evolved, learned from error, and value our brotherhood', adds mature and reflective facets to Vishaal's personality profile. 'He, fiery mustard, tempered by me, the sweet-edged balsamic,' is an amusing, delectable analogy, as is the description of both brothers, 'mellow and mature', like a slow-maturing cheddar.

Vishaal has used a familiar story of the challenges faced in sibling relationships to connect with readers and, in the process, revealed much about himself. The essay is a masterful extended metaphor on his relationship with his brother. We come away, seeing admiringly how, in his case, differences ultimately layered and united two dichotomous personalities. And the essay's conclusion with a well-chosen spicing of Buddhist spirituality ('You cause me to be, and I cause you to be') is entirely fitting.

RIYA SANKHE

Stanford, Class of 2023

Major: Computer Science and Economics
School: Dhirubhai Ambani International School, Mumbai, India
Hometown: Mumbai, India

RUCHI'S ADVENTURE BOOKS

Scattered stamps and stray pieces of paper littered the hardwood floor in a chaotic mosaic of color. The scene almost resembled a ritual sacrifice to the Gods of Stationery. A young girl sat in the middle of the room, blissfully oblivious of the disarray that lay at her feet. In her head, the cherry-blossom paper at the far corner of the room had already risen and begun aligning with the cascading cornflower-blue ribbon she held reverently in her fingers, ready to grace the cover of this year's *Ruchi's Adventure Book*.

Three months remained for Mother's Day, and the preparations for my mother Ruchi's annual book had just begun! Third in the bilingual adventure series I created for her, these were no ordinary storybooks. They comprised irresistible adventures, captivating verses, and enigmatic riddles, all specifically designed to enthrall Mom on this special day.

After weeks of planning, I set to work. In the secrecy of my room, I constructed breathtaking worlds and riveting adventures: Ruchi slaying a wicked dragon, saving Planet Earth from the terrifying man-eating virus Alpha543, and solving the mystery of the Blue Lady's death at night, all while working at a magical circus by day. In homage to Mom's North-Indian heritage, I even wrote about her crime-solving adventures in Hindi. The books encapsulated a foreign, mesmerizing world, allowing me to explore eclectic writing styles and wild ideas. My imagination ran free, creativity my sole assistant.

The adventure book always came with a matching gift. The gifts were my own creations: carefully curated but low-cost. That year, I envisioned a personalized perfume. Searching, I scavenged an old bottle from an international-flight overnight bag. This became my muse. Ribbons salvaged from birthday gifts were delicately sculpted around its walls to form a dappled perfume bottle. To perfect the fragrance, I then experimented with various flowers and spice concoctions from the kitchen. After five unsatisfactory attempts, I got it. The perfect fusion of scents occurred when floral notes from the Arabian Jasmine flowers blossoming in the veranda mingled with salt-water. Almost there! Now the packaging. Dexterously molding clay from my 'toy cabinet', I cradled the bottle in a perfume case built with scrap cardboard—and the gift was complete. And not a moment too soon—it was the night before Mother's Day!

Looking back, these early experiments with the gifts formed the foundation for my penchant—and later passion—for imagining, innovating and creating. Gifting wasn't about purchasing items; it was about demonstrating love through careful planning and artful innovation. Unbeknownst to me, these gifts would become my earliest mentors, guiding me in transforming ingenious visions into realities.

Gradually, the gifts re-contoured into projects of greater complexity. Creation was no longer limited to festive occasions; it expanded to my interest in theater, writing and entrepreneurship. My social venture, Weave Nation, grew from watching bags full of scrap-cloth carelessly discarded. Combining my love for the environment and innovation, I decided to produce my own grocery cloth-bags to replace plastic ones. Months later, sitting on the same hardwood floor amongst myriad scrap-cloths of varied textures and hues, I worked instinctively, piecing bits together to create imaginative bags. Scarlet handloom danced with brilliant ochre string before melding with streaks of the coffee scrap-cloth that lay beside me. And the design for the first cloth-bag was ready! Then came manufacturing and sales. Leveraging those same planning skills, I sourced the scrap fabric from local factories and got over 500 pieces stitched in two months. Luckily, the dates for my sales campaign even coincided with the plastic bags ban in Maharashtra state! The entire production was sold out in two days.

So, on the top shelf of the teak cabinet in my mother's room, lie five books and five gift boxes, tenderly wrapped in muslin. Messy, colorful, and dated exactly a year apart, these are no ordinary gifts; they are the veiled architects of who I am today.

OUR THOUGHTS ON RIYA'S ESSAY

Riya's essay is a deeply personal narrative of who she is. This is one of those essays where 'show, not tell' is rendered to vibrant perfection. The first paragraph's third person narrative reads like the opening of one of the stories she wrote for her mother. It is extremely revealing. In a few short lines, we see someone who loves stationery, texture, color, the arts, and crafts; someone who has a vivid imagination.

The annual Mother's Day gifts that Riya creates for her mother each year track the evolution of Riya's personality and what is important to her. Creative processes, for example—the thought and detail that go into developing a bespoke perfume and short story are far more meaningful than the expense of a store-bought gift. She also clearly shares a special relationship with her mother, rooted in storytelling, and evoked through Mother's Day gifts. The creation and development of these gifts provide context and background. Riya's early creative pursuits built a foundation that gave her the confidence to take them further afield to other domains—she hints at what these are, and then deep-dives into her entrepreneurship project.

The first half of this essay is the backdrop against which Weave Nation is so meaningful. In the latter part of this essay, we see Riya grow wings—her credible transformation from conjuring dragons and cardboard gift boxes to creating tangible impact. What was once a labor of love and imagination became a propellant for social good by reducing plastic waste. A daughter's perception of her mother's superhero tendencies lifted off the pages of a book and soft-lands into real life. That Riya's patchwork bags sold out in an extremely short period of time is almost beside the point. The charm of this essay lies in Riya's depiction of her colorful pursuits and even more colorful personality: her influences, and values as they were at the time of writing. It is clear that all of these will continue to evolve.

NITYA HINDUJA

Columbia, Class of 2020

Major: Biomedical Engineering
School: International School of Geneva, Switzerland
Hometown: Geneva, Switzerland

TWINS

'How do we tell you apart?'

This question encapsulates the quest for superficial differences to appease the common person's curiosity at the deviance of identical twins. A response of, 'Well, I'm half a centimeter taller' adequately satisfies the low appetite of the average inquirer. Few grasp our frustration: how can I explain that Ninya and I are the antithesis of each other? That it is this balancing act of juxtaposition that makes us a pair?

My sister is a mirror that costs me a lot.
There is not a difference between us; not a spot.
Visitors admire us as a pair:
Our matching noses and identical hair.
She reads my mind I read hers too.
I wouldn't believe it if I were you.

At nine, I composed these words for a poetry competition. Bound by rules of rhyme and limited vocabulary, this was the best I could do to portray the inexplicability of being a twin. Today, eight years thereafter, my perception is drastically different and despite it all, it is to my womb-mate that I owe my current identity.

Being monozygotic, I am accustomed to hearing, 'Which one are you?', which initiates a round of 'guess-the-twin'. 'You're Ninya. No... you're Nitya!' I have two names: one that I was designated at birth, and the other that was thrust upon me arbitrarily by those who never made the effort to search past our skin-deep likeness. Worse, some are indolent enough to brand us collectively as 'NinyaNitya'. For years, we were bracketed as one individual delineated by two identical bodies. It never seemed fair to me that while everyone else had their individual identities, I merited half of one.

It would be extremely rare for two individuals to grow up as closely as I did to my sister. We shared our home, school, friends, room, toothpaste... everything down to a cramped fetal 'apartment' for nine months. Inseparable we were, but out of no choice of our own. Too close for comfort? There is a line that exists between every two inhabitants of this planet. However, in our case, this line was drawn to be crossed.

How did we, despite our commensurate genes and proximity develop into aggressive opposites?

As we grew, we jettisoned the matching outfits that give us away. The questions changed to, 'Are you twins?' Variations were noticed, and the comparisons began. 'She's the fun twin' and 'you're the smart twin', or 'she's the sporty twin' and 'you're the artistic twin'. Physically, we were in-differentiable. Consequently, an endless cycle of labels was used to distinguish us, igniting fiery competition.

Eventually, we got tired of fighting our way out of each other's shadows. The competition faded, and collaboration formed: an unspoken agreement that we each had pre-assigned roles. Believing our labels, we started assuming our supposed characters. I'm the quiet one? As soon as Ninya and I were together, I would jump into character as the under-spoken sister. When it came to academics, Ninya would enact the 'dumb twin'. For a while, we abided by the unspoken rules, as if we were only allowed to excel in certain areas in order to enable the other to shine in hers.

We fought to be different. Then, scrimmaged to establish equality. We pushed and shoved forgetting that while we needed our space, this relationship was allowing us to flourish. Comparisons accentuated our differences. If I excelled in an area, I had to push this strength to sustain myself, and to compensate for my sister's 'shortcomings'. Subsequently, she returned the favor. It was an unfolding plot and drama that had us alternate between being the star of the movie and the supporting actor.

When I finally get the chance to steal the spotlight, I know that I would not be on stage without the support of my 'other half'. If it were not for our late-night run-throughs, I wouldn't even know my lines.

OUR THOUGHTS ON NITYA'S ESSAY

Nitya's essay might have backfired with an unsympathetic reader. However, it makes up for its tenor of exasperation with its unapologetic glimpse into the mind and life of an identical twin. Nitya is candid about the frustration of living with someone who looks exactly like her but is still nothing like her. In doing so she takes us on a journey of self-discovery and an acceptance of the irony that her identity as an individual is inextricably linked to her twin.

The essay begins with deep frustration—it is not a reflection of frustration; it is frustration in its quintessence. Hence the jab at the 'low appetite of the average inquirer', and the perhaps sarcastic response to said inquirer (the casual observer would not care to scrutinize a half-centimeter difference in height). A superficial reader may interpret this as the rant of a petulant child, but something deeper runs between the lines. Nitya is giving voice to the challenge of communicating her separateness from her twin in a nice, tidy package, when all visible evidence points to the contrary. How indeed does one process the experience of living with a mirror image for almost two decades, and then share it with the outside world in a way that it will understand?

Nitya attempts to do just this. She describes the casual, perhaps joking, or unwitting confusion of people struggling to tell 'NityaNinya' apart, and how it would grate, as things repeated often do. She invites us into her reality with a biting rawness that is not mellowed with hindsight or time, because there is none—it is still her reality, and always will be. But through this, she describes and shows us her evolution, taking cues from the labels she and her twin were given, and from the tension inherent in sharing a life and womb with a doppelganger. The conclusion, that so much of who Nitya is, is linked to her twin, is foregone—what matters is the story of how Nitya became unapologetically herself. University essay prompts ask students to elaborate on their lives and circumstances, and Nitya has done so with boldness and candor, speaking both to her evolution and her character.

HIMANSSH PETTIE

Brown, Class of 2024

Major: Engineering
School: The Aga Khan Academy, Hyderabad, India
Hometown: Hyderabad, India

'*Oye madu!*' my friend called out to me teasingly as I was bargaining with the auto-rickshaw driver. See, money-saving is an innate quality for us Marwadis (colloquially 'madus'). I believe and live by our saying, 'Every penny saved is a penny earned.' I embrace this quality and all others that accompany my culture. I am proud to be a Marwadi.

Historically, Marwadis are a community native to the modern Jodhpur region of Rajasthan in India. By trade, we have been migratory merchants supported by several North Indian rulers because of our skill with numbers and banking. Mathematics has been my favorite subject since the fifth grade leading me to take challenges like accelerated additional math, wherein we finished four years' portion of Mathematics in two years, head on. Another outlet for my passion for STEM subjects has been the STEM society I founded in my school which organized several factory visits, invited guest speakers and mentored other students.

We first left the state of Marwar due to the extremely harsh climate and arid conditions. After all, the term 'Marwar' means 'the region of death' in English for a reason! This proves something my grandmother told me all the time: '*Jahan na jaaye gaadi, wahan jaaye Marwadi*,' roughly translating to, 'Marwadis go even where no one dares to tread.' I have shown this trait of my culture by adapting to a new school in the last two years of high school. In fact, I fit in so well that a lot of new students thought I've been in the school for years! I even adapted to several different work atmospheres such as that in Cerebra, one of India's largest E-waste processors and TIBCON, a worldwide leader in capacitor manufacturing, and conducted research there.

The circumstances of our birth also engrain an adventurous spirit in our DNA. It makes us natural risk-takers, but of course the risks we take are calculated because we just love numbers so much! Personally, this comes out in the form of my love for adventure sports like scuba diving and bungee jumping. The thrill I seek from these sports equates to my love for all things mathematics just like how e ^ (i*pi) equates to -1.

Us Marwadis are also known to be highly resilient and hard-working. We don't stop working until we are satisfied, and Marwadis are never satisfied. Just like Arjuna (from the epic *Mahabharata*), when I have a target, that's all I can see. I don't back down from any challenge that comes my way and if it knocks me down, I make it a point to get back up and rise higher than ever. We are also excellent negotiators and debaters as seen, alongside my hard work, in my substantial experience with Model United Nations and in the fact that I am the house captain for Maurya House in my school's batch of eighty.

Our most characteristic traits, however, are our helpfulness and respect, especially for our elders. We are known all over the world to be helpful and kind to everyone and our respect for our elders is unmatched by any other culture. I have been taught, since my childhood, that respecting others is paramount no matter the situation. This value has been cultivated and nurtured in me and I have learnt that, finally, the respect we give is the respect we get.

Being a Marwadi plays an extraordinary role in my life. It describes my role in society and perhaps even gives me an identity. I am who I am today because of my culture and what my elders taught me, and I have boundless love and respect for them because they have made me adaptable, hardworking, respectful, and much more than mere words can describe. The lessons I learnt from them are invaluable and unforgettable. This makes me proud to be a part of the virtuous Marwadi community. So, when my friend called out, '*Oye madu!*' I answered, 'Yes that's me!'

OUR THOUGHTS ON HIMANSSH'S ESSAY

Who we are is often a function of the communities we are born into, or those that we choose. Himanssh's essay exemplifies this, in that it expresses his individual identity by celebrating his connection to his core group, the Marwadi community.

Mixing oral history with external perceptions and his own experiences, Himanssh presents himself as a proud Marwadi representative, unabashedly personifying the values that make the community his home. Beginning the essay with a candid confrontation of one of the most common stereotypes associated with the community and their innate thriftiness, he embraces his conscious spending (or not) habits as a welcome inheritance from his identity. This overt acceptance sets the tone for the rest of the essay, as Himanssh traces his mathematical prowess, his resilience, his ability to adjust to new surroundings, and his supportive nature to the values imparted by his famously hardworking and philanthropic community. He goes on to discuss the migration, historic development, and business acumen of the traditional trading group: he identifies with this history in which he finds his own affinity for numbers and calculations.

While attributing much of who he is to this group identity, Himanssh introduces content that reveals nuggets about himself beyond his strong bond with the culture: we see his passion for STEM subjects and adventure sports, his affable personality and fierce loyalty to the teachings of his elders. There is also a keen sense that these qualities of respect, kindness and focus are more important than the achievements that they fostered—from house captaincy to internships at Cerebra and TEBCON. Stitched through the stories he chooses to tell us, an image of Himanssh emerges, especially as the essay derives from *his* understanding of what it means to be Marwadi. Apart from his grandmother's statement about the culture's adventurous and adaptable spirit, our understanding of the community (and him) comes from what he tells us, and is borne from his abiding admiration for and adherence to its tenets. The lessons he has learnt are 'invaluable' and 'unforgettable', and will clearly stand him in good stead in college and beyond.

ARYAN JOSHI
Brown, Class of 2025

Major: Economics
School: Mallya Aditi International School, Bengaluru, India
Hometown: Bengaluru, India

EDGBASTON, 12 JUNE 1996

India is in trouble. Sachin Tendulkar, batting 63, is racing to a century when his partner's wicket falls. Sachin needs someone to anchor the other end. Left-arm spinner Sunil Joshi, nursing a fractured left index finger, takes guard. Sachin scores 122. In crippling pain, Joshi scores a humble 12 but holds firm against the ferocious English pace attack.

Sunil Joshi is my dad, my hero, teacher and muse.

Whatever the laurels he's won to date, he considers his Edgbaston innings his finest hour. When asked how he withstood the pain of bat hitting ball at 100 mph, he nonchalantly replied, 'I couldn't wish it away, so I ignored it and played on.'

Years later, playing an inter-school fixture, fielding a hard shot, I ended up with a serious hand injury. Calling time out, I rushed to our team tent only to be told to leave the field. I was the captain so this was not an option. Drawing on his paradigm, I too completed the day-long match by taping the torn webbing on my hand (that warranted stitching) and playing through the pain. My father's grit inspired me to tap into my own inner strength.

I recall the day my grandmother passed away—Dad was playing for India in Kenya; he completed the tour and conducted her last rites only on his return.

From these instances, I learned the imperatives of mental strength in sport. Looking to transit the lessons learned to all sportsmen, I initiated my print and social media campaign, 'Mental Strength Matters', that arranged and promoted dialogue with accomplished athletes across disciplines, centered on building and developing mental fortitude by elucidating how sportspersons triumphed in 'hopeless' situations. Sadly, the 'mind over matter' maxim has too long been ignored by sportsmen. I want to remedy that.

My father draws from humble beginnings and tread the hard road—from playing on village tracks to playing for India, coaching a national team and, more recently, being appointed chief selector for India's apex cricket body. He'd seen hard times—he was injured at Edgbaston as, unable to afford left-hand batting gloves, he batted wearing conventional ones. Reminiscing, he'd often lament that boundless talent in India languishes due to resource and opportunity constraints.

Recently, while visiting an orphanage I noticed kids playing cricket with makeshift gear, including a boxwood cricket bat! When I mentioned this to Dad, he suggested I act rather than comment!

I did!

I connected with and visited a flagship sports goods manufacturer in Jalandhar. While sympathetic, they had no spare bats to offer (due to backed-up demand). However, while leaving, I noticed discarded willow logs. Querying their purpose, I learned that they'd been rejected for mainstream manufacture. I thought they'd admirably serve my purpose and asked for them. After some cajoling, they agreed. Next, I negotiated a piece rate for crafting with local artisans. Similarly, I contacted other manufacturers and acquired diverse 'seconds' but perfectly functional cricket gear. Two weeks later I delivered the accumulated booty! Watching a padded-up youngster holding a game-standard albeit unbranded cricket bat take guard, I was thrilled. The orphanage will play the Karnataka School League this year. I'll be cheering them on.

'Win, it's a team triumph, lose and the buck stops at you,' my father warned when I was appointed school cricket captain.

I learned early on that captaincy is a two-edged sword. During an inter-school tournament, my teammate Anish's stellar batting took us from 'mission impossible' to 'in-with-a-chance' to the cusp of victory. With just a run left to win, I took strike but just held wicket. I wanted Anish to score the winning run; that glory was rightfully his.

Sports field maxims and coping traits are equally relevant in academics. As in batting, timing is everything, be it in completing assignments or revisions. Sports field discipline saw me through the vicissitudes of new learning systems while maintaining perfect grades, something that will endure through University and beyond.

OUR THOUGHTS ON ARYAN'S ESSAY

Aryan's essay stitches together two narratives—he layers his father's experiences with his own to convey the values that shape him. Even as sport, especially cricket, takes pole position in both accounts and connects Aryan with his father, it also provides a vehicle for significant learnings. Much like a book of fables, the essay uses his father's life as a reservoir from which one might draw strength and commitment: this provides commentary for Aryan's experiences.

Describing his father as his 'hero, teacher and muse', Aryan makes the rare choice of beginning the essay with another's achievement. Recalling his father's defiant batting in the face of seemingly insurmountable odds at Edgbaston, Aryan puts himself on the outside-looking-in, joining the reader and spectators in shared awe. In the very next paragraph, he switches perspectives, showing himself as a man-of-action by emulating his father when faced with a match-stopping injury.

This switch between Aryan's experiences and his father's life and advice is not jarring or disconcerting, as he has adroitly italicized for clarity. We think it works in an admissions essay: while the description of his father's life prima facie portrays Aryan as a spectator and listener, neither are passive roles. Aryan is shown to be an active listener imbibing inspiration (playing through his injury) and values (mental strength) from his father, a famous cricketer, and drawing on these to follow through (acting rather than commenting) as his most avid student. Additionally, as the essay progresses so does the overlay of his father's commentary evolve, from descriptive stories to involved conversations to advice. Moving parallelly to Aryan's growth as a sportsperson, citizen and individual, his father's guiding role anticipates Aryan's leadership and mentorship forays. There is an almost poetic connection between his father's role and the kind of compassionate and responsible leadership Aryan projects through his 'Mental Strength Matters' project and association with an orphanage.

The essay transits smoothly to the final paragraph, with Aryan resisting the obvious route of a detailed application of sports to academics. Thus, it succeeds in presenting Aryan as his own person, ready to tackle a new universe with sound, old learnings.

VIRAJ RAI

Columbia, Class of 2019

Major: Computer Science
School: Singapore International School, Mumbai, India
Hometown: Mumbai, India

'Methinks you are my glass, and not my brother.'

—William Shakespeare, *Comedy of Errors*

Well, what did Shakespeare know about having a twin brother! I am Viraj, although I'm known and addressed with my twin as Sahil-Viraj and spoken to and of as a single entity, even by my parents. In fact, I am expected to answer even if addressed as 'Sahil', for expediency! Though not identical, we baffled teachers, with one of us being punished for the other's transgressions.

It wasn't fun. I had this one constant with whom I'd work, play and eat. I tried to distance myself, but he was omnipresent, staking his claim on my life and efforts. When I enrolled in classes and activities in which I could work independent of him, my overprotective parents moved in, insisting on his participation.

As we grew, our paths started diverging. I began exploring my individuality first tentatively, then boldly. I strummed the guitar, played in bands; he played the piano. I leaned towards engineering, the sciences, and robotics; he focused on finance. Mundane as they seem, these were big, audacious steps at autonomy. We tried to make separate friends, but since we were always together, my friends soon became 'ours'. They preferred to have us as a package.

Determinedly taking steps to carve out a separate identity, I conceptualized and built projects—a Sound Controlled Electronic Circuit, for example, for Science fairs; performed on stage with *Live like your Last* and *The Musketeers*, but the road was uphill. We were still Sahil-Viraj for our family, friends and faculty. The name followed me, chased me, and haunted me.

The Berkeley Engineering Program was another significant step towards independence. I was ecstatic when we were assigned different groups—finally I was Viraj, unhyphenated. I thought, finally, a life different from his! A few days into the program, my palpable excitement waned as I found myself turning in CAD class to ask, 'So can you integrate a Google sketchup in Maya 3D?' Or twice, to pass a quip. But he wasn't there.

Working for the Navjyoti Foundation in Bawana village, outside New Delhi, was a step towards independence. The talent show 'Udaan'—a smorgasbord of dance, song and drama—teased out hidden talent because I believe I did things differently. Noting the inputs of a precocious eleven-year-old Pratik, I made him de facto director. This empowered him to choose a team. And while the play they wrote—drawn from their daily life which featured drunkenness and abuse—we brainstormed another paradigm and broke through stereotypes. It felt good that the accolades were for my efforts, and not the entity, Sahil-Viraj. I had finally etched a separate identity for myself.

Then, the reckoning: I would have enjoyed it more with him! I am not saying I couldn't function efficiently alone, but something was amiss. I might not admit it to him, but I missed sharing it with him. The buzz was missing. That's when I understood that I'd taken the perks of 'twin-dom' for granted: My playmate, my friend, my confidant.

So now, I'm finally Viraj. I participate in quizzes, MUNs, robotics programs and online courses separate from him; yet, ironically, we are more expanded and enriched through interactions. Though we explored totally different subjects for our extended essay, mine in Math and his in Economics, we constantly discuss our themes and conclusions. Having lost the dependency, we connect, in fact, more profoundly.

Today, as we set out for college my grandfather's words ring true: *'Tame be bhai agar saathe kaam kar sone toh puri duniya ne ullu banavi shako cho.'* (If you two brothers stick together, you can tackle the whole world.) Sahil will always be alongside, even if we are in different fields and different universities.

Of course, we did fight about who would write the twin essay; I won.

OUR THOUGHTS ON VIRAJ'S ESSAY

Viraj has written a breezy, introspective piece that paints a picture of his life, his struggle for his own identity and shows him to be open to change. Like the other essay in this book about being one half of a twin pair (see Nitya Hinduja's essay, p. 10), this one highlights the challenges of maintaining an identity separate from the twin, and Viraj's eventual realization that being part of a pair, beyond forging his identity, made him all the stronger for it.

In insisting on his separateness from his brother Sahil, Viraj takes us through his interests, key moments (and some confusions) in his life: getting in trouble at school for his brother's transgressions, being musically inclined, developing a passion for Engineering and Math, and the inevitable existential obligation to share friends. These provide backdrop and context.

And then we see two key snippets wherein Viraj enjoys resounding success and experiences on his own terms, but also comes face-to-face with the bitter-sweetness of not having his twin along for the ride. Significantly, Viraj appears to be startlingly self-aware when he says that he missed having his brother's companionship, even though he might not admit it to him. Here, again, we witness a glimpse of Viraj's inner life and monologue as it processes sibling rivalry. The essay ends predictably with resolution, with the two brothers finding an equilibrium in their sameness and their differences. This is an essay about identity and growth. Viraj's accomplishments are intriguingly an aside to the main event—his growing, nuanced understanding of the complexities of being a twin.

With that said, the *Comedy of Errors* quote at the beginning is never explicitly explained—yet it intuitively and tantalizingly links to the last sentence in the first paragraph ('Though not identical, we baffled teachers, with one of us being punished for the other's transgressions'). It flows seamlessly with the essay in natural progression, making clear that his twin, given their disparate interests, is de facto his alter ego, a fact indistinguishable to all but him. That said, we must not assume that the reader understands the context and meaning behind every literary reference—placement and explanation might either be intuitive, else, in order!

ARYAMAN JALOTA

Princeton, Class of 2018

Major: Operations Research and Engineering
School: Singapore International School, Mumbai, India
Hometown: Mumbai, India

'Aryaman, your mother is not well,' said my father to me when I was four and curious about why I had not seen her in a month. My innocent mind did not comprehend this extreme understatement. As I grew older, I saw her in a weaker and more fragile incarnation, and understood that she suffered from cardiomyopathy, a terminal heart disease. I realized that she had spent two years in the United States awaiting a heart transplant, a wait that allowed my father, her devoted husband and an Indian classical musician, to earn enough to afford the transplant during the time they both spent away from me.

My childhood was initially bereft of parental care, and subsequently blessed with a patient for a mother and a stranger for a father. Not many would label it ideal. Contrarily, my upbringing is actually analogous to a Shakespearean tragedy in reverse. It was founded in a state of despondency, but it eventually forged a markedly uplifting identity.

The nascent development of my identity arose from my disconnected relationship with my father, who became a workaholic to finance my mother's medical care. I struggled to understand his transformation and yearned for an orthodox father-son relationship, but was this possible after years of detachment? My flailing self-worth was further exacerbated by my disinclination towards music, an anomalous trait in a family of two national award-winning musicians. Frustrated and guilt-struck, I resolved that if we could not bond on the stage of a concert, I could reach out to him by somehow embodying his ethos to success: devotion. He brought his devotion to the stage, whereas I brought mine to the podium. Initially, my desperation helped me win my first debate at fourteen. Subsequently, I won numerous debating accolades, extended my devotion to Model UN, and eventually served as the secretary general of my school's conference twice. During these years, my father and I saw little of each other. Ultimately, the endless evenings I spent in school leaving no stone unturned for the conferences paid off. They had just the cathartic implication I desired: my father watched me deliver the secretary general address with an unflinching proud smile on his face.

The most significant aspect of my identity, however, was sculpted when I received the hapless news that my mother's kidneys had failed. I was apprehensive whether, as a recently resuscitated fighter, she could withstand another merciless blow. She has since been undergoing renal dialysis four times a week. Her medical history complicates donor compatibility; yet, the hunt for a kidney continues, and I often stare at the timer on her dialysis machine at Hinduja Hospital for hours, fearfully wondering where the ticker on the timer of her life is. At one of these moments, an idea was conceived. Last summer, my cousin and I gave birth to the NGO ORGAN to mitigate resistance towards organ donation in India. Through this initiative we strived to increase the number of donor pledges in Delhi and set up a network of hospitals that connects donors to recipients through software. Travelling from Apollo to Fortis Hospital, I gathered data on transplants and visited their dialysis units. I noticed patients with the same anticipative look as my mother's; they too were awaiting a kidney in a country where only two percent of those in need receive one. Yet, it wasn't this statistic, but their expressions that solidified my resolve to help others find organs. I recognized that beyond a service, ORGAN is the route that connects me to my mother's plight today and the network that will find her a kidney tomorrow.

Working for ORGAN reminded me of something my father told me: 'Circumstances are great resources. You can easily build a meaningful life around any circumstances.' I initially refused to accept his platitude, but have slowly realized that my identity is the quintessential manifestation of his words.

OUR THOUGHTS ON ARYAMAN'S ESSAY

Aryaman's story is a raw, authentic telling of his circumstances and how he coped with them. While his style is matter-of-fact, he creates a vivid picture of what it was like to live in a home with one terminally ill parent, another who was compelled into absence by that terminal illness, and how Aryaman expanded as a result—he uses the word 'blessed' literally. He is open about his then distant relationship with his father, and his identity crisis. Through this narrative, we collect pieces of information on what holds Aryaman's interest, what does not, what motivates him and how he navigated his circumstances.

This essay is particularly contemplative—Aryaman distils his insights from the turmoil clearly. For example, he works through the existential angst of realizing that music is not for him, despite his parents' talents, but ultimately arrives at acceptance and finds his métier. He wonders, almost as if through a stream of consciousness, if he can find common ground with his father, and despite their apparent distance, he finds that he can. The successes he met with through debates and his subsequent appointment as secretary general of Model UN were essentially by-products of cathartic, dogged, hard work. He shows the reader that he coped with difficult circumstances by channeling his energy into a project and excelling—'devotion', as he calls it, learnt from his dad, perhaps. This trait is also apparent in his founding of ORGAN, directly inspired by his mother's predicament.

Through ORGAN, Aryaman realizes that his grief, though significant, is not exceptional. Recognizing the emotion which he feels for his mother mirrored in other families and patients, he finally makes sense of his long-term trauma. ORGAN gives him more than a purpose, it gives him a connection with his mother. In assisting the larger community, he serves her. This becomes a turning point—the hope that comes from Aryaman's work enables reconnections with his family.

Importantly, this essay is not self-pitying. It highlights Aryaman's strengths, his comfort with being vulnerable, his clarity of thought and his learning that he can, and must, make the most of his circumstances.

2

THE ANALOGISTS

'Life is like a box of chocolates –
you never know what you're gonna get.'

—Forrest Gump

Analogies, for most of us, trigger flashbacks to middle school grammar or high school lessons on literary devices in poetry. We might think of simple, popular similes like 'As sly as a fox', or the timeless opening of Shakespeare's 'Sonnet 18': 'Shall I compare thee to a summer's day?'

The essayists in this section, however, use comparisons and representations to create vivid, visceral, and three-dimensional portraitures of their personalities. Some use multi-sensory imagery to evoke near-physical response, others borrow lexical elements and corporeal connects from analogous objects to recreate their own life-changing moments for their readers.

Are you ready to surf the tidal waves of their experiences?

ANJINI KHANNA

Cornell, Class of 2023

Major: Economics
School: Sanskriti School, New Delhi, India
Hometown: New Delhi, India

At dawn, I hear birds chirping, while standing, hands folded, thinking about the Grade 9 Mathematics final examination. My body faces East, towards the Sun, honoring Him and seeking his blessings to achieve the milestones I've set for the day. I am in my first pose of Sun Salutation or *Surya Namaskar.*

I bend backwards, arms outstretched, pause, and follow it by a forward bend, my thoughts lost in the variable methods I used to conquer the trigonometry problem the previous night. It's the elasticity of mind versus body. I am reminded of the adage my Mathematics teacher quoted: 'Every great and deep difficulty bears in itself its own solution. It forces us to change our thinking in order to find it.' These words resonated when I received a standing ovation for an Excellence Award in Mathematics in Grade 9.

Yoga, a daily ritual, is an integral part of my life and was inculcated in me by my parents at age fourteen. Within yoga, Sun Salutation, to me, is its soul, awakening my body and mind and creating positive energy that I transmit onward to add buoyancy in my life. Every posture of Sun Salutation echoed events and experiences of my youth. In fact, I was taking something away from the Sun every day. I feel the Sun imbues me with attributes of discipline, dedication, resilience and humbleness.

Yoga has provided me with the strength to handle life's uncertainties. In January 2017, my grandfather lost his fight against cancer in Bangalore. As I approached the first term exams of Grade 11, I started doubting myself, and my grades dipped slightly. The transition from tenth to eleventh grade in every student's academic career is challenging. Subjects are unfamiliar, and course work dramatically increases. I was also upset at my grandfather's demise which impacted my performance. These thoughts ran through my mind, as I slowly bent performing Sun Salutation, my torso touching the ground. I feel the stretch and agony more intensely this time around—difficulty and pain must be endured to reach my goals, seemed to be the message.

I harbored a dream to be part of the School Council in Grade 12 and decided that I would leave no stone unturned to realize my ambition. Having applied to the committee headed by the school principal, I awaited a final interview that would seal my fate. I felt exuberant when, after the interview, I exited the principal's office with an acceptance letter in my hand. I was a proud member of the School Discipline Council. My mind at this jubilant moment goes back to my posture of Sun Salutation where my body is levitating in the air, supported steadily by my hands and toes. The highlight of my new job was the Discipline Awareness Movement that aimed to imbibe values of discipline in every sphere of life.

My self-belief and determination, largely due to yoga, was evident when I orchestrated the Annual Day play called *Who am I to Who I am* based on bullying and body-shaming. As an assistant director, I administered the theatrical performance with grace. On the academic front, I bounced back, with my supremacy in Accountancy and Mathematics in the first term examinations of Grade 12. Coincidently, this thought emanated while I maneuvered towards my ascending posture of Sun Salutation, slowly lifting my chest off the floor, my head and neck held high, legs energized and, with one last stretch, I was back on my feet. I was feeling optimistic and confident once more.

Doing the twelve steps of Sun Salutation, my life had replayed itself and come a full circle. I felt fulfilled and gratified. I fold my hands yet again and, gazing towards the Sun, perform the final posture to thank Him and seek His blessings, this time not to desire success, but success with humility.

OUR THOUGHTS ON ANJINI'S ESSAY

Surya Namaskar is a yoga sequence structured by a set of twelve interlinked postures or *asanas* that are traditionally practised as an acknowledgement of the beginning (sunrise) and the end (sunset) of each day. Seen as an offering to the sun for its life-giving and life-preserving properties, the salutations that primarily symbolize things coming full circle also represent the effort, discipline, and practice of conscious-thinking that flow through the movements. These themes emerge powerfully and parallel Anjini's life through her interweaving of notable moments from her adolescence with her performance of the sequence.

Anjini dexterously uses the flow of sequence protocols to structure her essay. Her descriptions of mindfully contorting her body provide vivid imagery to tangibly express and access her headspace. For instance, her description of the initial stretch connects with her recollection of winning an excellence award in Mathematics, elucidating that both feats were factored by the 'elasticity' of her mind. Similarly, she expresses her buoyancy by vividly describing how her body 'levitates' when she realizes her ambition of becoming a member of the Student Council and, equally graphically, describes her 'agony' when recollecting difficult times. As Anjini explains, the salutations seem to 'echo' experiences from her life as much as provide her with the tools and mental fortitude required to deal with challenges. Significantly, each event Anjini discusses has both, an element of reflection and an outlook to the future. While viewing the difficulties she struggled with in the crucial transition period between Class 10 and Class 11, we viscerally feel Anjini's emotions as she faces dual challenges: the grief of her grandfather's death and the pressure of entering unfamiliar academic domains. However, her focus and discipline result in her overcoming both and realizing that difficult moments and her achievements are equally a part of her reality.

Almost in echo, Anjini completes the first half of *Surya Namaskar*. The rigor it represents is apparent. Her claim is not one of effortless excellence or genius but one of conscious and mindful success born from sustained practice. Even as she completes her 'ascent', we are left with the knowledge that the peak is yet to come.

SANJANA MITTAL

Yale, Class of 2025

Major: Electrical Engineering
School: Dubai College, Dubai, UAE
Hometown: Dubai, UAE

Following my humble beginnings as a seven-year-old fascinated by Betty Crocker mixes, I soon set my eyes on the more elegant renderings of the baking universe: macarons—their delicacy, their components, their detailing, their colors... and their feet.

Now the 'foot' of a macaron is an enigmatic concept; who'd imagine that dainty French delicacies have 'feet'? Yet, the 'foot' of a macaron is its defining metric of quality, and crafting perfect macaron feet is a coveted goal chased by bakers worldwide.

'Macaron-feet' is the term ascribed to the elegant ruffles lining the bottom of a macaron-shell. Look when you next visit a French bakery. They form due to air within the shell rising through its base when baking, forming tiny uniform air pockets—the foot. A symbol of beautiful, understated excellence that I longed to achieve.

However, macaron-feet are notoriously elusive; one wrong move in the baking process, I learned, and 'my' feet fell flat. Minuscule errors consistently kept me teetering on the edge of success. Frustration set in and my inadequacy irked.

But challenge has always been my poison of choice. Even as footless macaron batches sneered at me in smug pretention, I narrowed my eyes on the goal: reaching that coveted macaron-feet haven. Week after week, I toiled and troubled to bake new macaron batches, fiercely experimenting and testing daring recipe ideas, all at the expense of my all-too-willing family's swelling waistlines.

Meanwhile, accompanying my macaron-feet conundrums, my EPQ brought forth another profoundly intriguing project: building a robotic pen-plotter—a Raspberry-Pi powered robot that can (or should) draw. This academic undertaking supplemented my macaron-induced ravings and, over several months, I let the two tasks consume me, pouring everything I had into chasing these twin goals.

Both tasks demanded constant focus and dedication—each macaron recipe demanded analysis as much as each circuit connection necessitated evaluation. While I carefully whipped eggs into precise meringues in the kitchen, I maintained similar accuracy when soldering GPIO headers onto microcontrollers in my room; while the scientist in me rigorously calculated machine dimensions and parameters, in glorious tandem, the same analytical mind determined the effects of sugar and flour proportions.

Gradually, my robotic pen-plotter took shape, and the long nights spent poring over faulty connections and broken motors finally paid off. My code started working (thank you, Python gods!) and my pen-plotter drew its first rudimentary images. Pride washed over me in waves, but a heavy cloud yet loomed: I still hadn't achieved my macaron-feet. Every time I saw more footless macarons sniggering at me, my resolve hardened. I vowed to wipe those smirks off their footless faces. I had to. I had succeeded this way with the robotics project; my approach had to work here too.

Months passed, and I remained fixated on my macaron-feet. But blinded by purpose, I didn't see that my parents now shared my macarons with friends, or that my brother demolished each batch quicker than the last, or the innumerable compliments bestowed by all guests who tasted them.

Apparently, the only person who did not like my macarons, was me.

Then gradually, it dawned on me. I can't apply the same approach and mindset to every task. My detail-oriented and ruthlessly resilient nature had served me well for my pen-plotter project, but perhaps baking was a different beast. I was pursuing perfection in something meant to bring warmth. My short-sightedness had blinded me from the reasons I loved baking: its comfort, the affection it brings, and the joy it can spread.

Finally, I saw the love within the imperfections. The feet weren't perfect, but every bite brought smiles, laughter and joy. That's what truly mattered.

I'll always hold on to my love for a good challenge, but with it now, a balanced outlook. Those macaron-feet weren't taunting but teaching me—that the principal universal characteristics of success are growth, adaptability and perspective.

OUR THOUGHTS ON SANJANA'S ESSAY

In this captivating essay, Sanjana regales readers with two of her seemingly unrelated challenge-driven exploits—mastering macaron-feet and building a Raspberry-Pi-powered robotic pen-plotter. Using gastronomic metaphors, anecdotes and references are a guaranteed subliminal 'hook' for the admission commissioners' full attention. Human taste-bud memory responds involuntarily to descriptions of food, delivering a quick dopamine hit, and ensuring positive regard. Adding familiarity—Who doesn't know Betty Crocker mixes and cakes? Who hasn't heard of MasterChef?—the mould is ready, the oven is warm.

Next, Sanjana takes readers through the intricacies of the 'notoriously elusive', 'enigmatic concept' of French macaron-feet almost scientifically. Even as she tickles the taste buds, she flavors her telling with animated, sometimes self-deprecating humor—'footless macaron batches sneered at me in smug pretention'—while she 'toiled and troubled', 'fiercely experimenting' at 'the expense of my all-too-willing family's swelling waistlines.'

Thus, Sanjana masterfully involves readers and their curiosity in her culinary conundrums, all the while weaving in aspects of her thoughts, emotions, reasoning, and actions. A memorable example from the essay quotes, '...challenge has always been my poison of choice.'

Sanjana continues stirring her skills, strengths, and character traits into the mix, drawing parallels between her two stories—'constant focus and dedication—each... demanded analysis... necessitated evaluation'; 'scientist in me rigorously calculated... the same analytical mind determined...'

Once her coding challenge is accomplished, Sanjana shows perseverance, bringing readers' attention back to her still-unresolved dilemma—through gut and giggles. 'Every time I saw more footless macarons sniggering at me, my resolve hardened. I vowed to wipe those smirks off their footless faces.'

Unable to see the wood for the trees and accept the oh-so-evident popularity of her macarons, Sanjana questions whether her 'detail-oriented and ruthlessly resilient nature' could take on 'baking... a different beast'. She gradually reflects and finally sees that 'those macaron-feet weren't taunting but teaching me' and acknowledges 'the love within the imperfections' that drew mirth and joy. This, she reflects conclusively, is what truly mattered.

Sanjana ends by exhibiting a regained 'balanced outlook of [her] principal universal characteristics... [her own] growth, adaptability and perspective', while still salivating over and relishing a good challenge.

SHIVIN UPPAL

UPenn, Class of 2022

Major: Computer Science and Business Analytics (Wharton)
School: Delhi Public School, R.K. Puram, New Delhi, India
Hometown: New Delhi, India

In a Mediterranean pine forest in late January, the beagles followed the pungent, intense fragrance that led to several dead-ends and one precious discovery: the elusive, inconspicuous truffle. This fruity fungus, the size of a walnut and covered in red mud, hardly appeared attractive, but as it was shaved over the bowl of *tagliàtelle* and garnished with a crisp of *grana padano*, it evolved into a delight for everyone. Like the toadstool, I, too, am an acquired taste that metamorphoses everything that I complement.

With Heston (instead of Hulk) as my childhood hero, I played into my fascination with flambé and fondue. I threw my spaghetti on the wall to test *al dente* and held my Pavlova bowl of whipped egg whites over my head to test their stiffness. My enthusiasm spilled over outside the kitchen, as I tried to make popping candy toothpowder—my first patentable recipe!

Hours of watching molecular gastronomy inspired me to whip up brilliant dishes out of nowhere. Ideas like poaching pears in pomegranate juice, pairing them with arugula and goat's cheese and sorbet made fizzy using excess dry ice were vital to my entry into the kitchen. At home, my mother, a chef by profession, spent half her days in the kitchen, and I spent that time with her. Tablespoonfuls of my childhood went into designing my mother's home-catering menu, comprising delicacies from Rosemary and Cream Cheese *Kebabs* to baked *Conchiglie* pasta.

While my friends were blowing up test tubes, I was making soda by putting water in a siphon in the Chemistry lab; while they were kicking balls around the soccer pitch, I was scooping balls of *Stracciatella.* Not everyone was receptive to the idea of a boy my age playing with whisks and spatulas, just as some will never appreciate the rare but unforgettable truffle.

Like the truffle that infinitely elevates a dish, I threw myself into every avenue that came my way. I found myself at the auditions of Junior MasterChef India amidst over hundred thousand children from across the country, and then among the top 36. This exposure at such an early age certainly impacted my personality and life in an unimaginable manner. I went on to head my school's Culinary Club as its president, whipping up desserts and selling them at bake sales, and attending masterclass lessons. I shared my signature recipes—*arrabiata*, *béchamel*, and *velouté*—while conducting a culinary workshop. While I didn't know it then, the drama from my foodie creations has infused life into everything else I have done, making my efforts animated, suspenseful, and expressive.

Inspired by icing a cake to make it more appealing, I put on my whites to better lives around me. The essence of sharing that cooking embodies led me to start Golden Ager, a portal that links retired people to start-ups, which can benefit from a pinch of business experience. I make this process work in reverse, too, by using my knowledge of Linear Programming to optimize the dietary components of my recipes. Juggling to combine all of cooking's components has led me to fold in connections between seemingly disparate areas of learning, scale my perspectives, and celebrate the resulting fusion of tastes.

I have spent many invaluable years focusing on and gaining wonderful new ideas, and wandering down exciting new avenues. And not everything has worked out as planned or been appreciated all around. I tell myself that I am just another truffle, covered in red earthy soil, speckled black over white, with a smell some may not like. Yet, I strive to enhance every mix, eliciting the best from the dish of the day. My life is a cycle of being foraged from the depths of rainforests and journeying through the refinery. Using the best of ingredients and techniques, I end up on the connoisseur's plate, closing the evening banquet with a '*Voila!*'

OUR THOUGHTS ON SHIVIN'S ESSAY

With a single whiff of pine, Shivin vividly illuminates readers' real or imagined memories, transporting them right into the forest, running in the wake of the furiously sniffing beagles—in search of the 'elusive, inconspicuous', yet globally coveted exotic truffle.

There are so many incredible sensory elements and metaphorical references in Shivin's first three introductory sentences, that readers are already hooked by a full-on multisensory experience of where this story is going. Even if one does not know who Heston is, it is amply obvious where Shivin's tastes and talents lie. Shivin uses the truffle mushroom as a metaphor for himself—'an acquired taste that metamorphoses everything that I complement'. He is playful and at ease with his fascination for, and foray into all things food, while still establishing the seriousness of his interest in the science of 'molecular gastronomy'.

Shivin is clearly an expert on the prominence of olfactory memory in human sensory perception, and literally leads readers by the nose, or rather their receptors, through his culinary life journey—repeatedly titillating their tastebuds by 'poaching pears in pomegranate juice', thereby illustrating various aspects of his fun, creative personality while also giving readers some bright ideas. Behind the humor of the 'tablespoonfuls of [his] childhood' stands a gifted chef, knowing exactly how readers will respond to the mouth-watering 'Rosemary and Cream

Cheese *Kebabs*' and 'baked *Conchiglie* pasta,' perhaps even attempting to make them at the first available opportunity.

Shivin touches upon how his interest in 'playing with whisks and spatulas' were seen as being different from social expectations but remains undeterred by stereotypes. He presents his confidence in his ability to 'infinitely elevate' and 'metamorphose everything that I complement'. He takes great pride in his passion and progress through Junior MasterChef India, on 'to head my school's Culinary Club'. Realizing how 'the drama from my foodie creations has infused life into everything else I have done, making my efforts animated, suspenseful, and expressive', he decides to share his joy for food—through his initiatives. He creatively aligns his other skill sets, like 'Linear Programming to optimize the dietary components of my recipes'.

While candidly admitting how things did not always pan out as expected, Shivin yet strives to 'enhance every mix, eliciting the best' in everything he attempts. And ends up 'on the connoisseur's plate' certain that his value is appreciated by those who matter; he is who he is, and proud of it.

Shivin's essay immediately commands interest in that it focuses on a topic of universal interest – food – and skillfully uses it to draw analogies, while keeping us riveted and drawn to his spirited and communicative persona.

MEHEK VOHRA

Brown and Rhode Island School of Design, Class of 2024

Major: Cognitive Neuroscience and Graphic Design
School: Dubai College, Dubai, UAE
Hometown: Dubai, UAE

THE ART OF SUSHI

It was during the Singaporean Summer of 2007 that I had my first tryst with chopsticks. I remember my fingers effortlessly guiding them, finding it no different to painting with a brush. My growing infatuation drove me to fearlessly order platters of sushi topped with salmon, octopus, and squid; while my parents grimaced, I would sweep maki into my mouth, diving straight into the depths of unknown flavors and textures.

Three years later, I bid adieu to those fresh salmon rolls, leaving Singapore's street food for Dubai's Arabian flavors. In a city where sushi was only a distant memory, I took up the challenge of re-creating those perfectly crafted sushi rolls. For weeks, I persisted through numerous failed attempts, simultaneously elevating my patience quotient.

After many months of blood, sweat and lopsided maki rolls, my parents challenged me to prepare a meal in the spirit of their 21st anniversary. My creativity and precision were about to be put to the test. In preparation, I spent hours polishing blades and measuring out ingredients; my methodical mindset was micromanaging every detail. I dusted off my apron, locked my hair into a bun, and began...

With surgical precision, I sliced open its soft skin. My fingers grazed over the exposed meat, mentally calculating the number of incisions to be made. As the blade sank down, the scent of fresh salmon sliced the air, intertwining with the tangy fragrance of vinegar, and the honeyed hints of sugar.

Four hours later, exhausted, and with salmon skin stuck to my fingers, I reflected on my chef-d'oeuvre. I had mastered the art of precise portions of mayonnaise, Sriracha, and lime juice, and consequently created the most delectable spicy mayo. Although pleased with the maki, my mission had not yet concluded; my masterpiece was yet to be skillfully unveiled. I got back to work. My acumen for detailing came to the fore as I positioned the delicate china on the dining table; on each platter were six pieces of maki separated in twos by equal quantities of wasabi, ginger, and soy sauce. Wooden chopsticks were placed tangential to the plates, and the tableau illuminated by candlelight.

As my family savored every morsel, rice grain and salmon sliver, their appreciation brought to light the importance of giving and creating art with a purpose. Those hours of creation and labor were well worth it, for from them I learned that beyond what you say or give, it is the intent that truly matters. I transited this insight into my artworks, intricately layering my canvases with context and emotion, much as I layered salmon on rice.

In time, sushi-making became my guiding light. With new-found confidence, I ventured forth into undiscovered realms of flavors, textures and ingredients. Beyond the basic avocado and cucumber, I began experimenting with finely sliced crab and freshly seasoned seabass. While as an artist, I started straying from pre-set formulae and recipes, and began to follow my own path, thus allowing my creativity and intuition to guide me. Life in the Middle East inspired me to create my signature sushi, 'The Intercontinental Wonder' ... the wrapping of tomato and parsley, essential ingredients of Arabian salads, around Japanese seaweed, combined and beautifully balanced flavors from two diverse cultures.

I also devoted hours to developing my own mentoring methodology; I passed on my knowledge to my younger brother, a trainee. With every sushi roll, we grew closer, and petty disputes were settled through fervent cook-offs.

As I continuously seek new challenges, whether it is re-inventing the flavors of Singapore, skydiving above Dubai's architectural anomalies, or traversing oceans in pursuit of new opportunities, I will pack my essential ingredients... creativity, risk-taking proclivity, meticulousness, patience, and soy sauce. My journey as a novice *Itamae* (Japanese cook) has inspired me to complete each *task to the t*; I have learned that how you do anything, is how you do everything.

OUR THOUGHTS ON MEHEK'S ESSAY

Mehek's essay and title dexterously yet naturally combine art and Sushi to set the stage for readers' expectations. Then she employs the popular strategy of metaphorically and literally describing one 'thing'—in this case, aspects of her personality, strengths, skills, and mindset—using another defining and distinctive 'thing'—sushi-making. It works spectacularly in helping the reader relate to the hard-to-define, unquantifiable and 'unseeable' features of her abilities, work ethic and potential. Mehek takes our focus away from the obvious explanations of her 'academics' and chooses instead to entertain and engage with an unexpected sensory experience, demonstrating her ingenuity.

Maya Angelou's famous quote ends with: '...people will never forget how you made them feel.' Mehek has hit upon a very clever age-old strategy of using the primal human response to food, to make readers 'feel' something. The mere aroma, and then taste, of food provoke the most intense memories and stimulate responses. Mehek also uses detailed descriptions of its visual appearance and umami flavors to entertain and invigorate the imagination.

Art often features food. Mehek flips this, using food to feature her artistry. Sushi is about art as much as food—and to the non-Far Easterner, it is also about novel, scintillating tastes, and courage. Representing culinary elegance, sushi-making is an intensive, process-driven challenge that requires learning through dedication and persistence. Slicing the fish in sushi preparation has been compared to performing surgery. A precise balance between the ingredients—condiments, rice and fish is the quintessential prerequisite for attaining respectable results. We feel we are alongside Mehek in her kitchen as she prepares, and explains the process, even as she experiments with sushi's aesthetic multisensory appeal, precision, and visual elegance.

All of which reveal Mehek's many layers and showcase Mehek, the artist. Mehek smartly and willfully helps readers attribute her personality and her art to sushi-making's artistry and complexities—demonstrating her overriding originality, determination, and capacity for hard work. Later, her mouth-watering creative combinations of different Middle Eastern ingredients demonstrate adaptability, taking readers and their olfactory cells and taste buds on a journey possibly remembered beyond the Common App process!

Finally, Mehek astonishes readers with deep insights into how sushi-making helped her engage positively with her family: '*...petty disputes were settled through fervent cook-offs.*' She concludes by taking that one step further towards an amazing and wise realization for one so young ('*I have learnt that how you do anything, is how you do everything*'), causing readers to reflect upon their own lives.

ANONYMOUS

Princeton, Class of 2023

Major: Physics
School: Dhirubhai Ambani International School, Mumbai, India
Hometown: Mumbai, India

The plastic glimmers in the sunlight. The first thing I see each morning are his milky-white eyes, his red and blue tights, and the big black spider painted on his chest. Waking up next to my Spider-Man action figure may seem somewhat unusual, but I'm often unsettled if I don't. He brings a smile on my face and gives me the comfort of knowing that I always have a sympathetic someone who'll listen and appreciate my point when no one else does, ranging from the fascinatingly intuitive calculus behind special relativity to rants on *Brooklyn Nine-Nine*.

When I sit up, I see my two-dimensional poster Superman, arms folded, smiling brightly and reassuringly: his twinkling eyes give me hope that today will be a better day, that today I will learn something new, something interesting, that today I will finally catch my school bus on time. No, who am I kidding? In no alternate universe would that ever happen.

I drowsily stumble across my room to my favorite Flash comic on the table—he's trying to escape a black hole. You'll have to outrun light for that, Flash. Physics does not allow that, does it? I relook at the comic book. The depiction of the black hole—the power of the human mind. To imagine that. I look out the window at the rising Sun—it's beautiful. The idea that it's a cosmic entity deep in space, that billions of these stars constitute our galaxy, how several billion galaxies grace our Universe, and the consequent possibilities. The insignificance of my being humbles me, and is... actually very liberating.

I walk to my bathroom, seeing the varied Deadpool stickers on my mirror. He's unhinged, eccentric, but there's more to him. It's the expression. It's the freedom and ability to speak and act at will, unfettered by external opinion. He helps me take a leap of faith—to navigate life with the same eccentricity, to bring my unique perspective to problems, be it global issues at Model UN or a Newtonian mechanics system in Physics class.

I zealously apply laws governing international waters to solve a space privatization crisis, and build science toys to demonstrate principles of electromagnetism at the Astronomy class I conduct for students from underserved government schools. I smile. I keep focused on the future, but time and again reflect on the past—just to keep things in perspective.

I turn to my domain. It is just a room, but it's mine. And I have an audience. All my superheroes. With toothbrush as mic, I practise a few jokes—observations about the inexplicable need for shoelaces and semicolons. Or perhaps biting political commentary about the government where I pick up on all the wrong issues to deal with (I don't understand this obsession with cow slaughter). They may not get more than a few laughs at a stand-up set, but at least Thor cannot stop smiling.

As I dress in an animated rush, I spot the Batman emblem I etched on the wall as a twelve-year-old. It's a different language, one that traverses time and speaks to the polyglot in me. I can communicate with a younger me, who reminds me that, like for Bruce Wayne, things will not always go my way. But I have to make it happen. I know that running that one Astronomy class won't bring about a revolution, but I still have to go out there every Sunday and do what I have to, because in the end, I have to know that I was there, catalyzing change.

As I'm leaving, my heroes come to life. They jump off the walls, out of the plastic, and into my brain. Over the years, their ideals and attributes—Spider-Man, Superman, Batman and countless others—have coalesced in me, defining my unique identity.

Reality is mine to shape—and fiction is my tool.

OUR THOUGHTS ON THE ESSAY

'The plastic glimmers in the sunlight.' The essay starts with clear humorous intent, unabashedly admitting a dependence on action figures for security. This is not unusual; most of our childhood heroes and their stories expose us to important values through play.

These role models might stay with us through adulthood, serving as benchmarks for our principles and actions. Like for the narrator, they are also confidantes who listen stoically as we reveal our deepest thoughts and feelings. No boundaries, no judgement. The reassuring 'two-dimensional' simplicity of a poster superhero promises hope in the seemingly direst of circumstances. Here, humor laces self-acceptance as the essay continues in conversation with idols, freely speculating and exploring the galaxies of inner 'universes'—humbled and liberated by the connections between physics and human existence.

This is a fast-paced, propulsive essay, taking readers on a roller coaster from the heights of imagination to the very mundane—the bathroom, and a suitably paired 'unhinged, eccentric' and unapologetically expressive Deadpool. We gain insight into the narrator's approach in applying a 'unique perspective to problems'—from global issues and politics to physics and astronomy, to social work. The superhero role models, mentors, confidantes serve as a ready audience and partners-in-crime when picking 'on all the wrong issues to deal with'.

The structure—a spinning, action-packed odyssey—has a superhero waiting round every corner, a pillar of support at every hurdle, waiting to guide the narrator across all the difficulties. Showing belief in the smallest of tasks—'...running that one Astronomy class won't bring about a revolution, but...' the narrator proves to be an agent of change.

We've barely followed the narrator out his front door (late!), and already it has been an exhilarating adventure, flying through their minds, clutching onto the capes, webs, and winged boots of 'superheroes', understanding their 'ideals and attributes'—all facets of the student's own personality, a source of courage for each day. We are convinced; so, we enter and accept his reality. As the essay reminds us, in its brilliant and effective closing line, 'Reality is mine to shape—and fiction is my tool'.

SIDDHANTH LATH

Columbia, Class of 2023

Major: Mechanical Engineering
School: Dhirubhai Ambani International School, Mumbai, India
Hometown: Mumbai, India

Gardener. Academician. Scientist. Carpenter. Altruist.

My balcony garden shows me that all things are possible. Four storeys above the toxic car fumes and cacophony of a Mumbai thoroughfare, I enter my microcosm of pristine greenery nestling in a 1x4-meter balcony and tend my garden, an oasis of color, scent and texture in the urban sprawl. I weave through the basil, okra, tomatoes, lemongrass and pepper plants, my path guided by the morning glory that interlaces them into a tight family. I focus on each, deeply inhaling the vivid scents—fragrant jasmine and pungent onion, heady peppers and bitter gourd.

In this Eden sits my mother's gift of a basil sapling whose overwhelming aroma and resilience inspired me to delve into growing vegetables and herbs. Tellingly, a month later, I gleefully garnished my hallmark pizza Margherita with fresh basil whose aroma and turgidity beggared outsourced leaves. Oregano followed. And thus began my journey: I lovingly curated this balcony garden, foraying into vermicompost, cocopeat and other enablers of growth, reveling in the primal satisfaction of growing food. The results opened a whole new palette I didn't know existed. Soon enough I was packing organic herbs weekly, to friends' demands.

That garden so viscerally embodies me, be it out-of-season scallions braving the blistering Mumbai summer's heat, sunflowers which rival an eponymous painting, or the proliferating morning glory. They thrive in concord, in a cramped balcony relegated to the shadows by towering, abutting skyscrapers. Seeing my plants confined to shadows for nineteen hours a day, I pondered, then introduced curved foil reflectors retrofitted at angles calibrated for maximal sunshine, supplemented by specialist 650 nanometer lights and tilted pots. I then engaged vertically, harnessing my nascent carpentry skills and building a bamboo trellis to ensure my plants' vertical growth by absorbing maximum sunlight in close confines.

My garden in the urban wilderness is a constant reminder that even in an inhospitable milieu, I can, given the will, foster the ingredients for growth and prosperity. Does not the lotus bloom best in thickest, muddiest water? Of course, it was the seemingly delicate but hardy *Ocimumbasilicumaka* Basil that was, overarchingly, the motivator. It's resilience and consistent growth in poor soil, polluted air and inadequate sunshine emboldened me: this shows me that I too with grit and determination can blossom and grow, no matter the odds.

Walking through the garden is a walk down memory lane, a lane replete with milestones: the white jasmine I planted on the day I was appointed Student Council coordinator; the crimson hibiscus I planted to mark the day my sister left for university. Brilliant-hued sunflowers revive memories of teaching computer skills at a school for underprivileged boys like Aman, the sprightly schoolboy whose singular aspiration was to disrupt the class. Despite him being the weakest student in the class, I relentlessly persevered with him and now his passion for computers blooms as bright as the sunflowers.

My vermillion cherry tomatoes remind me of Geography: once hated, now adored. Planted the day I was declared India topper in Geography, its growth from struggling shrub to provider of sweet miniature tomatoes analogizes my progress from considering the subject a repository of monotonous map work to an enduring fascination sparked by my new Geography teacher Mr Kimweli. Much as I tended to my saplings, Mr Kimweli focused on me and evolved an animated passion for Geography. My cherry tomatoes stubbornly molded for two months but remembering how Mr Kimweli had labored to change my perceptions, I too navigated the obstacles, fertilizing, weeding and pruning. The fruits of my labor paid off handsomely, both in tomatoes and in Geography.

I see each day how cultivating my garden is indistinguishable to cultivating my life and I can proudly say my garden has shown me that I can be

Gardener. Academician. Scientist. Carpenter. Altruist and so much more…

OUR THOUGHTS ON SIDDHANTH'S ESSAY

The garden and Siddhanth feed into each other in this redolent sample. Imaginative, sensitive, and filled with symbolism and imagery from nature, his essay seems to fall within a romantic aesthetic reminiscent of Shelley and Keats.

Siddhanth's essay is notably reflective. Instead of focusing on a single, defining incident or discovery, he strings together a mix of non-linear learnings, memories, and undertakings much like the winding 'morning glory that interlaces them (his plants) into a tight family'. The denotation of his balcony garden as a place that makes 'all things possible' is emphasized by its multi-sensory representation. Described as 'an oasis of color, scent and texture in the urban sprawl', notwithstanding its balcony domicile, we are drawn into the garden, and more specifically, into Siddhanth's experience of it. These visualizations and his active experience of the garden (inhaling, weaving, curating) hold our attention through his meandering storytelling structure, much like a rambling creeper, nudging us to revisit our own plant-triggered memories.

Beyond its evocative aspect, Siddhanth's aesthetic flourishes contrast with the physical, hands-on aspect of gardening—the sheer commitment it takes to cultivate an urban garden. Coaxing growth from foreign, nutrient-poor soil, 'in the shadow of Mumbai's skyscrapers', the 'calibration', 'harnessing' and 'building' to nurture his plants show Siddhanth to be both dreamer waxing poetic in introspection, and doer who invests in the work to manifest results. The stream of garden activities speaks intriguingly of Siddhanth's perseverance, and mirrors his milestones, that appear to flow in tandem with plant runners and perfectly timed blooms. Instead of sounding like a self-congratulatory inventory of achievements, the value lent by the gardening metaphor showcases the work (including Applied Physics learnings) that went into Siddhanth's success. 'I too navigated the obstacles, fertilizing, weeding and pruning', he tells us. We can imagine he did this both in the garden, and outside of it. His growth as a Geography student is testimony.

Overarchingly, Siddhanth's essay stands out for its open embracement of non-traditional activities. Gardening, cooking, pausing to smell the roses, Siddhant is not limited. As he himself states in an addendum to his opening list of adjectives, he is all this, and more.

AYESHA MANGALDAS

Harvard, Class of 2017

Major: Psychology
School: B.D. Somani International School, Mumbai, India
Hometown: Mumbai, India

MY LEXICON

I have been in love with words for as long as I can remember. Growing up in a home enveloped by books, where the biggest treat was being allowed a few extra stories at bedtime, how could I not be? We read books on art, famous people, lady robbers and feminist princesses. By the age of five, I could appreciate the nuances of words. I knew that red could be crimson or scarlet or even vermillion. Even today, while expressing myself, I am thrilled by the use of an appropriate word, which makes the entire sentence dance.

Here are some of my favorites:

Pulchritude, for the paradox it possesses—it means beauty but is shrouded by one of the most odious sounding words. It reminds me of my city—Bombay. Although the filth, the fetor and the fragmentation engender constant carping, for me, it is the paragon of perfection. It is home to every caste, creed and color. It is home to fearless and resilient Indians trying to make a living. It is home to, and defines, me.

Ennui, for it gracefully rolls together utter boredom and dissatisfaction. It is the curse of my generation, and also the underlying theme of my two favorite books: Camus's *L'Étranger* and Beckett's *Waiting for Godot*.

Sciolism, because I searched long and hard to find a word to illustrate the cadre of pseudo-intellectuals the 21st century is breeding, and finally found it in David Foster Wallace's list of favorite words. All the spurious parading of knowledge on sites like Facebook and Twitter truly irks me. For heaven's sake, get real!

Freudian Slip because it's life's way of getting the truth told. I don't agree with everything Sigmund Freud theorizes about, but the subconscious intrigues me. My way of understanding a person is not through listening to him talk, but through catching every slip of his tongue, and watching him fumble to mask his error.

Serendipity—'Happy accidents' play such an important role in my life. Coincidences intrigue and enthrall me—surely they are a reminder by the universe that life will always remain mysterious and uncontrollable?

Visceral is a word my English teacher constantly uses. He is Irish and the way he enunciates the word makes me really feel things in my gut. I relate to English literature viscerally—'The Genius of the Crowd' by Bukowski, rather than stirring my intellect, rouses something deep-seated inside me.

Trup—I concocted the word *trup* after spending ten hours straight on an Art exam because sometimes, existing words are just not enough. If Roald Dahl could invent the language 'Gobblefunk' for his book *BFG*, so can I! *Trup* is a hooting laugh, belted out during a conniption brought on by exhaustion.

Et tu, Brute? is not a word, but a phrase that helped me get through a betrayal by my two best friends. During that time, alone, I'd stab my finger at an invisible figure, fling my head back and vocalize each impassioned word of Shakespeare's.

Embrace. I love this word for both its connotations—of the body and of the mind. In the literal sense, I love to hug and be hugged. In the metaphorical sense, I love it when my mind embraces ideas and I embrace life itself and all its myriad opportunities.

My passion for words defines me. It is the way I make sense of the world. With a pen in my hand and a word in my mind, I am invincible.

OUR THOUGHTS ON AYESHA'S ESSAY

Ayesha's essay imprints a vibrant and authentic three-dimensional sense of who she is on its readers. Channeling her love for language and lexis, it offers a carefully composed mini dictionary of her favorite words as a vehicle for self-expression without indulging in wiser-than-thou posturing.

Bringing into play memories from her childhood, the opening paragraph provides a rich, albeit brief look into Ayesha's world. The reader can imagine her as a precocious five-year-old in a home brimming with books and warmed by a shared love for literature. Wistful and proud in equal parts, the paragraph serves as the introduction for an essay with a somewhat unorthodox structure. Apart from her impressive reading habits, Ayesha's deference to the nuances of vocabulary is particularly noteworthy. Her evocative description of the shades of red which 'could be crimson or scarlet or even vermillion' prefaces her choice to use select words to structure her essay, assuring the reader of the refinement and consideration underpinning each decision, both in her essay, and in her life.

The true quality of Ayesha's essay comes with the association of her chosen words with events, emotions and experiences while revealing flashes of her personality and history. We get glimpses of her strong connection to Mumbai, the city she considers home, her love for Albert Camus, Samuel Beckett and Charles Bukowski, her disdain for social-media intellectualism and her belief in slips of language as caveats and intent. There are no uniting themes for these factoids apart from Ayesha herself, whose unique thumbprint marks the essay much like her coinage of 'trup'.

There is an underlying acknowledgement of the breadth of reading Ayesha willingly undertakes. From Roald Dahl's animated stories to classic Shakespeare plays to David Foster Wallace's involved philosophy, the influences are diverse. However, the essay delivers the message through matter-of-fact narration rather than exaggeration: Ayesha's reading is a key and impressive part of who she is, but not all that she is. Instead, there is a wholeness and dimensionality to the information revealed, however unconnected they may appear. From her childhood reading to her adult openness to learning, we are left with a distinct after-image, one that is thoughtful and memorable.

TANYA SHAH

Dartmouth, Class of 2020

Major: Computer Science and Studio Art
School: German Swiss International School, Hong Kong
Hometown: Hong Kong

In slow motion, the tape starts to peel. The artist is unaware. At the microscopic scale, the adhesion is giving in. Suddenly, twenty strings swing out of nowhere. Momentum. The day's work was now a tangled mess.

I was left with a week until the art exhibition and I was spending every second possible building my first installation. I was suspending metal pieces, each on individual strings, from a large frame fixed to the ceiling. My aim was to depict an object being blown to pieces, to capture a frozen moment of fragments bursting out from the center. So, there I was, with hundreds of nuts and bolts sitting in front of me, patiently waiting to be transformed into art.

Perched on a ladder, I was thinking of dimension, of the viewer's perspective. I finished tying a knot, and there hung a heavy bolt, but there was too much stress on the string. It was seconds away from snapping. I had been using the thinnest fishing line to keep it as invisible as possible, but this bolt needed something stronger. I rummaged through a drawer filled with various rolls of string. I had no idea which to choose. I stared at the labels denoting their tensile strengths.

Suddenly, a formula came to mind and I scribbled it down. T equals MG plus MA. A is zero but G is constant. 'When T goes up, M goes up,' I muttered to myself. I needed wire with slightly higher tensile strength to hold the weights being used, and found the perfect one.

It was strange that simple physics had helped me with my art. The thought lingered.

With each knot, the awkwardly hanging blobs of metal slowly turned into a work of art. Subconsciously, though, I was looking at the piece in a different way. Was it balanced torque keeping the frame stable? Was each bolt affecting its state of rotational equilibrium? Was I unknowingly considering center of mass when I suspended each object? I realized I was creating art but thinking physics.

Looking through a new set of eyes, I was seeing connections that I had never noticed. We are trained to think in a linear manner—art is art and physics is physics, two distinct fields—but suddenly, the intersection was becoming clear. The overlap was slowly revealing itself and the two realms were coming together, perhaps encapsulating the essence of creation.

I am beginning to consider the notion that nothing in life is entirely discrete; it is only when we merge and blend different channels of thought that everything begins to make sense. Perhaps there is no such thing as pure art, and all art is intertwined with something—be it history, culture, or physics. Maybe viewing the same situation through different lenses paints a truly complete picture.

Eventually, the installation was complete and ready for display. The hundreds of suspended fragments conveyed the idea that when broken down, everything is more complex than what we see on the surface. I am starting to believe that.

OUR THOUGHTS ON TANYA'S ESSAY

Tanya's essay is all about perspectives. The third-person viewpoint she employs as her writing style in her first paragraph. The several perspectives of viewers she considers while creating installations as an artist. The invaluable perspective and resulting shift, added to by bringing physics into the equation. And perhaps, most significantly, the many perspectives she is yet to discover.

Communicating abstract concepts in writing can be especially tricky. The elusiveness of intangible changes can lead to convoluted and rambling prose. Tanya efficiently deals with this problem by manifesting her internal change through externalized art. Her project, which 'aims to depict an object being blown to pieces, to capture a frozen moment of fragments bursting out from the center' offers enticing prospects to consider its meaning from multiple viewpoints. Apart from the artistic logic of the piece, diverse in its interpretations, Tanya writes about the technical challenge of suspending stand-alone pieces of metal while giving the impression that they had burst forth violently from an original center. The use of physics-related concepts like tensile strength, center of mass and rotational strength in her artwork, awakens her to the way disparate perspectives work together to create a whole. 'Creating art but thinking physics', Tanya's realization adds a novel dimension to her artwork, and its deconstruction cogently symbolizes her awareness of the distinct and complex logics that converge to create reality.

This essay presents Tanya as an ideal Liberal Arts candidate. Her openness to discovering new facets of herself, even if they are at odds with what she already knows is apparent throughout. As is her ability to critically evaluate and think through complex structures calmly and logically. Most importantly, the essay portrays Tanya as someone who can easily adapt to new ways of looking at the world, while maintaining her unique perspective.

DEVANSH KHANNA

Cornell, Class of 2024

Major: Hotel Administration
School: Vasant Valley School, New Delhi, India
Hometown: New Delhi, India

On days there's cereal at breakfast, my face wears a fiercely accommodating smile. However, on weekends, when the air in heavy with the smell of pure *ghee* smeared on fluffy *parathas*, I know I can win the world. Brought up in a joint family with over three generations under the same roof, our biggest discussions have always revolved around the Sunday lunch, and seasonal specialties. Even though the dining table can barely accommodate all of us in one go, every once a year, post-Diwali, we ensure we go to the Golden Temple, Amritsar, together.

Our visit to the holy Sikh temple has its purpose and meaning. Not only do we offer prayers but also serve the *langar*, i.e., the community lunch. It is a strange joy to see the eldest in our family supervising the long queue and the youngest handing out freshly made *rotis* to the innumerable strangers, all equal in the house of God. After the *seva*, we head for an early dinner, usually to one of our favorite restaurants. Not this year. As heavily recommended by our Uber driver, this time, we went to try a new place named 'Sarhad' (Urdu for frontier).

I was mildly surprised to find that Sarhad appeared like just any other pitstop on a highway that fueled rumbling stomachs. Standing on the Wagah–Attari border of India and Pakistan, countries with a common history of trauma arising out of Partition, the atmosphere inside Sarhad was little short of a carnival! I was astonished to see no signs of the infamous animosity, and amazed to witness people enthusiastically interacting with each other, sharing life experiences, families and traditions over steaming cups of tea, generously spiced *kebabs* and fresh *tandoori rotis.* It felt as if the border was merely a line on the atlas, otherwise non-existent.

On my way back, I couldn't stop introspecting that as part of the subcontinent with similar languages and lineage, why were we so estranged from people across few kilometers away? Observing the guests in Sarhad, I wondered if the current heightened political tension between the two countries stemming from the Uri attacks and Article 370 could be amicably neutralized if the dialogue took place over a hearty meal of *Rogan Josh*, *Haleem* and cold *Lassi*?

When my friend from Oxford Summer School visited India with his family, I was unable to show him around and desperately looked for a local guide instead of a tour company that followed a rigid itinerary. Inspired by the concept of locally guarded secrets, I knew there must be thousands of such treasure troves tucked away in the lanes and by-lanes of India's many states, each a diverse country in itself. I wanted to connect with local guides who would show them around their city, and not just take them to tourist-heavy locations. I wanted to connect people with the off-track, with the essence, with the flavor of a city and its cuisine.

Having discussed the financial viability of Tour Buddy with my parents, I researched with the marketing team, and worked my skill-set up the digital analytics way. For the numerous meetings with reputed travel agencies I could hold, there were several others which refused meeting me because of my age. Every time there was a review on the app, the response came within a record five seconds. While it has gained over a hundred users, I plan to expand it to neighboring cities and eventually, beyond borders.

I look forward to retaining tradition and imbibing global fusions in my outlook, just as food as a cultural identity has undergone. While creating the app I realized how democratic it was, not discriminating its user-base on the basis of nationality, religion or gender. The crucial 'salt to taste' will always act as the guiding template for my actions—to respect divergent preferences. Having diverse options helps satiate my hunger for service, at the table, and that of humanity.

OUR THOUGHTS ON DEVANSH'S ESSAY

What is it about food that lends itself to being a perfect analogy for many things? Food is transported in and words are transported out via the mouth. Tasting and talking are the tongue's two main functions. Only natural then, that food metaphors spice up our language.* Aromas ('when the air is heavy with the smell of pure *ghee* smeared on fluffy *parathas*') summon instant mouth-watering multisensory memories.

In many cultures, food brings people together and connects them on multiple levels. The most common example is the tradition of eating with the family around the table, second only to serving food to the larger community—representing communication and communion. That is exactly where Devansh starts—delicious Sunday breakfast and lunch at home. He lulls readers into a comfortable food-induced trance, to sit back and enjoy the ride. His mind-train of thought takes them through to his community and social service, chugging its way to the Golden Temple and the geo-political 'Wagah–Attari border of India and Pakistan'. Food is often used, and, in this case by Devansh, to symbolize something greater than the meal itself.

Pausing for a 'pit-stop on a highway to fuel rumbling stomachs,' the bonhomie between citizens from India and Pakistan stuns Devansh.

**source-* *https://www.epicurious.com/archive/blogs/editor/2006/10/food_as_languag.html*

Still, he manages to convey the spirit of the moment beautifully, using colorful analogies ('the atmosphere inside Sarhad was little short of a carnival!') to communicate the vastness of this single moment. As he puts it, 'It felt as if the border was merely a line on the atlas, otherwise non-existent.'

Devansh's introspection takes readers on a tour of his inner and outer experiences, explaining the motivations behind his innovation of 'Tour Buddy'. The connection between travel, friendship, and food that he establishes flows organically from what he has shown us to be important to him.

This would include helping readers connect with his personal development, by revealing his values through careful deliberation on issues—not the least of them being his desire to have the world share food on a table of his making!

3

THE VIRTUOSOS

*'There should be no boundaries to human endeavor.
We are all different.'*

—Stephen Hawking, *The Theory of Everything*

Musicians. Artists. Physicists. Bakers. Inventors.

Our student virtuosos are masters of a variety of instruments: describing their compelling journeys to their dreams, pin-pointing dramatic 'Aha!' moments and weaving tales that convey their complete immersion when in their 'zone'. These essays take unique routes to represent their talents—and their personas.

Achievements are the fountainhead for the essays in this section—virtuoso achievements, one might add. Growing from this fold are learnings, observations and vivid sketches that leave their imprints. Marked by a penchant to persevere and arrive at the pinnacle, these maestros showcase not just their talent, but also, their evolution.

GITIKA BOSE

Columbia, Class of 2021

Major: Computer Science
School: International School Manila, Manila, Philippines
Hometown: Kolkata, India

I would not call it déjà vu. It was more a sweet feeling of remembrance and identification. All my experiences and accomplishments seemed to foreshadow a future here, or so I hoped. The stars seemed to be aligning in my favor. Today, I am standing at the pinnacle of each of my past experiences. I dream of being a researcher at NASA. This is not simply a whim of today, but a culmination of my dream from yesterday, the preceding year, and I will go on a limb here and say, the preceding decade. But let me focus on my passions presently, as a function of three specific, time-separated, critical experiences in my life.

With each step at the Kennedy Space Centre in Florida, I feel increasingly at home. I am overwhelmed as I see an image of Kalpana Chawla on the memorial wall. I have always been in awe of her boldness. My idol. I smile and reflect on the strength I have derived from her words, 'The path from dreams to success does exist. May you have the vision to find it, the courage to get on to it, and the perseverance to follow it.'

Rewinding back in time, I remember my experiences at the Mind Museum, a world-class interactive science museum in Philippines.

'Hi, my name is Gitika Bose. I really appreciate your time and hope this new youth space research program excites you as much as it does me. I propose that....' My presentation deck is detailed and professional. Despite the museum director's heavy breathing, I remain confident and enthusiastic. The program is accepted.

I snap out of the past as the hour-long wait for NASA's 'Shuttle Launch Experience' comes to an end. I experience a rush of adrenaline that reminds me of when I first stumbled across space exploration as a curious fourteen-year-old. My brother took a break from his studies to go for a swim. I saw his senior year Physics textbook open, and instinctively perused its pages. Expecting a minimal level of interest, I was surprised to find my eyes glued to a chapter on Astrophysics. The future lay in the most advanced space technology and cutting-edge research. I naturally pursued the topic, nagging my brother for direction and consuming any information on the internet. Vast expanses of stars, black holes, supernovae, asteroids led me to contextualize my existence in a different perspective.

A challenge is what I call the modus operandi of growth. I faced one such challenge only moments after my successful pitch at the museum. On a fundamental level, the nature and origin of stars revolve around elementary scientific reactions. I am finally under the spotlight with my unique set of equipment, introducing one such reaction to 121 eager students. I finish the explanation with '...the brown coating is the copper deposited on the iron nail as it displaces iron.' Amidst the confused silence, I could hear my racing heartbeat. My first live demonstration. And there is no brown coating.

I stumble back on the podium, unnaturally smiling while murmuring a few 'umms'. I review all the steps and suddenly my eyes fall on the sandpaper lying on the ground. Of course! The nail had not rusted during my practice demonstration! Taking absolute responsibility, I apologize and repeat the process, this time successfully. It may have been an unusual first impression, but it forever solidified my ability to pay attention to details. As I proudly accept the Mind Museum's invitation to return and facilitate workshops, I bring with me a great longstanding passion, an experience-driven skill set, and a detail-oriented mindset.

The preceding three scenes are seemingly disconnected and yet they tie in very neatly into my dreams and aspirations.

Fast forward—let's drift back to the NASA tour. All my experiences and accomplishments seemed to foreshadow a future here, or so I hoped. I was looking at F-1 engines, command modules, space suits—the Apollo/Saturn V centre. The guide was describing the shuttle terminal velocity. My attention piqued, and I raised my hand instinctively with a question. All eyes turned towards me. I could just feel the tour guide think, 'Ugh, not another question from her again...'

OUR THOUGHTS ON GITIKA'S ESSAY

Drawing from her idol Kalpana Chawla's wish for others to materialize and live their boldest dreams, Gitika confidently expresses her NASA-centered calling by recollecting the discovery of her 'vision' and displaying the 'courage' to try. Keeping the reader engaged through her zigzags across the time continuum by cleverly employing signposting ('a function of three specific, time-separated, critical experiences'), she cleverly deploys non-sequential movements through time. Shooting off to critical moments in the past and looping back to her present at the Kennedy Space Centre, the essay's temporality encapsulates Gitika's belief that her life has been a largely intentional, sometime serendipitous lead-up to this moment.

We feel the anticipation and excitement on Gitika's part increasing, the closer she gets to the 'Shuttle Launch Experience'. The adrenaline triggers her memory of discovering Astrophysics; and we are transported. Coincidental as it is, the impact of reading her brother's Physics textbook has a mind-altering effect. Gitika finds purpose, as Astrophysics helps her understand her place in the universe. Her grand vision constitutes science and research, both in terms of her professional future *and* as the predicator for mankind's future. This early sense of belonging, discovery and belief power her endeavors as a patron and practitioner of science—from dreaming and thinking at home in Manila, to participating hands-on at the Mind Museum in Philippines and, ultimately, at NASA.

Gitika also comes across as spirited and gutsy. She is unabashed in asking questions, undaunted by the vastness of the unknown and unshrinking in the face of challenges. Her experience facilitating a workshop at the Mind Museum is a particularly well-chosen example of character. It demonstrates her ability to take initiative, her tenacious passion for science and her mercurial thought process. Faced with a public mistake, Gitika gets a hold of herself and owns up to her omission. She revisits her experiment, finds traction and gains a life lesson on the importance of detail.

As Gitika drifts back to the present for the final time, her faith in the vision she embraced and her courage to forge ahead are palpable. And as she persists with yet another question, Gitika leaves us with a reassurance of her tenacity and curiosity; and with the knowledge that soon, she will make a mark in the universe.

MANAN GOENKA

Princeton, Class of 2022

Major: Computer Science Engineering
School: Sishya School, Chennai, India
Hometown: Chennai, India

'Mom.... towel,' I called reflexively. Silence. I was alone in an Air BNB in Bangalore, far from home.

'We would love to introduce you to the concepts of rocket science, and you can learn by working with the team and getting some hands-on experience,' read the letter from Team Indus, the only Bangalore-based Indian team competing in the Google Lunar X-Prize competition (GLXP). This vindicated five months of effort. Though apprehensive, I was beyond thrilled that I, a sixteen-year-old, would work with world-class scientists and engineers to send a space rover to the moon.

So, what were they like? Up close and personal—cordial and totally dedicated. For Team Indus, engagements transcended 'office hours and rooms'. Heated volleys on colonizing Mars, SpaceX, artificial intelligence, space technologies, etc., the obsession for all things 'space' manifested through Star Wars-inspired nicknames and designations. I was R2D2 (someday I'll know why), the men's bathroom was Darth Vader. The bonding was priceless. Perhaps they saw their younger selves re-animate in us. Their infectious zeal had us exceed our briefs. Introduced to engineering software—SolidWorks, CATIA, CAD; I thrilled at their research on black holes and gravitational waves, their winning submissions for international competitions like Can Sat. Nights, in my

BNB, I'd contemplate the night sky; the stars became my destinations.

Their Axiom Research Lab, Northern Bangalore, resembled a sci-fi movie set with artificial moon terrain, 3D printing machines and prototype testing labs. Priceless platinum sheets, titanium cones and carbon fiber rods, once textbook concepts, emerged as spacecraft constituents. I was in my element.

Importantly, my approach to complex problems changed. Mr Srinivasan Hegde, a latter day Wehrner von Braun and ex-mission director of ISRO's lunar orbiter mission, mentored my final project. His journey from poverty to space legend, his unique teaching methods inspired me. He'd set a problem statement, no hints, unlimited time. The internet and aerospace engineering textbooks were my resources. On joining, I'd been provided with the GLXP competition parameters and tasked to curate a mission as Team Indus had. Daunted, I pondered, 'Where do I start?' Following four days of intense research, I designed a comprehensive plan that impressed all.

Moving onto GMAT (General Mission Analysis Tool) and STK (Systems Tool Kit) software for my final individual project, he continued setting problem statements; gratuitously, I engineered solutions consistently.

One day, I asked, 'Sir, if you explained the solutions, wouldn't things be expedited?'

'I took three months to resolve them,' he replied, driving home the point that complex problems often had simple solutions.

Working on designing a Lunar Transfer Trajectory, I obsessed over why the satellite wasn't getting captured in the moon's orbit. Seeing my distress, Hegde revealed that India's first satellite, Aryabhata, reached the launch site in a bullock cart as wood absorbs radiation. I learnt that adaptability defines successful engineering: no quick-fixes and paradoxically no analysis-paralysis. I revisited the issue, Eureka! The solution lay in a concept learned in 11th grade: Escape Velocity. The spacecraft's velocity needed to be below the moon's escape velocity to be captured. I reversed the thrust direction, mission accomplished. Simple!

Working with their mechanical, aerospace and chemical engineers, I forayed into each field and discovered my métier. A Team Indus friend and I conceived a unique spacecraft design, applied for patent, submitted it in a national competition. Returning, I created a YouTube series on orbital mechanics and the GMAT software I'd learned. Selection for the Rocket Simulator project at IITM was consequent to my GMAT/STK skills. At school, I questioned more, improving my grades significantly.

Beyond these 'spaced out' engagements, living alone was a crash course in growing up. Budgeting, cooking (noodles and adventures with tiered sandwiches), dusting, washing clothes, keeping abreast with schoolwork previewed adulthood. And Team Indus's engagement seemed easier than navigating heritage potholes through Bangalore streets and conducting heated cost-benefit analysis with fruit vendors.

And back home, I amazed Mom with my new-found culinary skills: tiered sandwiches for dinner, every Friday!

OUR THOUGHTS ON MANAN'S ESSAY

Growth often hinges on moments where we find ourselves isolated from our comfort zone, living far away from familiar ideas, people, and places. While Manan's essay adheres to this convention and begins with the realization that the ecosystem in which he finds himself is alien, his description of time spent as a member of Team Indus projects him reveling in being outside familiar territory. Told through a spirited, animated account filled with dialogue, learnings and witty nooks of narration, the account brings to fore Manan's playful and adventurous spirit.

This essay revolves around Manan's passion for Astronomy. While never overtly stated, his selection for a team chosen for the Google

Lunar X competition speaks volumes about his early expertise in cosmology and his commitment to the scientific exploration of space. Manan takes the risk of delving into somewhat esoteric and advanced conceptual topics and discussing technical project-related details sans explanations and signposting. However, his narrative voice is so well placed in his essay that these details are revelatory instead of seeming obfuscating or technically condescending. Retellings of discussions on the ethical and technical challenges of space exploration are balanced with relatable references to Star Wars (R2D2 and Darth Vader) and existential culinary adventurism (tiered sandwiches and two-minute noodles). Most effective of all is Manan himself, who communicates each new challenge and interaction wrapped in genuine wonder and curiosity ('resembling a sci-fi movie set'), effectively making space for a reader's potential unfamiliarity.

Consequently, the essay reads like a (space) voyage of self-discovery, launched by his passion, sustained through holistic growth, and guided by the relationships he builds along the way. There are planetary influences—the defining mentorship offered by Mr Srinivasan Hegde who encourages Manan to solve problems himself rather than providing him answers, for example. We also see his burgeoning partnership and camaraderie with an unnamed teammate who he goes on to work with on patenting an original spacecraft design. Most importantly, however, we see Manan find his métier and emerge as a more evolved and settled version of himself, one that has found 'his element' by stepping out of his secure milieu.

RIYAAN BAKHDA

Columbia, Class of 2024

Major: Computer Science
School: Dhirubhai Ambani International School, Mumbai, India
Hometown: Mumbai, India

THIS BOMBAY BIRDER'S BANANA REPUBLIC

'As a child I learned to spell "banana". I didn't know when to stop.'—R. Bakhda

Greetings from Mumbai, India's cultural melting pot, famed for inclusion, pollution, and ridiculously boisterous traffic! Encircling this vibrant concrete jungle is another albeit verdant jungle, the Sanjay Gandhi National Park, lungs of the metropolis and natural safe haven for those sharing my love for the green and tranquil—and for breathing!

Returning triumphant from an Australian robotics expedition awash with algorithms, wiring and computers, I hit the forests with packed breakfast, bird-encyclopedia, binoculars and impeccable cartography knowledge to continue my self-given mission of scribing my nature almanac:

'The Bombay Nature's Booklet'.

Cresting a hill, I perched atop a boulder and gazed at distant dumping grounds and ancient rivers stilled by city waste. Grimacing at this plastic overuse, I drew from my backpack, somewhat inappropriately, a plastic-wrapped repast of tomato sandwiches. Feasting amongst banana trees, I recalled 'sadhya', a South Indian tradition wherein food was packed in banana leaves, and instinctively Googled the premise behind this age-old praxis. And thereby hangs a tale.

Hornbills, Owlets, Woodpeckers, Bulbuls, and Drongos chirped curiously at my overly-human-self, invading their feral neighbourhood. I stumbled across studies explaining how banana leaves' durability, water-resistance and anti-bacterial properties made them ideal food packaging of yore. I also discovered 106 million tons of banana leaves were slashed annually in India. Like Newton's iconic apple chronicle, a banana-inspired epiphany struck:

Can leaves replace plastic in food packaging?

Perhaps it sounds preposterous but linger awhile... Humans use invisible communication waves, fly heavier-than-air machines; sounds absurd, but it works! As a veteran of countless similar innovations, I knew technology could bring resolve. Once home, I resumed toiling: using CAD to visualize numerous versions of a food-wrapping machine. Weeks of sleepless nights followed as I struggled to make the CAD rendering a reality.

I started at base level: using Lego pieces that built my childhood to construct a 'framework prototype' before upgrading to aluminum and 3D-printing. Bringing into play image-processing algorithms learned while leading the programming troupe of my FIRST Robotics Competition team, I implemented a diseased leaf identifier. Machine Learning knowledge from my four-year-long automated speech pathology initiative optimized my leaf-cutting procedures. The Raspberry Pi circuitry skill set acquired while building my landslide detection prototype helped me code a large array of sensors. And thus, pursuing this packaging machine, I forged Frankenstein's Tech-Monster: a patchwork body assimilating assorted skills I'd mastered as a self-proclaimed technology guru.

And then, the day of the first trial arrived. Alas, in operation, the prototype failed repeatedly as leaves tore when bent 90 degrees.

I simply didn't know how to proceed and sulked for weeks, before swallowing my pride and accepting that bringing in other hands and minds could help.

Soon enough, I assembled a team and mentor for my crusade. I delegated work to my teammates—two Biochemistry students whose initial expressions of skepticism yet haunt me. We spent weeks devising a chemical method to strengthen and sterilize leaves before finally succeeding. After fine-tuning, the prototype took leaves, processed and cut them with surgical precision, input food, and dispensed a single sealed package. The prototype, christened EverGreen, had evolved from chimera fiction into an 'Automated Organic Food Packaging System'.

We signed up for the World Robotics Olympiad and, fortuitously, my 'banana dream' conjured on a trek won the Gold Medal at the national level, and Rank 6 at the international level. And the saga continued! After being featured as 'Children of the Planet' in an exclusive newspaper article, my team awoke one day to an acquisition offer from the company designing packages for Uber-Eats in Mumbai.

Sometimes, it bothers me that worldly problems are infinite, that things rarely harmonize with human ambition. But then, I remember that the passion and ingenuity we employ to solve such problems transformed us from cave-dwellers to moon-walkers.

Now if I could find use for banana skins...

OUR THOUGHTS ON RIYAAN'S ESSAY

Five key elements of storytelling intermingle in Riyaan's enthralling essay: Setting, Character, Plot, Conflict and Resolution, and these jointly and severally communicate his riveting profile.

The title, to begin with, is an engaging framing device. Whimsical and alliterative, the idea of a 'Bombay Birder' running a 'Banana Republic' is a great hook, and the absurdist humor that makes it so is expertly emphasized by Riyaan's quote in the beginning—refreshingly, his own. Playing on the 'na' repetition at the end of the banana, we understand that his zany writing style is representative of who he is, and not just a writing tool. This is the first inkling of character we get before we even get to the body of the essay!

Setting and character blend in the essay's first half: we, the readers, are irresistibly introduced to Riyaan as the titular 'Bombay Birder' and bird watcher. Introducing his connection to nature, he, almost diffidently, introduces us to his expertise in robotics in the same breath as his routine of escaping city life to bird-watch (and breathe). Riyaan's atmospheric descriptions of the flora and setting surrounding him convey his investment in environmentalism, which manifests as a tangible anchor for his later efforts.

As the banana leaves that surround him get the wheels in Riyaan's mind turning, we have the rumblings of a plot. The absurdity of him discovering this while crouched silently on a hill advances his colorful account, a curious counter to the tech-centric aspect of Riyaan's other work. All of this keeps the essay alive and accessible. As the narrative advances, his belief in science's limitless capacity adds gravitas to his character and explains his ability to imagine the impossible, and then act on it. Through this, the essay's conflict is strikingly believable. There are days of reckoning and doubt, but the resolution demonstrates Riyaan's growth. In his attempts to build a functioning banana-wrap machine, he recognizes the value of diverse perspectives and teamwork in his Banana Republic.

The Bombay Birder and his Banana Republic exist in a finite universe, with a beginning, middle and end. And even as it concludes with an engaging continuum to his opening line, we know that Riyaan and his I-can-fix-it universe is ever-expanding.

VARUN VENKATESH

Yale, Class of 2023

Major: Economics
School: Tanglin Trust School, Singapore
Hometown: Singapore

I'm sitting at my piano. On it rests a catalogue of sheet music spanning time and genre (Tchaikovsky to The Weeknd), a metronome, and a photo-frame. In that frame is a photo of me dancing in a diaper, in brazen defiance of public decorum. My parents say it was to Miles Davis's *Blues by Five*. Its textured, modal richness continues to enamor me all these years later; it also happens to be the piece that I'm going to play for you today.

I begin with a medium swing to get your foot tapping. My fingers have a mind of their own, but if you watch them closely, you'll notice that my left and right hands are responsible for distinct halves of the piece: one is prescriptive and the other subjective.

In the bass clef, I play the chord voicings notated on my score. I spend as much time studying jazz as I do playing it. I marvel at the mathematical beauty of the twelve bar blues progression and the influence of indigenous West African cultures on jazz scales, and I reflect on how the genre is a product of contextual patterns as much as empirical ones. You may think that notation limits me, but this isn't true; in fact, it helps me appreciate the melodies on a profound level, motivating me to keep improving so that I can do them justice.

My right hand, however, takes the liberty to improvize and innovate.

It took me a while to feel confident enough in my understanding of technique to step out of the shadow of sheet music. Take the chromatic scale: I've been playing it since I was five years old but applying it in a novel way to express or elicit emotion is a different challenge altogether. In this way, jazz has pushed me both intellectually and personally, helping me realize that I can take a jazz standard, season it with my own flavor, and it will still be appreciated and enjoyed. When I'm bored after a long day, I'm in the mood for something crispy: I'll take a normal chord and sharpen the ninth, just like a Nutella milkshake made crunchy by the addition of some cornflakes (the Varun Special). When I'm feeling down, I fool around with the Coltrane changes: much like adding miso to a chicken soup, it's warm and comforting.

OOPS.

My fingers slip from a Db to a D. I hear some dreaded dissonance and feel a glimmer of panic—like being caught off guard by a point of information at a debate. But it's in these moments that my fingers—and my ideas—feel most alive. Every piece is a new conversation with the composer, the piano, and myself. Can I turn this around with a chord modulation? Or is this 'mistake' a new avenue to explore?

My band joins in with a *Billie's Bounce* interlude after my solo. I feel the beat in my pulse, but the syncopation keeps throwing me off. Tom jumps in with a sax run, and Guiliano glorifies my mistiming with a virtuosic drum fill. Intuitively, we riff off of each other's ideas and critique each other's solos; there's nothing quite like our symbiosis. For the last four years, we have been musical explorers: The Miles Davis quintet for the unacquainted.

The piece ends. The room is silent. I hope you enjoyed it. I know it might not have been perfect, but perfection wasn't my goal: I was only looking to exist in that liminal space between my left and right hand, the prescribed and the emotive, where mistakes turn into melodies and the line between the individual and ensemble is blurred. Most of all, I was trying to show you that while I'm an eighteen-year-old pianist on the outside, jazz makes me feel the euphoric glee of a two-year-old dancing in a diaper on the inside.

OUR THOUGHTS ON VARUN'S ESSAY

Varun builds up instant reader interest with the first two sentences of his essay in a unique way. What will he choose? The photo-frame! Indicating a childhood story is coming up, he then describes himself 'dancing in a diaper… to Miles Davis's *Blues by Five*'. THE ART OF CUTE! He hooks his reader's emotions right from the start. He establishes his sustained joy and interest in jazz music, as also his pursuit, and possible mastery of the medium. '…in brazen defiance of public decorum', hinting at what we just might hear about his personality.

Varun uses sensory vocabulary like 'textured, modal richness' to get readers further invested in what he promises he is 'going to play for you today'. And proceeds to lead readers into a detailed and physical tour through his musical process 'if you watch closely'. It soon enough becomes clear that Varun is using his music-making as a metaphor for his general thinking process—a fusion of 'prescriptive and… subjective'; 'mathematical beauty'; 'product of contextual patterns as much as empirical ones'. These, he tells us lightly, he spends 'as much time studying… as [I] do playing'.

Varun continues in this vein, explaining how jazz pushes him as an individual. Academically, jazz is his respite and fuel, enabling him 'to step out of the shadow of [prescriptive] sheet music'. He shows readers how he has learnt to enrich a jazz standard, perhaps a metaphor for traditional thinking, adding his own emotional 'flavor'. Then, steps up the sensory experience with a comparison to his experimental mix of foods—sharpening a 9th like adding crunchy cornflakes to a Nutella milkshake, or Coltrane changes like adding a miso kick to chicken soup.

He brings you back to the present with an 'OOPS', like he has gone too far, and flubbed—'caught off guard by a point of information at a debate'—which, however, leads to inventiveness and 'ideas [that] feel most alive'. There are the inevitable and exciting errors which provide new routes to explore, giving us a sense of his campus self. He also takes care to display his symbiotic teamwork skills with like-minded peers who 'intuitively... riff off of each other's ideas and critique each other's solos'. Finally reminding readers that the 'eighteen-year-old pianist on the outside' is still 'the euphoric... two-year-old dancing in a diaper on the inside', Varun deftly connects his conclusion to his introduction. Similarly, his ideas connect to action, and even blunders that inevitably underpin new learning, thereby demonstrating an inherent lively mastery over his own learning process.

YAASHREE HIMATSINGKA

Princeton, Class of 2023

Major: Public and International Affairs
School: The Cathedral & John Connon School, Mumbai, India
Hometown: Mumbai, India

DIVING INTO COLOR

Brushes, dirty rags, 300 GSM cold-pressed paper and my *Schmincke* watercolors lie scattered on the dining table I have commandeered, despite my family's protests.

This is my comfort zone.

But there is a world beyond Schmincke and cold-pressed paper. Art has led me to take risks, so antithetical to the girl who was once obsessed with perfect gradients, straight lines and full stops. Terrified of making mistakes, I'd shy away from lively colors, experimentation and working directly on canvas. My art thrived in an excruciatingly detailed realm of black, white and grey.

All of that changed—and still is changing. It wasn't brought about by a sudden revelation, but by little ongoing challenges—drawing without a reference, preserving the 'rawness' of an observational piece by leaving off a finishing coat or working extempore.

Daring strips of intense color in unexpected places yet contributing a fine balance to the whole, unconventional media (Jenga blocks? Scrap metal?) and gestural, Impressionist strokes that capture the light bouncing off water—these are now defining features of my work. I've learned that Art isn't necessarily a function of technical ability, superb visualization and spatial and tonal awareness; it needn't always be aesthetically appealing. Real art takes courage; it involves embracing uncertainty with excitement—the idea that something beautiful hidden within, paradoxically, will emerge after laying on *more* coats of paint!

Inspiration for pieces comes in personal, wacky and non-traditional flavors. Pulling stimulus from Sagan's *Pale Blue Dot*, 'Cog in the Wheel' involves viewers contributing to a growing doodle on a long roll of paper from a dispenser—the deeper message being that we're all part of something bigger than ourselves, like cogs in a wheel (and that's not a bad thing!). 'Necessary Evil'—a chessboard inspired by Star Wars and the *Gita* (a defining philosophical text) has pieces made of wooden pegs, embodying the equilibrium between harmony and chaos; 'Four Seasons II' features fresh seasonal flowers nailed to wooden chopping boards, a synesthetic representation of Vivaldi's *The Four Seasons*.

And Art can be a powerful explanatory tool. While simplifying complex ecological concepts from Dr Ulanowicz's book, *A Third Window*, I used illustrations to deconstruct challenging ideas. Can't autocatalytic centripetal-ity be explained through a cyclone converging the surrounding ecosystem resources inwards? Isn't the interplay between ascendency and overhead very much like the dynamic between members of a soccer team?

Art led me to explore the interconnectivity between different interests and disciplines. Studying chemical equilibria inspired film-based renditions of the cobalt-chloride reaction. Studying Nazi propaganda in History compelled me to delve deeper into 'degenerate art', provoking an entire extended essay on the topic. An exhibition on Escher drew me to tessellations and hyperbolic geometry, sparking an exploration that mathematically analyzed three of his works. Experimentation with black felt-tip pens and water, causing the pigments to bleed, led me to investigate the use of paper chromatography in paint-media analysis and art conservation. An interest in global affairs and the fragile geopolitical balance provoked 'Troubled Waters' – a representation of 21st century international diplomacy.

And through Art, I expressed my insecurities. Angry, uncontrolled sketches with sticks of charcoal gave body to intangible anxieties and abstract emotions. Tearing the paper up after releasing those feelings. 'Scattered' is a representation of the days I feel overwhelmed, torn between priorities. After a week of stressful administration devising a suitable exam timetable, I sought refuge in painting. Norah Jones's *Shoot the Moon* and soft pastels provided a space for me to vent locked-up frustrations and shore up emotional strength.

Art heals and nurtures. It completes me, permeating every facet of my being. My works evolve as I do, with experimentation and discovery. My set of *Shmincke* watercolors will remain a constant—a point of comforting familiarity; but I won't forget to take with me everything else I have derived from Art—curiosity, strength and the courage to walk on the edge.

OUR THOUGHTS ON YAASHREE'S ESSAY

This vivid, raw piece of writing opens a window into Yaashree's soul—the best essays we have seen are vulnerable and reflective, and this is one of them. Yaashree seamlessly uses art as a lens to tell the reader about herself. We particularly like how she begins the essay with a vulnerability, describing herself as someone who shies away from risk, because it projects a confidence and, paradoxically, an openness to change and embracing the unknown. The risk aversion is manifested through art. It also changes through art.

Yaashree's foray out of her comfort zone of muted greys and neutrals did not happen with a 'leap', but rather through progressive baby steps. Most changes in life happen in this way, but the compelling fact is that she made a conscious effort to change, incorporating color or unorthodox methods. She shows her progress through the shifts in her approach to art and admits to this progress being ongoing. The power of her essay lies in the understanding that meaningful change is a process, not a destination, and often, the process is, in itself, rewarding.

We also see how Yaashree uses art as a medium to understand and engage with the world. Chemistry and lessons from history can be deconstructed and sublimated into paintings and installations. The sources for these artworks are varied, indicating that while Yaashree is focused on nurturing her craft, she draws inspiration from all things, however disparate they may be. We can assume that the art pieces she discusses were included in her application, and so her already vivid descriptions would be amplified with the portfolio as a reference.

And finally, art is catharsis. It is a way to de-stress, process difficult feelings and counter angst. It is a way to reflect, and it is, potentially, a constant in a changing world. This essay leaves the reader with the sense that they know who Yaashree is—a dynamic, curious, thoughtful artist who will never stop learning and evolving, and will likely continue to use art, to reflect and process change. While Yaashree and her art may shift in tandem, the existence of art itself will not, a surety for someone for whom art is both an anchor, and a tool.

GAYATRI MESWANI

Harvard, Class of 2024

Major: Psychology
School: Dhirubhai Ambani International School, Mumbai, India
Hometown: Mumbai, India

'Ms Meswani,' cried the hotel security guard, 'Please open the door! There's smoke in the hallway and the alarm has been tripped!'

Let me explain.

My culinary journey began with measured quantities. When I started baking cookies, cakes, and Indian *mithai*, I learnt that precision was paramount. Exactly half a teaspoon of vanilla: any less would be imperceptible and any more would make the batter bitter.

The mechanical aspect of baking enticed me: measured inputs produced logical outcomes. Whether I was folding *galettes* at French preschool or rolling *gulab jamun* at my grandmother's, the predictability of the process put me at ease. This gave me the confidence to experiment within the safety of my formulaic bubble, substituting a new flour in my cookies or a mix-in for my brownies. In this binary mindset, switching one ingredient at a time for an alternative, I etched the 'successful' variations into my recipe book and discarded everything else.

As I matured, so did my palate. I encountered new flavors and dishes presented in ways the traditional baker in me feared anarchic. Yet, I began to suspect that my binary swaps limited, rather than enabled, innovation. My inelastic view of what defined good and bad food kept me from generating my own ideas. Sticking within the confines of a recipe restricted the skills I could learn and the creativity that culinary expression could evoke.

I turned to Nanima, my grandmother and an incredible cook, to help me escape the monotony. Our weekly lunches included my favorite, *sukha batata*, squares of potato sautéed in spices, which I resolved to make as my first venture beyond baking. I began by adding spices to the oil. They sunk to the bottom, congealing in a way that never happened when Nanima made them. I called her for help. Her diagnosis? The oil was too cold. I started over, this time waiting for the oil to heat up. As soon as I added my spices, the oil sizzled and spat like a rabid dog. I plopped my potatoes into this hellfire as oil droplets scalded my forearm. Overwhelmed, I emptied the atrocity into the sink. A mushroom-cloud of smoke filled the kitchen as the scorching oil collided with the cold tap-water.

I kept trying. Eventually, I achieved edibility, but my *sukha batata* just wasn't what Nanima makes. 'Gaya,' she sighed, 'you'll never cook this dish as well as I do,' she said frankly, deflating my aspirations like a sunken soufflé. 'This is my masterpiece; you need to find yours.' She was right. Her *sukha batata* is the culmination of decades spent perfecting her masala blend, the foundation of the dish. What was my foundation?

I had begun by baking, focusing on precision. It dawned on me that precision, which I had considered a limiting factor, was my foundation. My potato recipe had to play to my strengths: knife skills and presentation. I devoured recipes for mashed potatoes, rösti, potatoes *dauphinoise*, *aligot*, gnocchi, *batata harra*, any variant of this ostensibly pedestrian, yet versatile ingredient I could find. I began testing. I tried scoring the potato, increasing the surface area to allow the spices to infuse the flesh. Next, I experimented with frying oils and spice blends. My potatoes burnt in olive oil because of its low smoke point (simultaneously teaching me that hotel room kitchenettes are horrible sites for such experimentation). Eventually, I stopped discarding my dishes because cooking is about progress, not perfection. I learned to adapt rather than regress.

Failure taught me more about cooking than any book ever could. The deceptively difficult task of cooking a potato pushed me to look at my 'failures' as starting points for success rather than outcomes to be avoided. I began extracting what I could from each attempt. Yes, eventually I achieved a potato recipe I was proud of, but by then, that was hardly the point.

OUR THOUGHTS ON GAYATRI'S ESSAY

Gayatri invites us into her kitchen. Beyond the meticulous measure-and-make baking that centers her, and Nanima's stellar melt-in-mouth *sukha batata* that frustrates her every effort, she invites us to taste her vulnerabilities and successes in food-related avatars. Accessing a particular kind of culinary realism where the right temperature of the oil long remains elusive and aspirations can deflate like 'sunken soufflés', Gayatri tells us an engaging story of her happy trysts with failure.

Witnessing Gayatri's quest for 'successful' recipes where she doggedly experiments for the method that will deliver and 'discards the rest', we get the sense that she will settle for nothing less than perfection. She thrives in the structured and ordered universe where she knows that *galettes* are folded and *gulab jamuns* are rolled. Gayatri communicates this through her well-expounded cooking methods, which are neat, precise, and comfortable in their predictability. However, as her tastes evolve and expand, the premise that there ever can be a definitive universe of ingredients and methods, and a static understanding of quality is repudiated. Challenging her idea of a 'successful' dish, this moves the narrative to Gayatri's Nanima whose elusive *sukha batatas* prove to be a red herring if not a nemesis. Convinced that the recipe holds the key to elevating her cooking, Gayatri tries, and tries again, to make the potatoes just like her grandmother. We can feel her frustration here, deftly expressed through a sizzling pan and a smoke-filled kitchen, and her attempts to figure out where she has gone wrong.

Some of the most important life lessons come from a shift in perspective, a new way of framing things that makes everything seem like they have fallen into place. The transformation is subtle, helped by Gayatri's Nanima asking her to stop trying to be the best version of someone else and 'find her own masterpiece'. Accepting this, Gayatri goes back to what she knows and rediscovers her love for cooking. Again, we feel the change in the culinary imagery she employs, as 'congealing' and 'plopping' give way to 'scoring' and 'infusion'.

By accepting her limitations and the inevitability of failure, Gayatri evolves. The experimentation might continue, but the focus is on the process now, rather than perfection.

PRANAV CHANDRASEKARAN

Yale, Class of 2020

Major: Computer Science and Psychology
School: B.D. Somani International School, Mumbai, India
Hometown: Mumbai, India

Our Lady of Salvation Church with its striking green walls and its beautiful yet minimalist bell tower stands apart from the cookie-cutter shoebox apartments surrounding it. Known affectionately as 'Portuguese Church' by all, it is a recognizable landmark. Every Sunday at six, the church bells peal, calling the faithful to mass. My teacher, Ms Bridget, lives in a small apartment crowded by an ancient upright piano and two chairs. Her apartment building, opposite the Portuguese Church, in its pedestrian aesthetic, starkly contrasts with the church's majesty.

Awaiting my call to stage, I gaze at my concert program and consider the influence of the pealing of the bells on my music. As I entered the building every Sunday, the bells would usher me to sit before the altar of my art.

Scanning the program, an *Allegro*, the first movement of Dussek's Sonatina Op. 20 No. 6 floats before my eyes. Its speed and majesty echo as I stare at my left hand's ring finger, slightly crooked from a fracture I had incurred while learning the piece. Though minor, it apparently necessitated surgery. Through the ever-present pain, I worried I'd be unable to play the demanding *Allegro* with the precision it required. Nonetheless, I tried. A week later the doctor, surprised, declared that the correctional surgery was unnecessary. The keyboard acrobatics required to play the *Allegro* had moved the bone neatly into position; my fractured finger had healed on the long road to excellence. Resounding applause and appreciative nods from my audience brought the knowledge that my performance had been flawless.

As a pianist, my music is my medium to communicate with the audience. A slow, nostalgic jazz piece transports listeners to a dreamy world and the riveting notes of the tango keep audiences enthralled. I share a silent bond with the audience, punctuated by the lilting notes of Mozart and sometimes the masterly symphonic poems of Liszt. The headiness of a standing ovation is ineffable, the elation of congratulation irreplaceable. And you know you have brought at least an hour's happiness to many.

I glance down and see the first movement of Mozart's Sonata k. 545; learning this taught me true happiness, and knowledge that fulfillment comes only through assiduous labor, in this case, perfect technique and dynamic control. This is compounded by the fact that playing a piece the easier way—at a slower pace than it warrants or eschewing some difficult technical elements—makes me feel inadequate. I now aspire to play complex pieces in the most challenging modes. I loved playing the magical Sonata at a slow pace. Yet, Ms Bridget played the piece for me at an accelerated speed that required considerable dexterity and expertise. Inspired, I played it faster, with perfect technique. Though my hands hurt and wrists swelled, I spent several hours weekly working on my technique until I could play at the same pace as her. The first time I played it immaculately at the increased tempo I was filled with a contentment that vindicated all the toil and practice it entailed. As a budding concert pianist, I immerse fully in my art and the months of disciplined practice leave no room for error. The notes are held in memory and I play effortlessly with them cueing in my mind's eye and my fingers stroking the keys. This, to me, is bliss! This 'expertise' taught by Ms Bridget through exercise and example brought me the happiness of achievement.

Sitting at the piano, lightly caressing its cold keys, I wondered if I had selected the pieces wisely and awaited my cue. Was the first movement of Mozart's Sonata k. 545 appropriate? I sighed and glanced at the front row. Seeing the expectant faces of my parents, the principal of my school and my teachers filled me with confidence. Ms Bridget entered the hall. I smiled and struck the first note.

OUR THOUGHTS ON PRANAV'S ESSAY

Pranav enjoys challenging himself and is an ardent worker, apparent in his beautifully wrought essay. His narrative describes how his traits and his defining moments manifested and progressed. While scribing this, Pranav takes care to describe his setting in vivid detail—the green-walled Portuguese Church, his piano teacher's spare lodgings, his broken finger—to enfold the reader in the telling of the tale.

Music evidently circumscribes much of Pranav's life in time and importance. He addresses the assortment of pieces he has learned, hinting at the diversity of what he has studied and zeroing in on the two that have deeply affected him. Dussek's Sonatina fractured his finger and brought him considerable existential angst—would he be able to play it with the speed and precision he wanted to post-surgery? Through this self-deprecatory yet humorous anecdote, Pranav reveals that he persists through pain, and all ends well—that all that ailed also healed, literally and figuratively. The happy denouement to the tale is that the music that brings joy to his audience, if only for a brief moment, also snapped his broken finger back into place.

The Dussek incident is a prelude to how Pranav labored to perfect his rendition of a Mozart's sonata. In describing how he learned to play the piece, he refrains from flaunting his undoubted talent but rather focuses on his philosophy and work ethic. He is ambitious and eager to take on more technically challenging pieces. However, there are no shortcuts—he practises feverishly, often through pain and fatigue, to master the piece. Yet, there is compassion, and a recognition that his playing for audiences provides happiness, something that Pranav clearly finds meaningful. We love that he does not shy from acknowledging his teacher's role in building his virtuosity—in the last paragraph when we see him awaiting his cue, we know viscerally that he is also awaiting his teacher's appearance to share his moment in the sun. We are left with the feeling that the kindness, perseverance, and confidence that music has imbued in Pranav will guide him through life's myriad challenges as well.

4

REFLECTORS AND MUSERS

'Life moves pretty fast. If you don't stop and look around once in a while, you could miss it.'

– Ferris Bueller

It is easy to get caught up in the crests and troughs of life. Especially in the maelstrom of fast-paced competitive college applications, where taking a moment to step back and process things can seem counter-intuitive. The essayists in this section take that risk. For them, success and failure are not to be recorded, but rather, experienced as moments of self-reflection and contemplation.

Determinedly asking why, the narrators turn inward, going back to examine the very criteria of success that they are judged by. Questioning positions, parameters and privilege, rich inner monologues ensue that distinguish their writing, revealing a sensitivity and dexterity of thought well beyond their years.

AKSHAY KANORIA

UPenn, Class of 2014

Major: International Studies and Economics (Huntsman Program)
School: Dhirubhai Ambani International School, Mumbai, India
Hometown: Mumbai, India

My introduction to meditation has had the deepest impact upon me. My teacher, Tashi, an avid meditator, was a forty-year-old convert to Buddhism, who was very glad to pass his knowledge on to me.

This past summer, I spent three weeks at a former Tibetan monastery, in the monastery town of Bir, nestled in the beautiful Himalayan mountain ranges of Northern India. It had been a Buddhist monastery until it could not accommodate any more monks and was subsequently converted into an institute for spreading Tibetan culture. I read about the town in a travel magazine. The monastery regularly accepted residents from the outside and, after some research, I decided it was something I had to do. The experience has left an indelible impact on me.

Over a period of several weeks, our practices evolved from simple breathing exercises to far more complex ones that required me to focus all my effort and concentration on the images that Tashi wanted me to conjure in my mind and hold there. The end of each session left me feeling calmer and happier, free of the daily worries that keep eating away at us.

Before visiting the institute, writing this essay or undertaking any task involving prolonged concentration, was hard for me. Earlier, I would have succumbed to a thousand wavering thoughts and environmental distractions; but now, all I have to do is close my eyes, breathe deeply for a few seconds, and restore my composition.

My daily schedule involved an hour and a half each morning and each evening devoted to silent meditation, under the direction of one of the permanent residents. We then spent time reading Buddhist philosophy at the monastery's library, followed by discussions with Tashi and the monastery's manager. In between, I did 'shraamdan' or community service in the form of cutting grass, teaching the kitchen boys English or whitewashing the kitchen walls.

One of the lessons that I particularly cherished was meditating with my eyes open, while walking around the temple in circles. As we walked around the temple barefoot in measured steps, Tashi would slowly tell us to become conscious of the things around us, while at the same time reminding us to keep our minds focused. I remember suddenly becoming aware for the first time of the precise texture and feel of the ground underneath me, in spite of having walked there for days, and noticing the many minuscule insects crawling on the ground in front of me, things I would not have noticed otherwise. I began taking in the intricate details present in everything around me and took special care not to step on the tiny ants which would easily have escaped my attention otherwise.

This heightened sensitivity to the environment was startling at first. I vividly remember frantically calling out to one of the other boys who had stepped on an ant when playing with his dog, and the immense satisfaction I felt when he lifted his leg, and the tiny ant was still alive. My meditation exercises instilled in me an appreciation for detail (my newfound appreciation for art, for example) and a serenity that has improved my interactions with others. Especially as a School Prefect and House Captain, my short temper often caused me to react non-commensurately to such situations.

Today, a great degree of objectivity and maturity allows me to calmly deal with otherwise trying issues. My experience at Bir has wrought a profound change upon my personal development. It has taught me to be more aware of and empathize with others. I have improved, not only as a communicator, but also as a human being. The memories of my time there will always be cherished, and the learning manifested every minute of every day.

OUR THOUGHTS ON AKSHAY'S ESSAY

Akshay's essay is a balm for the mind! The simplicity and fluidity of his writing touches and evokes a serenity, an almost meditative quality, not often found in Common App essays. His description of his time at the 'former Tibetan monastery, in the monastery town of Bir' effectively transports one to this tranquil hamlet 'nestled in the beautiful Himalayan mountain ranges of Northern India'. We visualize being there, with him.

Akshay talks about his past self, before Tashi, his mentor, passed 'his knowledge on to me', in tones that are gentle, almost apologetic—'Before visiting the institute, writing this essay or undertaking any task involving prolonged concentration, was hard for me.' This stands testimony to his much 'calmer and happier' overall disposition following his meditative journey of self-restoration.

Akshay's monastic experience seems to have done more than empower him with self-knowledge. He refers to daily 'shraamdan', selfless service towards others around him. He especially cherishes becoming 'conscious of the things around [us], while at the same time reminding [us] to keep our minds focused.'

He refers to how this practice in mindfulness has expanded his awareness to newly perceived information about 'the precise texture and feel of the ground underneath me, in spite of having walked there for days, and noticing the many minuscule insects crawling on the ground in front of me, things I would not have noticed otherwise... taking in the intricate details present in everything around me…'; lines that clearly convey how even the tiniest life-forms have taken on huge value for him. The humility with which Akshay recounts being startled by his own responses to this 'heightened sensitivity' is refreshing.

Akshay explains how his 'newfound appreciation' for detail was expansive, and enlarged his interests. Meditation lent objectivity and maturity—skills that are idyllic on a college campus. These, he reflected, seamlessly transited into school responsibilities, and his knee-jerk response to trying situations, where his 'short temper often caused [him] to react non-commensurately'.

Akshay presents his renewal persuasively, through demonstrating the 'profound change' in his 'personal development… not only as a communicator, but also as a human being'. Aspects of Akshay's character and strengths become crystalline, reflecting in the fluid grace of his words, as he relates his life-changing experience to the reader with such composure.

VISHWESH DESAI

UPenn, Class of 2024

Major: English
School: The Riverside School, Ahmedabad, India
Hometown: Ahmedabad, India

'So, Mr Desai, could you tell me about your new venture in more detail?' the journalist asked.

I was sipping chai in the Authors' Lounge at the Gujarat Literature Festival, immediately after my creative writing workshop, speaking to a local newspaper about my most ambitious project yet.

'Inklings Writing Center is India's first online writing center offering online courses, one-on-one mentoring, and editing services. Our courses on varied writing forms are conducted by experts in their field. Our Advisory Board includes eminent figures from literature, education, art and culture.'

I was teaching the short fiction course myself and had convinced experts to back an idea never before executed in the country. I considered it a major coup roping in instructors such as Kusum Choppra, who redefined a chapter in Maratha history, and award-winning theater artist Chintan Pandya, who performs in five languages across twenty countries.

'What made you think of doing this?'

'I've always wanted to give back to the community of writers that shaped me. Initially, I engaged with students and conducted workshops to mentor aspiring writers. However, I realized that the greatest problem fettering writers-in-the-making was the lack of learning platforms. And so, taking a cue from western writing centers, I resolved to create one of my own, tailored to Indian writers.'

I had long considered writing my calling, having published several short stories and a 135,000-word novel by the time I was fourteen. In June 2019, I edited and published an anthology of short stories written by students under my Project Bibliophilia. I regularly conducted creative writing workshops for participants ranging from four-year-olds to final-year university students.

The workshop model had limited reach and I wished for easier access to writing resources, allowing writers to pursue their passion unhindered by workaday obligations. This sparked the idea of an online writing center. I'd been promoting it at literature festivals, which was why I was here.

'What's your business model like?'

'We're a non-profit,' I explained. 'The instructors receive most of the course revenue and we retain a small percentage for administrative expenses.'

The Center is an initiative of Inklings Education Foundation, which I had founded and set up as a Section 8 company under the Indian Companies Act 2013 in October 2019. I'd spoken to tax and management experts to learn the process of registering a non-profit, the compliances, paperwork and legalities. I'd also met professors from India's flagship entrepreneurship school, EDII, to determine my business model. To save costs, I watched online tutorials and built the website on WordPress myself.

'Do you have a philosophy for the Center?'

I hesitated for a moment. I hadn't thought of a philosophy, but there was an ideal I wished to uphold.

'I find writing both an escape from and a bridge to reality, simultaneously creating new worlds and making better sense of ours. Writing is a vehicle of change, shaping perspective and building a sense of actualization. Writers like Franz Kafka and Fyodor Dostoevsky have influenced thinking and challenged societal norms, building a better world by exploring the human condition like none before them. I've always believed that a writer lies within every reader, and our mission is to provide that writer a path and platform to shine. We have something for every writer at every stage of their writing journey, drawing inspiration from the works of literary greats to move forward.'

'That's a wonderful sentiment. Lastly, why did you name it Inklings?'

'In the 1940s at Oxford, a literary discussion group of great authors including CS Lewis and JRR Tolkien called themselves the "Inklings". They discovered that they amplified their skills through sharing. The name is a salute to them.'

As usual, when I stepped out of the Authors' Lounge, I was greeted by workshop participants who ardently wished to take their writing forward but did not know how.

I was smiling—this time, I had just the thing for them.

OUR THOUGHTS ON VISHWESH'S ESSAY

We like Vishwesh's essay because it packs a punch without being convoluted or overly self-congratulatory. It reveals his passion for writing, his entrepreneurial spirit, community focus, creativity, inspirations, and vulnerability in clear, linear sentences.

The elliptical structure of this essay alone is evidence of creativity, and a reflection of the writer. It reads like a conversation between the reader and writer. Simultaneously it is a recollection of an interview. The questions posed by the interviewer anticipate those of the reader. Through the flow of this interview, Vishwesh revisits his entrepreneurial journey, and in the process reveals his love for the written word and his intent to bridge the resource gap for budding writers such as himself. In creating a writing resource, he benefits and elevates the community.

Vishwesh steps away from the interview for a moment to list his literary projects and workshops—the shortcomings of the latter being key to founding Inklings, given the scale and time constraints of the workshop model. This segue effectively provides background to his commitment to being a scribe. And then he brings us back to the interview for more pressing questions—the spirit of his venture. He expresses why writing is important to him and we see the sources of his inspiration: Lewis, Kafka, Dostoevsky, all counter-culture trailblazers—a vital nugget of information for an intended Literature major. Inexplicitly, we are told that he too suffered from writer's block—and the lack of timely guidance and mentorship in his life became an impetus for Inklings. His laudable goal: preempting other would-be writers feeling similar angst. Helping writers *write.* One can picture him as a TA in a UPenn class.

Concurrently, he reveals his vulnerability ('I had not thought of a philosophy')—which indicates an openness to being molded, and an awareness of his own shortcomings.

Overall, this essay speaks volumes of the student's personality using the lens of one project. That said, we loved how he described the nuances of setting up a company, and equally, would have loved for him to explore the specifics of how one or more of the writers he mentions influenced him, beyond broad brush strokes.

HARDIK PATIL

Stanford, Class of 2025

Major: Management Science and Engineering
School: Singapore International School, Mumbai
Hometown: Mumbai, India

It was 4 a.m., but I was yet awake, eyelids heavy, bone-weary, but fighting sleep. I envied the milkmen who ritually rose well before even roosters—they too were probably deep in slumber. Though I had hitherto logged seventy hours of sleeplessness, I yet had a task to do, and 'miles to go before I sleep.'

I scrolled the pages on my laptop screen, making sure yet again that all was in order, scanning the text and data with sleep-deprived eyes; but had you looked below their bloodshot surface you'd have discerned the bright glint of self-confidence and accomplishment there. I had done this before—thrice—and had emerged victorious every single time. I reread, for the final time, the section on *Hall-effect* thrusters, and finally leaned back in my chair, and declared to my teammates, 'It's ready!' There was no response. I swiveled around in the chair, only to see that all my four teammates were already fast asleep. I did not dare wake them up; they too had worked long hard hours on our entry to the Space Settlement Design Contest. I hit the submit button hard and immediately, if not sooner, fell asleep.

◆

Two months on: Once again, it was 4 a.m., and I was still awake. This time, it wasn't my cursor hovering over the submit button, it was the one on the judges' computer. Months of labor (including seventy hours of sleepless dedication) had boiled down to that one moment. I desperately wanted to know if we bagged the Grand Prize or 1st Prize. The results website went offline for about forty frustrating seconds, before the results flashed before my retinas. I searched end-to-end for my team's name, but it was nowhere to be found—not in the Grand Prize, not in the 1st Prize, not even in the 2nd or 3rd, or even in the honorable mentions! I hit refresh and perused again. I hit refresh once again, hoping that it was just some sort of technical glitch which stood between me and the Grand Prize—nada. Those months of labor seemed inconsequential.

◆

Sisyphus was an immoral, cruel Greek king who was notorious for having tricked death twice through craft and deceit. He ultimately got his comeuppance when Zeus sentenced him to the eternal punishment of forever rolling a boulder up a hill only to have it roll down again before reaching the summit. But was it really punishment? Was his inability to succeed really a curse? But let's hypothesize—suppose that (through craft, deceit, ingenuity or superhuman effort) he did get the boulder to the summit—what next? He'd probably enjoy the view that first time. What about the second time? And the third? There would not be much purpose to his existence then, would there? That Sisyphus was ordained to keep trying yet never succeed doesn't quite seem punishment to me.

Perhaps that is why I almost enjoy failure; failure affords you the opportunity to try again, to assess what went wrong and what didn't. With success, it's a done deal.

This has always bothered me. What will I do once I succeed? What next? Not difficult—there are other mountains and other boulders, other successes to build on failures. And admittedly, many, many of my successes were built on failure.

Time and again, many around me define me by my successes, but I believe that I'm better defined by the failures they were built on. The 5/5 on my AP Exam came after countless practice papers with 3s. That one game-winning layup I shot came after several hundred missed shots and bruised knees in practice. I have failed, and I have succeeded. I have failed more times than others have even tried. That's why I consider myself successful.

Those seventy sleepless hours weren't the first and they weren't the last. Sisyphus did it for eternity; why would I stop at just seventy hours?

OUR THOUGHTS ON HARDIK'S ESSAY

Hardik's essay is a rare gem that analyses and, in gentle rhetoric, ruminates and reflects in such 'successful' and insightful ways that the impact of its core message is amplified many times over.

One of the key devices the essay uses is disrupting the reader's expectations of the college application essay. His opening paragraph presents the perfect stage setting: we can imagine a hardworking team in the early dawn, having pulled through the final stretch in a series of all-nighters. The scene plays up our expectations of impending success. Surely, these herculean efforts will be rewarded!

However, in the very next passage he informs us of his team not featuring in the list of honorees.

The theme that plays through the essay is of the *expectations* of success in a system that rewards 'winners' but, more-often-than-not, glosses over the failures that underpin these victories. By all accounts, Hardik is successful in the conventional sense. He is hardworking, innovative, articulate and an achiever, all things that can be gauged from this essay alone. But he makes clear that he can march to the beat of his own drum and commit to his own parameters and definitions of success and failure. As he eloquently summarizes, 'I have failed, and I have succeeded. I have failed more times than others have even tried. That's why I consider myself successful.' This attribute, as embodied in his essay, would have set him apart in a sea of impressive profiles.

The myth of Sisyphus, eulogized as a philosophical parable explaining the human condition, is another incredibly effective tool that Hardik employs. Sisyphus was famously understood by existential philosophers as a stand-in for the absurdity and futility of human effort, but the essay reframes the condemned king's eternal punishment as something entirely distinct. For Hardik, Sisyphus stands as a symbol of effort; the gritty, thankless, and unending trying and failing, and trying again, which, even without the sought-after achievement, is, in itself, rewarding. For the Sisyphus in the essay, as for Hardik himself, the magic is in the striving and doing, pushing the boulder up the hill, rather than reaching the summit.

DEVISHI SARDA

UPenn, Class of 2021

Major: Economics and Cognitive Science
School: Modern School, Kolkata, India
Hometown: Kolkata, India

I was waiting in the splendidly breathtaking Rashtrapati Bhavan, residence of the President of India, to receive the Rashtrapati (President's) Award for my contribution to Girl Guiding by demonstrating advanced knowledge in first aid, camping, hiking, trekking, etc., serving the community and aiding environmental conservation.

Admiring the gardens through a window, I harked back to the beginnings, unravelling a kaleidoscope of memories. Strangely enough, rather than reminiscing about my early days as a Guide, I recalled the basketball court, my true training ground.

This is where it all began.

I remembered conversing with my opponents, Paulami and Saheli, about the role of basketball in our lives. Basketball was my passion, but their imperative. They hoped their basketball skills would secure them employment in the Railways or Police, guaranteeing their future. Despite our differences, basketball had brought us together. The following day, before playing them, I ruminated that we were each playing to win, but for different stakes. For them a win could foster employment, for me, well, I'd advance in the tournament. Even so, I gave my best. It's what a sportsperson does.

Basketball has enabled me to interact on diverse social platforms and traverse the Indian hinterland in non-air-conditioned sleeper trains, experiencing first-hand India's social and economic realities. And I learned compassion. Off-court, the empathy imbued through experiencing disparities in remote districts guides my actions today.

It led me to enroll as a Guide under the Bharat Scouts and Guides banner. I was determined 'to do my duty to God and my country,' to help people in need and always 'be prepared'. Guiding channelized the sensitivity I developed playing basketball into community outreach, working at a dialysis center, and organizing camps for underprivileged children.

Basketball molded my persona and taught me to persevere against the odds. I will never forget the 2014 semi-final match of the Indian School Basketball League. I had trained hard. Seven minutes into the first quarter, I tripped and tore an ankle ligament. Rendered hors de combat, I watched the game slip away from the sidelines. We were down 15 points at half time. My swollen foot throbbed painfully, yet I stepped in. Against our coach's advice, I strapped my foot and requested my coach play me. Ignoring the agony, I played limping. My teammates perforce adjusted their game—I couldn't run back for defence. By the fourth quarter, we'd cut the lead to 4. The game went into overtime and I took the game-winning shot. We'd entered the finals! After the adrenaline dissipated, my foot painfully reminded me that I had played 25 minutes with a torn ligament. That game imbued the will to never give up, encapsulated by an online portal in an article titled 'Made by Perseverance'.

A 'center' or 'pivot' in basketball is the player who directs the team's play. The last line of defence and, often, a team's attack spearhead, it necessitates vigilance and 360-degree vision. This discipline augmented my work as a Guide. 'Be Prepared', the Girl Guide's credo symbolizes being 'physically strong', 'mentally awake' and 'morally straight'. Playing basketball as a center ensures I follow that motto.

Basketball is a team sport that necessitates seamless coordination. Likewise, for Guide activities—improvizing stretchers to carry casualties, tying a bowline to save a drowning person, co-ordination is imperative. Basketball taught me this.

Yet, outside analogies, there were differences. When I needed to perfect my basketball maneuvers, I could approach my coaches or view drills online. However, when I needed help in Guiding protocols, either to ensure my knots integrity or to make sure my diagonal lashing was perfect, such enabling resources were absent. This led me to collate my six-year Guiding experiences into a teaching manual for my sister Guides.

Ascending onto stage, the irony struck me—I was being awarded for my services as a Guide, yet, the basketball court had been my guide. For service, and for life.

OUR THOUGHTS ON DEVISHI'S ESSAY

Devishi's essay showcases her remarkable intent and focus, making subtle and nimble connections between her work as a community leader and lessons drawn from her basketball training.

Using the basketball paradigm, as she awaits the President's award in an unexpected, regal stage setting—Delhi's Rashtrapati Bhavan—Devishi effectively reminiscences on what led her to 'Girl Guiding' and the development of characteristics that defined and distinguished her as a Guide. She draws parallels between the equity and camaraderie she found with her fellow sportspersons and the empathy she exhibits with people who come from backgrounds so different from hers, a founding motivation behind her community work. Her determination, ingenuity, and dedication to her roles off the field come from her commitment to basketball. This colorful casting of Devishi as a student and exponent of the sport is so viscerally descriptive that it is easy for the reader to imagine her as a lifelong learner.

Devishi's recollections as a sportsperson are all heart but her application of them as a Guide additionally demonstrate her ability to be deliberate and reflective, and lead from the front. For example, in a telling display of single-minded resolve, she plays through the intense pain of a torn ligament to pull her trailing team to victory. The commitment it takes to play under such strained circumstances is immeasurable, and perhaps, deserves its own separate essay. However, the manner in which Devishi describes her role as the 'center' gives us an insight into the sense of responsibility she must feel for her team and the resulting mental and physical strength she carries off the court.

Even though the recognition Devishi receives is for her stellar work as a Girl Guide, her thoughts are dominated by basketball. The authenticity of this connection is supported by her use of examples to substantiate each of the qualities which she believes stood her in good stead in her work as a Guide. Even when discussing the differences between the two worlds, in her initiative to provide 'enabling resources', we see the leader in Devishi who curates a booklet to help future Girl Guides. This ability to use basketball to explain who Devishi is, and the importance of those connections for community service, ultimately makes the essay engaging and successful.

To borrow from the title dedicated to her by an online portal, Devishi is 'Made by Perseverance'.

ANJALI AMBANI

Yale, Class of 2014

Major: Psychology
School: Sevenoaks School, Kent, UK
Hometown: Ahmedabad, India

The Indian-looking girl with the cascading hair who, when she speaks, has a hybrid American-Indian accent—that would be me. Born and raised in the suburbs of New York, we moved to Ahmedabad, India, when I was in the fifth grade. Lived there for six years, before shifting to 'Sevenoaks' in the United Kingdom to the 'the Sixth Form', where homework was 'prep' and dinner was 'supper'. Though I am now used to different ways of doing and seeing, while remaining true to myself, initially the move made me apprehensive. True, that it was an international school, but in terms of international exposure, I had seen the sights and met the people, but never lived with them.

I arrive. I unpack into one side of the cupboard in one side of the space with the sloping ceiling and sink in the corner. I go down, make-up on some faces, blank canvases for others. I tentatively walk up to them, introduce myself and we begin a polite exchange of names and hometowns. We bond over hot chocolate, discussing music and a shared love for *Friends*. The conversation, initially hesitant, grows animated. We learn about each others' cultures and viewpoints. Language was not a barrier I realized one English class, when my Chinese roommate unintentionally swore in German, the language of my other roommate. My closest friends are two Germans, an Austrian, an un-Chinese girl from Hong Kong, a Britisher from Libya, and several day students.

I find it incredible how easily I adapted to the diverse setting and divergent ways: where we come from did not matter, as once we started talking, I realized we all shared the same essential values. We each respect our parents; we all felt empathy and compassion when terrorists attacked Mumbai. We all rose at 4 a.m. to watch President Obama's inaugural speech. We shared the same sense of humor, a shared purpose: turning off lights in the common room to dance away our stress; grumbling that the Wednesday-night muffins had not been sent around. Together, we discussed existentialism, euthanasia, sexism and climate change issues into the night.

At Sevenoaks, I have been able to hone my lab skills with my extended essay—I had the chance to plan, conduct and write a research paper independently. As School Prefect, I help tour prospective international students and parents, which boosted my confidence in my ability to communicate with people from around the world. Studying Theory of Knowledge often resulted in very heated debates on issues, but we always came out thinking differently, keeping other perspectives in mind. We do not just read and remember, we also analyze and improve.

Initially, I felt like an Indian lotus being shipped off to the land of roses. Once the seed was planted, I realized I was in a botanical garden with cornflowers, edelweiss, orchids, and pomegranate blossoms where, though everything is different, each of us flourish. Diversity emphasizes individuality. I am confident that I can fit in anywhere yet stand out, no matter what the situation.

OUR THOUGHTS ON ANJALI'S ESSAY

The common application essay coaxes out the applicant's very personal, human side that lives behind the academic scores and achievements. The admissions committee wants to feel a 'personal connection' to you—how you think and feel about various situations, how you make decisions.

Anjali, 'The Indian-looking girl with…' a mixed identity revealed by her hybrid accent, responds by describing her 'transition': her experiences when adapting to a novel environment, finding her space, and fitting in as a teenager moving to a new high school in a new country. '…in terms of international exposure, I had seen the sights and met the people, but never lived with them.' Moving around to live in one country, then another, then a third can be extremely difficult, especially in a person's formative years. It challenges one's sense of identity. 'Though I am now used to different ways of doing and seeing, while remaining true to myself, initially the move made me apprehensive.'

Lessons learnt from these apprehensions, and indeed, from the difficulties we encounter are often fundamental to our future success as adults. Anjali's storyline is reflective and constructed from her 'now' responses. Her ideas flow clearly and naturally, forming a story arc centered in this one major experience in her life—high school. Through her exposition of her life-shaping experience in another country, we see aspects of her personality.

Anjali uses the simplicity of a fairly straightforward and casual, but personal narrative in the gentle, active and consistent tones of her authentic voice, humanizing her reality. With emotive vocabulary, she 'tentatively' walks up to the other girls, 'the conversation initially hesitant'. She addresses the core question: *Who am I?* '…I easily adapted to the diverse setting and divergent ways: where we come from did not matter… we all shared the same essential values.' Her personality traits, areas of interest, tangible academic skills and progress, delivered in stream of thought form a unique profile as she outlines settling into the new environment, and fitting in with all her multinational friends, sharing childlike joys, while understanding very mature issues.

Anjali concludes with what matters most to her. In stark contrast to the plainly narrated beginning of her story, she paints a wonderfully sensitive bouquet of similes and metaphors, that is an almost exotic multisensory experience, expressing her joy at blooming into a bright, young, and unique individual. 'Diversity emphasizes individuality. I am confident that I can fit in anywhere yet stand out, no matter what the situation,' is her confident conclusion.

ARMAAN GOYAL

Cornell, Class of 2022

Major: Hotel Administration
School: Sishya School, Chennai, India
Hometown: Chennai, India

MINUTIAE

My Science classroom is on the third floor of the high school building, right next to the Arts room. The Arts room is more of a storage room than anything, really, for pieces of art lost in time and memory. Between the thin walls of the adjoining rooms exists a small window—an architectural oversight that had occurred some forty years ago before the school's inception. On the first day of my life as an Eleventh Grade Science student, my teacher seated me right next to this window. As the weeks of studying Calculus, Quantum Physics and Shakespeare crept by, I found myself drawn to the room, gazing at the various paintings that decorated the walls of the mysterious space—paintings of war, portraits of old movie villains and some old comic sketches. And then I noticed it, painted across the inner wall of the room: a sentence in small blue letters—

'Focus on the minutiae, and the masterpiece is born.'

'Whoa.'

A plethora of thoughts swirled in my head: 'What does the quote really mean? How minute a detail must one get into? What truly qualifies as a masterpiece?'

My 'Aha!' moment came one night, as I tried to keep myself mentally afloat in a sea of numbers—average room rates, market penetration indices, and revenue ratios. I had spent weeks analyzing data from a hotel, but all my work had led up to that one moment. I proceeded to key in the final figures, and as I pressed 'Enter' on my laptop, my heart skipped a beat. Out came one pure, intangible, indisputable number: *Growth*. As I rewarded myself with a celebratory jar of Nutella, I thought about how entire business strategies are born based on the minutiae—seemingly trivial details that lead the way to growth; how the mystique of a masterpiece often rests on the trivia. I realized how significant details were to me; how I subsisted on the little things; the finer elements; the *minutiae*.

That musty classroom window was a gateway for my metamorphosis into an adventurous thinker. I began noticing details and relating the realms of Art and Science because I now recognized the subtle minutiae common to both. Sine waves on the blackboard reminded me of Hans Zimmer's 'Shepard Tone' in the movie *Dunkirk*. In Astrophysics class, my mind recalled physicist Robert Lang's use of origami in constructing a space telescope. I began enjoying these connections, for they fueled my sense of wonder at how beautifully synched Art and Math and Music can be. What I had thought to be momentary pleasures, turned out to be momentous.

My understanding of *minutiae* deepened at a village in Venkatapuram, where I volunteered to teach children Math at a school. I should have known the village children would alienate me—a tall, city boy who clearly did not belong. I could strive to overcome the language barrier, but culturally we were worlds apart. As I thought harder, Lang's origami crossed my mind. I picked up a newspaper and started making a paper boat. The apprehension in the air gave way to an accepting and jubilant spark as the students started building boats on their own, uninhibited—no-*folds*-barred. I looked at the students who had isolated themselves from me—they looked at me with twinkling eyes and cheeky grins. Something as humble as a paper boat had helped me connect with the children and became the inflexion point in my relationship with them. It was this seemingly inconsequential, mundane thing that gave me, and them, fathomless joy. The littlest act, it turned out, made the greatest impact.

We often delude ourselves by thinking that something is too minute to be noticed or taken seriously, but it's the smallest things that truly make us who we are—*that's* what the quote meant to me.

While I focus on the minutiae, a masterpiece is being born.

OUR THOUGHTS ON ARMAAN'S ESSAY

Armaan's essay is a contemplative and defining account of self-discovery—a remarkably self-aware narrative that evolves almost entirely in his own mind. Thoughts, musings, and recollections serve as currencies for travel, connecting seemingly disparate details and facilitating Armaan's movement from classroom to beyond, and back to classroom. In this essay, he ponders the enabling enormity of minutiae.

College essays can often have a sense of impatience about them, brimming with events and wrestling with the word limit. Armaan's essay bucks this trend to embody the spirit of focusing on small details. The essay offers a deep and active insight into the kind of thinker he is, without being weighed down by overt attempts to impress with signs of success. Instead, the essay focuses on specifics that matter to Armaan, such as his tendency to take a step back and contemplate the circumstances behind a successful business, even as he celebrates his epiphany by treating himself to Nutella. We are invited to experience his genuine sense of joy in making unexpected connections between Zimmer's score from *Dunkirk* and Sine waves that legitimize his love for Art *and* Math *and* Music. And even as we move through Armaan's life and observe his growth into an 'adventurous thinker', we sense the lucid calm that characterizes his internal narrative, one that suggests a robust and organized process of sifting through and evaluating information.

The central conflict of the essay comes in the form of him drawing on this internal narrative for the benefit of others. Before encountering the invisible barrier between him and his students in Venkatapuram, Armaan had been satisfied making connections quietly, crossing artificial borders of thoughts and disciplines merely for himself. However, when faced with the challenge of making a connection *beyond* himself, he sees the true value of the details he is drawn to, and the importance of small truths that make him who he is beyond language, religion, and creed. Armaan's crafting of a paper boat, and its subsequent success as a tool for connection serves as a metaphor for his transcendence from an adventurous thinker to a doer. In a single 'no-folds-barred' expression of minutiae, Armaan exemplifies the importance of details, his own masterpiece.

VIBHAV MARIWALA

Stanford, Class of 2020

Major: History
School: Bombay International School, Mumbai, India
Hometown: Mumbai, India

Force 7 winds, near gale conditions, and ten guests to be ferried across the bay to the Bombay Harbor. As I stood at the helm, my legs began turning to jelly. I wondered how I would safely bring them ashore. Taking a deep breath, I focused, with my eyes firmly on the sea, deftly steering the boat through the turbulent wind and choppy swell. As we entered the harbor, I heaved a heavy sigh of relief.

After all, there was a time when I was petrified of the sea. While my family loved the thrill of sailing in choppy waters, I would cringe with fear. But one day, while the boat was frighteningly crashing, my father asked me to take the helm. I trembled with nervousness as I started to steer. But as time went on, I grew more and more comfortable. My family had been sailors for generations; it was in my blood.

Last winter was special. Three generations—my grandfather, father, brother and I—sailed down the west coast of India to explore island forts and new kayaking routes. This was my first long sailing trip, and the first one that I was in charge of planning and organizing. As we left the shores of Bombay and soared with the wind down the stunning coast, I felt both calm and excited. I felt like a mature sailor.

Soon after we left the pollution of the Bombay Harbor, we were greeted by schools of dolphins, flying fish, and flocks of seagulls. It was bittersweet to see them, because I did not know how they could survive in a sea with such lax environmental laws. I was not even sure if future generations would be able to enjoy seeing such amazing fauna. I decided to do something. After the trip I volunteered with the World Wildlife Fund's conservation program and raised money—around $2500—to support the program by selling photographs of my voyage.

Later on during the trip, as I explored new kayaking routes around island forts, I understood the importance of maritime history. These forts were goldmines of history, with tales of traders and fishermen, pirates and smugglers, and epic naval battles between the Marathas, Mughals, and Europeans embedded within their walls. But they were neglected and dilapidated, with little written about them. I therefore found another project, and wrote my first article, documenting the maritime history and environmental problems of the area, for the Indian Yachting Magazine.

As I wrote my journal under the stars one night, our boat's deckhand Pandari began talking to me about life in his village. It was a hard life where neither he nor his fellow villagers had access to electricity, despite being only a few kilometers away from the bright lights of Bombay. This disturbing revelation made me take up an internship at a solar energy company called Frontier Markets to set up a distributor network of solar products in his village. Yet again, the sea had not only sensitized me towards something I had never experienced but had also made me impact someone's life.

Every day, I long to wake up to the sound of crashing waves. The sea has created some of my fondest memories and given me the thrill of discovery. But it has also helped me find my voice, be empathetic and responsible, and take initiative. Over my many encounters with it, I have learned how to respect the environment and the people that are a part of it, to document and explore the amazing history that lies along its periphery, and value the freedom and privileges that I have had while growing up with it.

Without the sea, I would not have been who I am today.

I gaze at the waves washing up on the shore, and hear the music of Miles Davis. I am ready to dive deeper and discover yet another adventure.

OUR THOUGHTS ON VIBHAV'S ESSAY

The way he writes it, Vibhav's connection with the sea is revelatory, and inspiring. Through vividly drawn descriptions, his essay captures the feel of a voyager navigating the ocean; steering to negotiate the waves' shifting moods, journaling to keep track of transformations. He discovers and chronicles its many facets and inhabitants in a metaphorical journey to understand his own place in the universe.

Coming of age at the helm of a yacht, Vibhav reflects on how his forays into both clear and muddy sea waters helped him grow into himself. He chronicles the deep feeling of kinship established with his family of sailors, the new perspectives and old histories he encountered, and the archives he founded through his adventures. As a third-generation sailor, an explorer, and a dedicated archivist, each of these facets tell us a little about who Vibhav chooses to be.

The sea is also Vibhav's entry point into the world at large. In writing avidly about his sea adventures, he recounts the deep waters as a place that 'helped [him] find [his] voice, be empathetic and responsible, and take initiative.' Away from his bustling life in Mumbai which, perhaps ironically, allows him to access the otherwise exclusive domains of yachting regulars, he encounters people and worlds that differ from what he knows. His immediate recognition of this difference, and willingness to accept responsibility as an agent of change reveal a commitment to using his life to help others.

In acknowledgement of all that he receives, Vibhav shows high regard for the sea: Respectful of its changing tides and troubled waters, appreciative of the diversity housed in its ambit and a willing learner of the lessons he encounters. He does not lay claim to his discoveries; instead, he emphasizes upon their collective ownership, by current and future generations, the mark of a leader. Vibhav's clever closure analogizes the music of trumpet legend Miles Davis (famed equally for his muted trumpet notes and exuberant fanfares) to the sea's many moods—from waves lapping gently, to surging waters crashing down: we get a whiff of the life he will lead.

As he embarks on a new adventure at the essay's close, the last line of Walt Whitman's immortal couplet springs to mind, 'Now voyager, sail thou forth to seek and find.'

SHIVEN DEWAN

UPenn, Class of 2024

Major: Finance and Behavioral Economics (Wharton)
School: The Doon School, Dehradun, India
Hometown: Meerut, India

'*Do you not think that our millennials like you are being over-schooled but under-educated?*' The words boomed on the speakers in the Durbar Hall of the Taj Palace Hotel.

When I was invited as a panelist to one of India's most celebrated think-fests, The Mindmine Summit, the opportunist in me yelped while the seventeen-year-old in me felt dwarfed by the aura of former Indian presidents and industrialists who would be present at the summit. I clearly remember every detail of my panel discussion on 'India's Millennials: Can they reshape Markets, Society and Governments?'; however, it was this question from one of the audience members that still rings in my ears. Smiling wryly, with a million thoughts in my head, I took a sip of water and picked up the microphone excruciatingly slowly. I noticed the ex-president's needle-eyed gaze scrutinize me in anticipation. A politician in the front row was unruffled and looked up while some journalists quickly got down to some indecipherable scribbling. No pressure!

A few minutes later, the audience's scrutiny eased, and I heard applause and heaved a huge sigh of relief! The rest of the panel discussion revolved around changing work environments, the millennial's desire for overhaul and the relevance of India's rich history in the Millennial

Age. However, it was this question that got me really riled up. Even weeks after The Mindmine Summit, the question refused to make peace with me. Therefore, to perhaps quench this burning desire, I launched my very own nationwide movement of 'Mindmine Chapters' in various schools. Sharing my knowledge base with my peers in an eternal search for a conclusive answer, I set up similar panels on 'India's Millennials'. The Millennial Dialogues have produced rich debate on education, millennial stereotypes, and experimental new-age parenting. I even compiled a policy paper comprising the salient points from all chapters; however, nothing brought me closer to solving this unending conflict between education and institutionalization.

Having been a student of two schools in different continents—Doon and Gordonstoun—has just added to the dilemma. I fondly recall my time, on exchange, at Gordonstoun when I immediately fell for the Scottish countryside, lush plains, the food (maybe not Haggis) and, of course, a rarity for an Indian—the snow. I never thought that I'd be getting rugby tackled on the muddiest of fields and follow it up by putting on my dancing shoes for a cabaret. It was torturous to decipher the Northern Scottish accent, and I recall sitting with my friend who illustrated the swap of the 'v' and 'w' sounds between my accent and the Scottish accent. Intrigued and enthralled, I even ended up swimming breaststroke for Gordonstoun in the month of January!

My experiences at Gordonstoun, coupled with the events at Mindmine, drive me to re-imagine education in the Millennial and Gen Z age. I'm half that mad kid signing up for slaughter on a frigid rugby evening and half that kid, clad in a suit, launching nationwide panel discussions back home. I want to be part of a community that, as my life does, till now, nurtures a farrago of chilly swimming and diverse perspectives. I don't just view higher education in the form of a tangible degree. So why university? College, for me, is not about landing a Fortune 500 job; it will, I hope, facilitate the discovery of my next cultural and paradigmatic shift.

Over-schooled or under-educated? Perhaps the person who asked me this question did not expect it to have such a profound impact. I now realize that perhaps there is no conflict between the two, so I don't need to respond. To me, education is the obsession strong enough to make me launch a nationwide movement just to look for a petty answer; it is the teamwork involved in the scrum on the rugby pitch and also the celebration of diversity while trying to figure out strange accents!

OUR THOUGHTS ON SHIVEN'S ESSAY

Shiven opens with a rhetorical question from 'one of the audience members', that sounds much like a jibe, a gauntlet thrown down in a clearly prominent public forum at the 'Durbar Hall of the Taj Palace Hotel', and hooks directly into the readers' thought process from the outset itself. It is undoubtedly a powerful device—compelling a thought-provoking internal debate in the reader: 'What was the question implying? Would the student be able to handle it? How would this student respond? Do they themselves agree? Disagree?'

Shiven thus sets the stage and then invites the readers to sit among the audience, physically experiencing the sensory impact as it 'boomed on the speakers....' 'No pressure!' He then dives right in, making every moment actively tell a story. Reading the essay becomes a pleasure, because it is interesting. And it is interesting because this is something Shiven genuinely wants to explain to the AdComs: '... this question that got me really riled up'. It has seeded in Shiven, a need to 'perhaps quench this burning desire'. It has taken him on a fairly unique, and engaging journey of initiatives and achievements 'in an eternal search for a conclusive answer...' to the enduring 'conflict between education and institutionalization'.

Shiven considers the life experiences—'getting rugby tackled on the muddiest of fields and follow it up by putting on my dancing shoes for a cabaret'—that have shaped his identity and personality. As also his 'diverse perspectives…'—'I don't just view higher education in the form of a tangible degree.' But rather as an obsession, a means to 'facilitate the discovery of my next cultural and paradigmatic shift'. Education, to Shiven, is clearly, about both harnessing and growing equally from schooling and experiences beyond classroom confines. Here, he processes these experiences.

Shiven told the admissions officers something about himself that he uncovered during his voyage of self-discovery, something that could not be expressed or quantified anywhere else on his application or his CV! His essay is a true and robust representation of who he is. The level of self-reflection makes him stand out from thousands of applicants.

5

COMING OF AGE

'She'll outgrow it, dear. It's just the age
... It's the age when nothing fits.'

—Rebel Without a Cause

Finding who we are and claiming our place in the world is a universal rite of passage. Literature, movies, songs are filled with references to people, places and moments that we associate the feeling of having discovered ourselves with. Capturing the awkwardness, the vulnerabilities and the possibilities of youth, the essays in this section harness the sentiments at the core of the most iconic coming-of-age moments, to present accounts that are both, highly relatable and deeply personal.

Public speaking, a magical hat, piano lessons, a poorly color-matched bald cap, John Mayer, cultural expectations of femininity and a few Gandhi-centered references await.

ANONYMOUS

Yale, Class of 2014

Major: Economics and Political Science
School: Dubai International Academy, Dubai, UAE
Hometown: Dubai, UAE

THE OVERSIZED HAT

I felt the anxiety flood every inch of my body. As a gawky adolescent, I could not suppress my nervousness of embarking upon the most anticipated, yet most frightening ten minutes of my thirteen-year existence. I was about to recite Dr Seuss' *The Cat in the Hat* in front of over a thousand schoolmates at my school's annual talent show. In line with the theme of my recitation, I had crafted a special hat for the occasion: the long red-and-white hat worn by *The Cat in the Hat* himself.

It was my mother who had always encouraged me to be outgoing and to move away from my introverted shyness, and it was she who had persuaded me to participate in the talent show as an elocutionist. Although at that time I had no idea of what the term 'elocution' meant, I eagerly signed up for an act at the talent show. Little did I know that I was not only the first, but also the school's only elocutionist.

At that moment, standing behind the crimson velvet curtains that draped over the stage, I dreaded the applause that was to follow my precursor's exotic flamenco dance: the applause that would signal the start of my solo act. I braced myself to perform an act poles apart from the succession of rock bands, dances, and comedian shows. Having assiduously memorized the book and repeatedly recited it to my infant brother—who, incidentally, never tired of hearing the story—I tried to convince myself that I was equipped to succeed, and that I could win the talent show. With every gust of air I exhaled, I felt more exposed and more unprepared than before. The grossly oversized hat that covered my forehead now overshadowed my confidence.

At last, summoned by the round of applause, I stumbled onto the stage; the same stage that I had walked on countless times in my primary school theatrical productions; the same stage that I had played the saxophone on with my school's orchestra; the same stage that I had danced on during International Day performances. I'd tread every inch of that stage in the past, but it suddenly seemed like an extra terrestrial planet to me. I could not recognize the wooden planks on the stage, my family and friends in the crowd, or any of the faces awaiting my performance.

In those milliseconds that went by, time came to a standstill. I could hear the thundering beat of my heart. I could feel the trickling beads of sweat on my head. I could see the glare of the stage lights on my forehead.

'The sun did not shine, it was too wet to play…' From somewhere within me, I summoned the strength to begin my animated recitation of *The Cat in the Hat*.

1626 words later, the roaring clap of the crowd resonated in my ears. I stood still on the stage, shocked by the appreciative applause from the audience. Detached from reality and elated by finishing my act, I ushered myself backstage.

It was only when the presenter began speaking again did my bubble burst. 'The winner for the 2005 Talent Show is…' I felt the butterflies flutter from side to side in my stomach. 'Act fourteen!' With my oversized hat, I stepped onto the stage once again, euphoric with the electric jolts jumping at me from every direction. Reaching forward to embrace the principal's congratulatory handshake, I shed the cocoon that had sheltered its reticent and withdrawn creature for so many years. I could never have anticipated that this moment would propel me to new stages to direct congregations of international youth at the United Nations Headquarters, address participants of Model United Nations Conferences as their Secretary General, and lead my school's diverse student body as the President of its Student Council and Head Boy.

Despite my sincerest intention to compete in the talent show as an elocutionist, I found that the next morning in school I had unwittingly become an overnight comedian. My eclectic ensemble and eccentric performance had become table conversation at the cafeteria during lunch. Although the hat had not shrunk, or my head had not expanded overnight, the oversized red-and-white hat now fit me perfectly.

OUR THOUGHTS ON THE ESSAY

A diffident youngster, barely in his teens, an impending talent show and an eccentric, comically large, homemade hat: the ingredients hold the captivating promise of an ever-familiar children's story about stepping out and the power of self-belief. His slice-of-life essay, 'The Oversized Hat', plays to our expectations of cherished familiarity. There is something cozy and warm about the essay's colorful narration of his rite of passage that skillfully conveys the limitless possibilities of early teenage years even as it highlights the vulnerabilities surrounding childhood.

The bulk of the essay, realistically, takes places within a thirty-minute window, stretching from his dreading his turn onstage, to winning the talent show. His essay is made impactful through writing that delivers on the essential qualities that make a successful elocutionist: engagement, modulation, and investment. It opens in action, but also in breathless anticipation, as well-placed, relatable pieces of visual imagery (thick, crimson velvet curtains, the glare of a too-bright spotlight) set the stage (literally and metaphorically), drawing the reader into the retelling. Skillfully employing emotion by linking first person narrative to impassioned and evocative verbs, nouns, and metaphors (I *felt* anxious/exposed, I *braced* myself, I *shed* the cocoon), he fluidly infuses the fluctuating intensities of performance. Moments of anxiety are balanced by clever bits of humor and commentary (an intently listening if uncomprehending infant, the eclectic array of acts at talent shows) that keep the reader engaged and acutely present in this narrative. By the time it is his turn on stage, we are invested in what happens next and his moment of panic is the required dramatic pause before the metamorphosis. By linking his future achievements to this watershed moment, he ensures investment there as well.

Out of all the devices he uses, however, the most impactful is the titular oversized hat, a nod to the iconic sartorial choice of Dr Seuss' enigmatic, anthropomorphic cat, and the source of the story's charm. Initially representing innocence and introversion in its incongruity and ill-fittingness, the almost magical resizing of the hat after the talent show speaks of his coming of age: all that he became flowed from that one act powered by daring and self-belief.

ISHA GUPTA

UPenn, Class of 2019

Major: Finance and Social Impact
School: Vasant Valley School, New Delhi, India
Hometown: New Delhi, India

Standing on the stage next to the Indian flag, I experienced a feeling of utmost pride. The opportunity to represent the orange, white and green *tiranga* (as we Indians fondly call it) was surreal. Wearing the traditional *salwar-kameez*, I felt unsurpassable accomplishment in being the face and voice of my nation. Selected as one of two students to represent India at the 2014 Asian Youth Development Program in Okinawa, I was honored to participate in this international leadership program along with students from fourteen countries.

Years ago, I could not have imagined myself on a stage in Japan. I've long been known as 'the delicate younger sister'. Indeed, I am petite of frame, but my head houses a mind that is quite loud and opinionated. Time and again, people would perceive me through the lens of my body, often underestimating me. With every new interaction, experience, or situation, society's perceptions remained the same. A sweet girl, they would say as if being 'sweet' was the only characteristic that defined me. The real problem, however, was that such views began to permeate my self-perception. I wondered if I was, in fact, that 'soft girl' who should conform to societal norms and not dare to speak out and say what I believed. Maybe I *was* what they thought of me.

Not willing to be defined by society, I yearned to find my true essence. In this journey, a significant turning point came early in high school, when I decided to take up debating. While apprehensive at first, I found debate the ideal platform to express myself. Suddenly, being underestimated was an advantage. At the podium during the 2014 Sherwood national-level debates, I heard some buzz and soon realized that it was about me. Some in the audience, seeing me in the lead speaker position, were predicting a 'one-sided' debate. According to them, the lead speaker of side opposition *looked* like he would be more emphatic and powerful. But I knew I had it in me to put up a good fight. Defeating him in the round – effectively rebutting every point he made – I realized that the audience had been right. It *was* a one-sided debate; they were just wrong about *which* side. As the applause died down, I smiled not because of coming first, but because of the confidence that came with it.

Other experiences have challenged my understanding of perceptions. Representing my school and India at a filmmaking competition in Lahore, Pakistan, in 2013, we worked to develop a film. Myriad thoughts emerged as we wrote countless ideas on a communal notepad. Fearing the views of the seemingly stern judges, though, we dismissed one idea after another. Presuming the judges to value somber documentaries, we strived to create a film that would resonate with them, forgetting the importance of it resonating with *us*.

Then it struck me, the greatest movies were the unexpected ones. Grabbing our ubiquitous notepad, I asked everyone to list their favorite movies. Soon, the now-tattered notepad contained a long list of interesting concepts and our creative juices flowed. We combined our ideas to develop a movie that was truly ours. And so, even though I wasn't the loudest or the tallest, I helped our team to find a collective vision that we could all call our own.

The way we look at things, or our perceptions of them, is just one part of what they actually are. Whether it was the *salwar-kameez* that I wore in Okinawa, the trophy I won in the Sherwood Tournament, or the tattered notepad I kept as a memento of our time in Pakistan, I've learned to look beyond what we initially believe to be true. For a while, I'd almost let other people's perceptions define me, but that same girl who was once understood only through the lens of her body, is today understood through so much more.

OUR THOUGHTS ON ISHA'S ESSAY

Few college applicants take the initiative to tackle the experience of a crisis of identity as unabashedly and unreservedly as Isha does. At an age where other people's perceptions of us often seem like the only source of external validation, Isha shows equanimity and grit that belies her years, muting the surrounding din to focus on her newly developing voice.

The idea of a non-confrontational, non-controversial, 'sweet' or 'soft girl' is often a gendered expectation deeply woven into Indian culture: Isha's 'petite' frame, though not actually indicative of much beyond its own description, is assumed to be the conclusive evidence of a quiet, docile nature. Skillfully structuring the essay, Isha refers to this only in passing, focusing instead on her resolve and actions aimed at moving beyond it. As such, we get a fuller understanding of her, who she is and how she thinks, rather than focusing on the crisis itself.

A large chunk of the essay is focused on debating as an avenue for Isha's evolution. Decidedly competitive and often cut-throat, debate offers the perfect stage for Isha to externalize the ongoing evolution within her. A concisely described anecdote demonstrates her growing confidence, and humorously observes how the assumption of 'softness' that once limited her now allows her to leverage popular misconceptions to emphatically dispel stereotypes. This inclusion allows us to see *why* debating and winning debates is important to Isha, instead of simply informing readers of her victory. As she states, 'I smiled not because of coming first, but because of the confidence that came with it.'

Armed with the confidence to be herself, Isha encourages others to do the same, using her lessons to create a uniting vision at an international filmmaking contest and further cement her transformation. This device of 'measuring' growth is effectively used in the essay, especially when we reflect on the opening visual of Isha standing next to the Indian flag in Okinawa. The progress this demonstrates, particularly when juxtaposed with her early doubts, emphasizes how far she has come, and how much further she can go, surprising a few debaters, unsuspecting peers and colleagues along the way.

ARNAV JOSHI

UPenn, Class of 2022

Major: Systems Engineering and Economics
School: Smt. Sulochanadevi Singhania School, Mumbai, India
Hometown: Mumbai, India

I was on top of the world when I came to know that I was the highest GPA holder in 8th standard. This was just my third year in the school and for a student of class eight, who had never addressed a large gathering of people before, an opportunity to deliver the welcome address at the Honor's Society Function as the standard 'topper' was invaluable.

I did not know if I was good at public speaking, but I did know that I was good at working hard. So, I put my heart and soul into creating a speech that would 'wow' the audience. I sought feedback from my teachers and worked on my pronunciations. The thought of standing at the podium having forgotten what I had to say made me break out in a cold sweat, but I was too much of a perfectionist to carry a crumpled piece of paper with me. So, I put every ounce of my energy into memorizing the speech. All I had to do now was to go up to the podium and start speaking.

A day before my 'ultimate test' I was told that the ranks were going to be allotted on the basis of the marks that the students had received and not the GPAs. Consequently, I was ranked second and, as was the tradition, had to give the 'Vote of Thanks' and not the 'Welcome Speech'. The teachers apologized for the mess-up, but politely told me that I had to give the 'Vote of Thanks'. My anger drowned in my anxiety and I had just a day to create a brand-new speech. I was suggested by my teachers to go ahead with the draft prepared by the student who was initially going to deliver the Vote of Thanks. While it sounded tempting, I was keen to make an impression and wanted the audience to see the real me.

I sat up preparing for my speech late into the night, scribbling 'catchy' lines on my notepad. I am a humorous person and I always like to pepper my discourse with witty remarks. So, while my gratitude for receiving a chance to address an audience and for the appreciation I had received for my academic endeavors was earnest, I had to sprinkle moments of laughter in my speech. I rehearsed before the mirror, giggling at my jokes and clapping at the sweeping statements I made. When I felt I was ready, I went off to sleep hoping that I would do alright the next day.

I walked up to the podium in the brightly lit Malhar Hall and my legs were shaking. Thankfully the upper half of my body—that was visible—was very still. I looked across the auditorium and started speaking—'A great man once said that feeling gratitude and not expressing it is like wrapping up a present and not giving it.' Every member of the audience had a pleasant smile on their face. I felt comfortable and I started making eye contact with people in the auditorium. I was no longer conscious of my diction and pronunciations—I spoke the way I naturally speak. The words were simple and the sentences were short, but everything I said came from the bottom of my heart. I poured my heart out and received a thundering applause in return.

When the official report for the event came out, in the four sentences that described the event, two of them talked about how I, with the sparkle in my eyes, had captivated the audience. This 'seemingly unfortunate' event gave me my greatest asset as a public speaker—authenticity. To this day, I do not carry a paper to guide me on the podium.

OUR THOUGHTS ON ARNAV'S ESSAY

While our achievements can be important markers of our personality, it is our reaction to life's vicissitudes and adversities that truly proves our mettle. Arnav's essay centers on one such defining moment of wresting triumph from the jaws of disappointment, something that taught him a life lesson about the abilities that set him apart. Spoiler—it had nothing to do with being the highest GPA holder in class eight!

Set in school, the essay is rooted in the relatable context of feeling bereft on being denied something we may have felt we deserved. Arnav, after being assured of the position of Valedictorian, along with its coveted 'Welcome Address', is informed a mere day before the address that he has lost out based on a technicality. Reeling from the abrupt turn in events, the salutatorian 'Vote of Thanks' initially seems like cold comfort, a consolation prize at best. However, his commitment to giving it his all to express his genuine sense of gratitude powers him to write a whole new speech the night before its delivery, notwithstanding the temptation to recite one already written. Arnav paces these events well, dedicating the first half of the essay as a build-up to his speech, and providing insight into the mix of anger, anxiety, and excitement he felt in the lead up to this 'ultimate test'.

Describing the speech he delivers, Arnav says, 'The words were simple and the sentences were short, but everything I said came from the bottom of my heart.' We see that in his essay too, Arnav's writing style is composed of short sentences and simple, legible language that is still incredibly effective because it rings true. He isn't concerned with over-intellectualizing or justifying his feelings—whether in his overt shock and anger on being informed of his change in position, or his glee as he writes the 'Vote of Thanks'. This helps us understand his frame of mind and his willingness to give a fair shot to public speaking even if it wasn't in the circumstances he had originally hoped for. And he is rewarded for it.

On the face of it, the essay is about Arnav's inadvertent discovery of his nascent public speaking talents. But more so, it is a tribute to his grace, resilience, dedication and character.

MAHIRA JETHWANI

Stanford, Class of 2024

Major: Economics
School: Dubai College, Dubai, UAE
Hometown: Dubai, UAE

'Thank you, Gandhi,' I whispered.

Touched by my impact on those that I once did not believe I could reach, I clutched onto the award for my Cooling Vest Initiative.

◆

Before going on stage, my headmaster had warned me that the celebrity audience 'will be completely engrossed in their own conversations; expect little acknowledgement for your speech.' This prediction didn't play out. I had the audience's undivided attention. This had only happened once before; when I became Mahatma Gandhi.

I was selected to play Gandhi in the school play 'Exotic India', in fourth grade. I'd heard the chorus 'you're the only "brown" one, so you play Gandhi' from my classmates. Horrified by the supposed insult, yet proud to play the role, I seized the moment and have not looked back since.

On the day of the play, I walked into school trading my Barbie glasses, neat school uniform, and frilly socks for round glasses, a white bedsheet securely wrapped around me, and a bald cap (seven shades lighter than my skin tone—nothing else was available), while carrying a walking stick. I was quite the sight.

Since then, my classmates mockingly called out 'GANDHI'S COMING, LOOK OUT!' when playing 'tag'. This strangely derogatory comparison to an icon of humanity led me to question my cultural identity.

Born in Dubai, nurtured as British and sporting an accent similar to the Queen's, yet the only Indian in class, I wondered what I could claim to be. Curious, I began waking up earlier to do extra morning reading about my cultural origins. The widespread discrimination and injustice Gandhi faced when ordered to occupy a third-class train seat despite purchasing a first-class ticket was a grim reminder that the color of my skin could be used to judge me. Learning more about Gandhi, I began to write about my newfound knowledge in class, which led me to view my new nickname as more empowering than belittling.

My experiences merged with Gandhi's to empower my speeches and build my empathy for those discriminated against in real life. This was a watershed that caused me to grow a tongue and start finding my own voice to defend those mistreated for reasons beyond their control.

Over time, repeating the script embedded Gandhi's ethos within me until advocating social humanitarianism came instinctively. I continuously strive to experience that liberating euphoria I felt when 'being Gandhi', but now through action, as myself.

Since then, I have refused to stay silent before injustice; I believe that to be a true 'voice' for others requires more than sound; it requires expression to achieve impactful change. Having had opportunities to express myself through journalism, art, music, and speech, I want to share these skills with those unable to effectively communicate their own perspectives.

I began by taking action in my home, Dubai. The diversity outside the school gates is extraordinary and I have proactively worked to bridge the gaps between people in such a multi-cultural environment. Dubai's exponential growth intrigues me but its glaring inequalities have led me to seek reasons for their existence and create change in whatever way I can.

To fully understand Gandhi's origins, and mine, I visited an Indian village school. Here, the disparities I sought to reduce in Dubai seemed less consequential. I taught innovation and Economics to girls who believed domesticity was their calling, not Economics. I set out to change their perspective, as mine had been changed by Gandhi. Each time I returned, I gained a greater understanding of their lives, and was more determined to open their eyes to their potential.

◆

As I stepped offstage, teary-eyed strangers hugged me and handed me business cards that promised opportunities and support for my future endeavors. I knew I had Gandhi to thank. To paraphrase him, I intend to 'shake the world in a gentle way' as I continue my journey with humanity.

OUR THOUGHTS ON MAHIRA'S ESSAY

This is a case of identity crisis leading to greater understanding and transformation of the self. Mahira begins the essay with an award ceremony; what it is exactly, we do not know, but it seems inconsequential as Mahira, while looking back, revisits her formative years in Dubai. But not before she thanks MK Gandhi, the father of our nation, for being her muse. And here lies the tale. The reader feels the impact of the subtle reminders of perceived non-belonging—the audience that will not pay attention, the cap that was too light for her skin, the India that was 'exotic', and the incongruity of sporting a British accent yet identifying as Indian. All this gives you a glimpse into her life, in a series of snapshots. You can almost picture Mahira burning the midnight oil, doggedly digging through books on Gandhi, wiping the tears from her eyes.

It is made evident that her experiences sparked a real desire to learn about Gandhi's life and fight injustices to propagate change. That is the theme of this essay—a desire to do good in the world, which is used to highlight both, Mahira's activities outside school and her internal evolution (including 'Grow a tongue'). The spirit of this essay rings true and clear—we can guess that Mahira would have stretched herself in Dubai to catalyze 'change'. However, the inflection point lies in an internal transformation that leads Mahira to identify areas for improvement and transformation beyond herself. Her journey of self-discovery fosters a genuine appreciation for diversity and empowering others to find their voice, as relevant to both her homes—Dubai and India.

As Mahira steps off the stage, having grown, in the essay's course, into a young woman with convictions and purpose, we feel her sense of achievement and join in the deserved accolades. Her experiences serve as testament to her inner fortitude, and to her drive for social justice. Mahira's narrative closes with a nod to future pathways, a richly potted onward journey as a gentle, yet effective agent of change, like her muse.

SAMIR THAKORE

UPenn, Class of 2023

Major: Finance and Management (Wharton)
School: Canadian International School, Hong Kong
Hometown: Hong Kong

It started with a traffic jam! That too on a Sunday.

I remember looking out of the taxi in frustration, my hair wet from a swimming lesson, willing the cars ahead to clear. But no such luck: this was the start of Occupy Central, and I had inadvertently found myself with a front-row seat. Most Hong Kong residents will remember this period of pro-democracy, student-led protests as a logistical nightmare in which blocked streets in the heart of the city led to significant disruptions in daily life. For me, however, it marked the start of something bigger.

Of Indian descent and Maltese by nationality, I was born in Hong Kong. My outlook on life was grounded in the widely propagated, optimistic view that, while Hong Kong was a part of China, it would always retain its unique characteristics that make it different from China.

That changed when I walked through the makeshift camps of Occupy Central. There, as a thirteen-year-old, I saw history being created in the fight for an inclusive future. There, I watched student activists rally the city around them as the police used tear gas in attempts to clear the area. I saw courage in the faces of students standing tall, and I learnt about the fears, hopes, and dreams of a generation known more for its political apathy.

Caught up in the explosion of headlines focused on the leaders, I initially failed to recognize the real heroes of the movement. They were in fact everyday college students, the backbone of the movement, who worked feverishly on logistics, shelter, and clean-up. They arranged temporary study areas on the streets and carved out spaces for debate and discussion. I marveled at the ingenuity and commitment that drove them to sustain the movement for nearly eighty days. This is not a story about my leading the charge to safeguard Hong Kong's freedoms. Rather, this is about how the actions of those not much older than me inspired me to make changes. I found myself thinking about fairness, equality, the role of the government, and the future of Hong Kong. After all, what is political becomes personal and a matter that concerns everyone.

To start with, I engaged more with the community. I taught English and basic computer skills to young kids and coached pre-teens in the quintessential English game of cricket. I helped to feed the elderly living in coffin-sized dwellings made of wooden planks and wire mesh. In short, I learnt about life in Hong Kong. And to better understand the politics of it all, I secured an internship in the Legislative Council (LEGCO), Hong Kong's mini-parliament, working for the Democratic Party.

At LEGCO, my work focused on grassroots issues ranging from rising property prices and public bus schedules to situations of life and death involving the arrest of citizens in neighboring countries. I learned that 'politics is the art of the possible' and that success, even for a well-meaning politician, is often elusive. I discovered an appreciation for the work of legislators. Theirs is not just a world of grand speeches, television appearances, and policy initiatives. A credible politician must do all that and yet be ready to help constituents no matter the issue at hand.

Through the prism of hindsight, I view Occupy Central and my internship as two stops on my journey of education and maturity. The movement taught me about the big things in life: passion, courage, determination, and the need to stay firm to my beliefs. My internship reinforced the importance of compassion and sweating the details. Some people are born to be leaders and others learn to lead. I love that I have so much more to learn.

OUR THOUGHTS ON SAMIR'S ESSAY

Discussing the mainspring effects of Occupy Central on his awareness of the world, Samir muses upon the power of political action, stating, 'what is political becomes personal'. Emerging from the womanist faction of second-wave feminism, 'The personal is political' came to be a rallying cry for including personal, lived experiences in societal analysis. Samir's essay sings a paean for this cause, combining storytelling with moments of introspection and analysis to produce a powerful statement on his early learning years, occurring against the backdrop of Hong Kong's politically volatile 2000s.

Open, curious and all of thirteen, Samir begins the essay as a bystander watching the birth of a civil-disobedience movement for the right to self-determination. Coinciding with his age for discovery, the protests leave an indelible impact, catalyzing his maturity while opening his world in unexpected and unforeseen ways. Inspired by the young age and everydayness of the protesters, his own perspectives of his capabilities and power expand. Samir nimbly adds details of the introspection and engagement that followed, making space for the changes in him while respecting the largeness of the looming unrest. Demonstrating his conviction, he transits inspiration into action and begins learning more about Hong Kong. This leads him to the next avenue for change—an internship with the legislative wing of the region's largest pro-democracy party, LEGCO.

Through LEGCO, we see Samir familiarizing with the rarely televised, minute details crucial for electoral democracy, where the call for equality is enshrined but equally so is the need for workaday essentials, like a functional bus schedule. His willingness to invest in behind-the-scenes legwork is a testament to his conviction in the process. This world of details is the one Samir identifies with, even as he draws inspiration from the larger and perhaps braver qualities and commitment of marching protesters. And like them, he commits to putting in the work to live up to and keep alive their legacy.

There are many stories woven through Samir's essay, and the openness of its end suggests many more to come. At the heart of it all lies a young boy's awakening, mirrored by his home's struggle for self-determination and identity. That leadership is learned, and that he will continue seizing opportunities to learn is the passionate conclusion of this essay.

ZAHRA VAKIL

Harvard, Class of 2016

Major: Psychology
School: The Cathedral & John Connon School, Mumbai, India
Hometown: Mumbai, India

In the rat race that is the city of Mumbai, everyone is in a hurry to be someone, to make it somewhere. Students are pressured to get straight As, finish college and make six-figure salaries. Until recently it was easy for me to be part of this rat race. Things changed quite accidentally last year, when I went to Mani Bhavan, a museum and research center that was once Mahatma Gandhi's home in Mumbai.

My reason for going to Mani Bhavan was embarrassingly specific. I needed information for my Sociology project. I was so blinkered by my assignment that I managed to remain oblivious to the fact that it was from this historic site that Mahatma Gandhi had begun many path-breaking movements.

I spent my first day at the library with my head buried in a book. That evening I told my grandfather that I was doing research at Mani Bhavan. He was excited, telling me stories about this landmark institution. He ended with an apologetic 'But I'm sure you already know all of this.' It struck me then how little I really knew. I felt a sense of shame at my narrow-minded focus on academic gain.

The next day when I entered Mani Bhavan I looked at it differently. Set amongst the laburnum trees it breathed out something special. There I was, standing in my shorts with a laptop under my arm drifting my way into the past. Finally, I stumbled upon a collection of rare books that were in a terrible condition. My gaze fell upon one of the quotes hung up on the wall that said, 'What you do may be insignificant, but it is important that you do it anyway.' My thoughts returned to those pages of my country's history that were slowly being allowed to fade away. I felt I had to get involved in preserving these texts.

After finding out about the shortage of funds at Mani Bhavan, I spent the next few days researching ways to conserve the books. I decided to adapt the idea of the Adopt a Book Scheme. Under the scheme, a person could donate money to adopt one of the three hundred rare books to conserve and digitize them ensuring that they would be accessible and preserved for future generations.

It took some time to gain the confidence of the Mani Bhavan's trustees, but once I got their approval, they were amazingly supportive. I drafted the brochure, the certificates, book plates and the web page. I found a designer and a printer and campaigned for donors. The program was launched this year on October 2, the birth anniversary of Mahatma Gandhi. With the support of the media, a hoarding at a major junction in the city, and posters at appropriate locations, the campaign fell into place with ease. Within three months we were close to our target sum.

I have learnt more from Gandhi's spirit in these twelve months than I have learnt from textbooks over several years. I learnt that what I do may have a small impact, but it is important to do it anyway, with perseverance and optimism for the future.

OUR THOUGHTS ON ZAHRA'S ESSAY

India's past and Zahra's present blend and mix in the palette provided by the essay to produce bright, original shades that offer glimpses of her future. Using a museum as a vehicle, she accesses the annals of history to demonstrate that sometimes, living in the past is OKAY.

Zahra honestly admits, despite embarrassment, to being 'part of the rat race', and 'blinkered' until this life-changing experience has her question how she had 'managed to remain oblivious' of something of such historical importance.

It takes a significant figure in her life—her grandfather—to help her recognize the extent of her 'narrow-minded focus on academic gain'. By bringing him into the story, Zahra adroitly changes the tone of the essay, whisking readers back to indelible childhood memories of grandparents' stories. With this flashback, however, what might have been dismissed as an excusable oversight in the 'younger' generation, now becomes a matter of 'shame' in disappointing the excited expectations of a much-loved grandparent.

This experience helps Zahra view Mani Bhavan through new perspectives, with all her senses sharpened—how the building breathed 'amongst the laburnum trees'; the archives' impactful quotes, its deference to learners and the realization that within its walls, precious history was 'slowly being allowed to fade away'. Her descriptions, tinged with the weight of her learning, allow the reader to witness Zahra's growth.

Zahra's essay structure works like a time capsule—a slow musing ride into the past, and then—BAM! It slingshots readers back into the present. Zahra has transformed her thoughts into action at lightning speed, and decided to do her 'insignificant', but 'important' bit to preserve her country's priceless past, by adapting the ingenious and innovative 'Adopt a Book Scheme'.

She does not belabor the hard work and effort it probably took 'to gain the confidence of the Mani Bhavan's trustees', of the Mahatma Gandhi Memorial Trust. Zahra simply and matter-of-factly outlines the process she went through, as though the sustained efforts were warranted to ensure 'the campaign fell into place with ease'.

Zahra finally reflects on how valuable this one remarkable learning experience has been, reminding us of the Gandhi quote that spurred her to open up avenues for action. Zahra has taken her assignment into new domains by thinking well beyond herself, of the value of preserving a national treasure for future generations. Her reflections and actions define her strength of character much, much louder than any words.

ANGAD KAPUR

Dartmouth, Class of 2016

Major: Government
School: The Cathedral & John Connon School, Mumbai, India
Hometown: Mumbai, India

A framed Martin Luther King Jr poster hangs above my bed. A stack of political magazines lie on the bedside and a gavel won at some Model UN lies on my table. One glance into my room and my deep-rooted interest in politics and current affairs is evident. So, when one of my favorite contemporary artists wrote a song with political implications it immediately caught my attention.

Music pervades a teenager's life in so many tiny, almost inscrutable ways—as you hum a tune in the shower, let go of yourself dancing to heart-pounding chart toppers, or just listen to that one favorite song with only the ocean for company. Yet, how many of us actually spend just a minute reflecting on the meaning of a song or what it stands for.

I do. Apart from its infectious tune, 'Waiting on the World to Change' by John Mayer has politically and socially charged lyrics that made a lasting impression on me the first time I heard it back in the ninth grade. The song challenges the current generation's attitude towards politics with lines like, 'It's hard to beat the system when we're standing at a distance'. As absurd as it sounds, the song acted as a catalyst to my interest in politics and I gladly accepted the challenge. I was determined to prove Mayer wrong in his assumption about our generation. As a ninth grader it made me think about how I could get involved in whatever small way. About half a year later I co-founded a youth magazine on politics called *SPECTRUM*. Through interviews with the political and social leaders of India and the world, I attempted to understand the 'system'. To get close to it with an aspiration to someday change it and be part of it. Meeting these people face to face not only inspires me but also opens my mind to a whole new world of perspectives.

'One day our generation is gonna rule the population.'

The realization that I am part of the generation that is the future dawned upon me. What could I do as a fifteen-year-old? I could not vote or participate directly in the democratic system. What I could do was form an opinion on the political scenario and put it out there for people to read.

I find myself travelling across India, shooting questions at the men and women who lead this nation. Demanding answers to questions people my age have failed to ask. Forming thoughts. Creating opinions. And sharing these thoughts and opinions with as many as I possibly can.

My video camera is on record. I've just thrown Barkha Dutt (a prominent Indian journalist) a question that's critical for my interview. She says, 'The future belongs to you but it can only belong to you if you are interested, engaged and you take part and for all your cynicism you are too young to be cynical....' But somehow the rest of the answer slips my attention. Lyrics of a song start up in my head.

'They say we stand for nothing and
There's no way we ever could'

I sit there smiling to myself. Take that, John Mayer.

OUR THOUGHTS ON ANGAD'S ESSAY

Navigating young adulthood through thoughts, songs, and action, Angad tells the story of awakening to one's own potential and power.

Starting the essay, at all of fifteen, he is politically aware (MLK poster, magazines), but perhaps un-engaged (weren't we all, at fifteen!). However, upon hearing his favorite musician John Mayer's lyrical rebuke of his generation's perceived political apathy, Angad sets out to prove him wrong. Tackling Mayer's accusation of 'standing at a distance', he launches a magazine titled *SPECTRUM*, creating a forum for discourse. By deeming the song as a clarion call for action, Angad showcases his intent to encourage change. This explains his decision to opt for a platform where others too can be inspired to engage with social and political issues.

The essay goes on to deftly tie Angad's realizations and actions to the song's lyrics and thereby create a metaphorical context for the transformation taking place within him. He uses the line, 'One day our generation is gonna rule the population' to advantage and captures the responsibility that younger people have to society at large, the future, and to themselves. For Angad, the lyrics represent possibility and promise. At fifteen, it might seem there are few avenues that allow for political participation; he cannot vote nor stand for elections. But he can make his voice heard in anticipation of the day that he can and will be responsible for change.

This spurs Angad to broaden his horizons, travel around the country and hold those in power accountable. Asking questions of electors, politicians and journalists, he continues to share this knowledge through his magazine, ensuring that this revolution transcends self and his newfound awareness. The message is clear, Angad is not sitting in the wings, waiting for the world to change. He will change it.

PRERNA KAKAR

UPenn, Class of 2014

Major: Bio-Engineering and Finance (M&T Program)
School: American School of Dubai, Dubai, UAE
Hometown: Dubai, UAE

It was 8:30 a.m. on a Saturday morning, and I was in deep sleep. My mother suddenly burst into my room, pulled open the curtains, and said, 'Wake up, Prerna, or else you will miss your violin lesson!' At that phase of my childhood, my idea of music drastically differed from that of my mother. While I liked to listen to Madonna, she had a passion for Mozart. I had failed in my mission to convince her not to put me in violin lessons a few months ago, and since then I had acquired a violin teacher who came to my house twice a week to teach me how to play.

My teacher had a stern and serious disposition and did not believe in wasting a single moment. Each session of sixty minutes seemed like six hours to me. It was the same monotonous routine each time. Start with scales and arpeggios, practise a few pages from my 'technique book', and finish with rehearsing a simple melody. He was critical and would never hesitate to correct my mistakes. I wondered whether I ever did anything right. He would tell me that if I practised and played well, he would consider making me a part of his orchestra. During each of these command performances, I would smile respectfully and pretend to enjoy the lesson. However, at the end of it, all I wanted to do was to get away from that music. My fingers would hurt and I wondered how I could convince my mother to let me transition back to Madonna from Mozart! I certainly did not want to be a part of his orchestra.

Looking back, I think my violin teacher sensed my resistance. One day, he invited me to a performance by his orchestra of young musicians in Dubai. The concert was an eye-opener for me. What I had thought was dull music until then, suddenly sounded so melodious and enjoyable. I was surprised to see that some of the orchestra members were even younger than I was. They all seemed to be having fun too. When they finished their piece, the audience applauded, and the pride and happiness on their faces was palpable. I too felt something change inside me. I suddenly wanted to be a part of the orchestra.

I painfully realized then that I had wasted my violin lessons so far. Strangely, my pride, too, would not allow me to admit to my mother or my teacher that I desperately wanted to join the orchestra. But I was determined and knew that the only way to do so was by playing well, for which I needed to persevere and train passionately. I started concentrating more during my lessons, and also, diligently practised in my spare time. My fingers hurt even more than before. However, that did not deter me from my passion. I now enjoyed playing the violin. My effort was eventually rewarded when, one day, at the end of a difficult lesson, my teacher invited me to be a part of his orchestra. My joy knew no bounds! I realized that with hard work, a positive attitude, and perseverance, one can successfully achieve one's goals.

There was more to learn as I continued to practise hard to keep upgrading my skills on the violin as a member of the orchestra. I learned the power of teamwork and coordination, in addition to individual excellence. I realized that however well each of us plays individually, we cannot make harmony if we do not coordinate perfectly. It was not about winning against one another, instead it was all about winning together. And, additionally it was not about showing the audience how good we were as a group, but about engaging them in our performance. I have now learned that if we are passionate about involving all stakeholders in an activity, the results can be exponentially higher.

The learning did not end here. I noticed that when any of us made an error during a performance, my teacher, as the conductor, would compensate for it with a flick of his baton, so that the imperfection would be blended into the overall composition, unnoticed by the audience. This taught me the power of leadership through influence.

Our orchestra also takes a lead in performing for fund-raising and building awareness for charitable causes. This experience has further amazed me on how we, as individuals or as teams, with creativity and energy can make a significant difference to the lives of people and the larger community. I realize now that with dedication, focus, and passion even ordinary actions can lead to extraordinary results.

Over the years, my experience and achievements as a violinist have molded my personality and work ethic. Playing the violin has convinced me that there is 'no short cut to success'. I have now trained myself to think positively, work hard, and enjoy all that I do, so that I can make a real difference to the world.

OUR THOUGHTS ON PRERNA'S ESSAY

The abrupt and initially unwelcome introduction of violin lessons in Prerna's life leads to a period of adjustment where she struggles to get past her mental block for musical preferences. However, using this as a launching pad, she goes on to track an enthralling symphony of expanding worldviews and the lesson that sometimes, being proved wrong is an invaluable gift.

Prerna's essay rests on convincing us on the larger impact of the 180 degree turn in her appreciation for classical music. This means we must believe her initial apathy and relate to it. By opening her essay with her mother pulling open the curtains of her room as she sleeps, she succeeds in both. It is an oh-so-familiar act that aptly defines the always-well-meaning-but-sometimes-overreaching ambit of parental affection. We identify. We can understand Prerna's reluctance, her tiny rebellion, and the resulting obdurate 'I *will* not like my Violin lessons' mindset. This serves as a fantastic fulcrum for the essay to hinge its transformation on.

When she witnesses her first orchestra, however, the change that takes place is internal, and the resulting desire to do well is her decision, and hers alone. Now, all that confirmed and entrenched her bias against violin lessons—the hurting of her fingers, the unforgiving precision of her teacher, become signs of her investment and labor. Eventually, rewarded by her inclusion in the orchestra, she comes to value the amplifying emotions of belonging to a team, and truly witness how music is created, collaboratively. In including her learnings from the orchestra, she has us witness how she functions in a group setting, and in a community. Prerna additionally takes care to enunciate the values she gleans from these interactions. Her ability to move past her initial conviction that the violin is not for her, dissipate her adolescent stubbornness, and embrace her new world demonstrates her potential as a student and a leader.

Prerna's essay benefits from its cogent, well-planned structure, relatable messages, and cohesive use of narrative. It is clear that her ability to learn from the past will continue to light a pathway into a bright future.

BARKHA SETH

Columbia, Class of 2025

Major: Engineering
School: Dhirubhai Ambani International School, Mumbai, India
Hometown: Mumbai, India

BOTTOM'S DREAM

'I had a most rare vision,' I whisper my lines to myself as I wait. Onstage, the lovers continue their dance, stepping and turning and gliding as they quarrel with one another. I glance at my partner—the formidable Queen Titania—standing tall, the earthy greens of her gown flowing in a stream behind her. Self-conscious, I turn away, clutching my hairy tail as I prepare myself.

I always loved new books. As a child, I would sit for hours at an end, flicking through the pages, soaking it all in. Fantasy novels, encyclopedias, comics, Enid Blyton, *Space: Discover the Universe*, *Calvin and Hobbes*, Shakespeare—anything I could get my hands on. Perhaps it was this love for reading that led to my varied interests.

Despite the diverse student body at school, I often found myself isolated in my love for both writing and science. 'Aren't you an English person?' the question followed me in science classes, but my friends in English class deemed me a 'science bot'. In my attempt to choose, I constantly shifted between the lab and the desk, the calculator and the pen, one friend group and another. Every step in either direction felt hesitant because what if I eventually chose to go the other way? When the time came, I rushed to my place, my equipment ready.

In the Physics lab, I stood with my partner at our usual counter. Add. Mix. Note. Calculate. The steam from the kettle rose steadily, fogging up my safety goggles. The ticking stopwatch matched my pulse as I took the measurements to calculate the specific heat capacity of the salt solution. A simple experiment really, but the first one of my own design. There, among the stacks of test tubes and beakers, I was performing, my partner and I working in a slow choreography, at a steady rhythm to add. Mix. Note. Calculate.

At my desk at home, I sat alone surrounded by the blank ruled sheets. Words poured out of me in an endless stream as I wrote, filling the empty spaces with adventures and ink stains. Though I stayed in one place, I travelled across worlds. Though I sat alone, I wasn't lonely. I wrote about times before land was surrounded by water. I wrote about a girl transformed into poison ivy. My thoughts took shape to form an intricately woven world until finally, I set my pen down. But each dream ended abruptly at the thought of losing the other.

The lovers exit stage. I scurry into position. Shoulders hunched, knees bent, face scrunched, my body betrays nothing but the aura of my character. My mind flickers with doubt. What if I fumble? What if people laugh? What if no one laughs? The audience stretches before me, eyes piercing through darkness. Examining... Scrutinizing! The bright white lights come on. I spring up and begin my song.

Many people speak of moments in their lives that transformed their own idea about themselves. My moment occurred as I scratched the hair on my face, braying at a crowd of unfamiliar faces. As the reverberating laughter of the audience echoes through the room, I forget who I am. I become Nick Bottom, the donkey, belching and snorting as I dance around my forest. My uncertainty transforms into adrenaline as I deliver line after line. 'Bottom's Dream,' the fans of *A Midsummer Night's Dream* called this scene.

'Bottom's Dream' had been an awakening. Amidst the thrill of performing, something clicked into place. The confidence that always lurked inside me surged ahead, and I realized that I did not have to choose one or the other. I was not simply a writer or a bot: I was both. I did not have to be Titania or Helena; I could be Bottom and make an impact. All of my interests made me who I was—and that person was well-appreciated.

OUR THOUGHTS ON BARKHA'S ESSAY

'I had the most rare vision. I have had a dream—past the wit of man to say what dream it was.' So goes the monologue called 'Bottom's Dream', describing a puckish bit of fairy magic that, amongst other capers, compels fairy queen Titania to fall in love with donkey-faced Bottom. As he wakes, Bottom struggles to reconcile the freedom and magic he has experienced with the limits of what is deemed acceptable by the more real world he will return to. Barkha's essay uses Bottom's dilemma to creatively communicate the limitations placed on her by her dread of scrutiny and the judgement she feels for her apparently incongruent passions for Physics and English.

Barkha's essay stands out because it works on several levels. Whereas her excellence in both English and Physics should not be mutually exclusive or revolutionary, in a school system that places definitive, qualitative distinctions between students pursuing the sciences and arts, she is an anomaly. Feeling the judgement of both of her disparate peer groups, Barkha grapples with her identity; however, her struggle finds expression in unique and insightful ways. She seeks solace in the sturdy, practiced choreography of Physics lab experiments even as she explores new terrain through her writings. As the essay meanders, delineating Barkha in her many roles, the reader can sense her comfort within her rich, diverse inner world and contrastingly, her paralyzing anxiety when faced with the possibility of exposure.

The moment of breakthrough comes at the moment when Barkha 'forgets who she thought she was'. Essaying the role of Bottom in a production of *A Midsummer Night's Dream* and giving into the whimsy the role necessitates, she finds freedom. Beyond her own ideas of who she should be, the reader witnesses Barkha's powerful acceptance of who she is, inconvenient dreams, et al.

'Bottom's Dream' begins with, 'When my cue comes, call me, and I will answer.' Indeed, through this essay, Barkha appears to be responding to her liberal arts calling, cued by her convictions, buoyed by her newly minted confidence, and delivered by a rebellion against limiting notions of self. A quiet rebellion, but nonetheless, a worthy, resonant one.

6

THE LEADERS

'There is a difference between knowing the path and walking the path.'

– Morpheus, The Matrix

Leadership is a popular theme in the Common App essay. While some of the other essays in this book have elements of leadership; the narratives in this section go beyond attaining leadership positions than demonstrating capabilities. The leaders here have reflected deeply on their experiences and their impact to describe and define what leadership means to them.

Discussing shortcomings, missteps and vulnerabilities with an openness usually reserved for laurels, these essays are evidence of the legacies their authors established, legacies that any academic community is sure to covet.

KANISHKH KANODIA

Princeton, Class of 2023

Major: Public Policy
School: The Doon School, Dehradun, India
Hometown: Gorakhpur, India

After an arduous day of working for *The Doon School Weekly*, debating, and directing a play, I returned to my room at midnight. As I looked around, William Henley implored me to be 'the captain of my soul'; Walt Whitman reminded me to 'publish myself on my personality'. All things seemed to be in place, but one.

A piece of paper, wrapped in tape, lay at my table, patiently waiting to hurl scathing words at me. That night my illusion of being a 'good' House Captain was shattered.

As the leader of the House, I had envisioned myself striking the perfect balance between being friendly and being firm. The former was essential to preserve the bonds with my juniors; the latter was crucial to uphold the public-school ethos of Doon. As my tenure began, I thought I had begun to embody the exemplary Captain. However, the letter proved otherwise.

A junior had criticized me for being too stern, blaming me for acting contrary to the ideals I had stood for. He even questioned if I was putting on a façade of a leader I had never intended to become. That junior perhaps spoke for the other boys, who had admired me as just Kanishkh, and not the strict House Captain.

I had not realized when my actions had alienated those who were even willing to elect me School Captain. Feeling estranged, I turned to my diary. The first page had a clutch of the advice I had received from my predecessors about how to best execute my role. I began to read, in an attempt to find how I could be Kanishkh and House Captain at the same time. The fourth quotation stopped me:

> *'Your rationality and compassion are your strengths. Do not try to overcome your weaknesses by compromising on your strengths.'*

It struck me that the answer was, after all, around me.

The answer was in the words of Henley and Whitman. All this while, I had mistaken my strengths for being weaknesses and suppressed them. I had confused being nice with being gullible. I regarded friendliness with the juniors as losing their respect. I had deemed a rational decision-making process to be slow and ineffective. I realized that instead, I just had to be myself.

The answer was in my role as the director. I had to listen to the juniors and get to know their perspective, like I did with the actors. Only then will I be successful in forging a bond with them.

The answer was hidden beneath the façade of my desperately trying to be the stereotypical leader one ought to be at Doon. Until that day, I had not realized that the façade had become my reality. It took a courageous attempt by someone two years younger than me to make me realize this.

After that day, I made an effort to peel off the mask.

I began to personally interact more with the juniors. I remember sitting in my school's amphitheater—*the Rose Bowl*—during play practices, and talking to the juniors about their favorite books, their aspirations, and even their lives. These conversations helped me connect better with my housemates and solved most of my problems, perhaps even theirs. I was amazed to see how, within a short span of time, the junior who had written the letter had begun to admire and respect me as not only his leader, but also as his mentor. Perhaps, he could now see that beneath the firmness, lay a person who was frank, trustworthy and caring.

Criticism from an unexpected source truly brought out the 'good' leader in me. I did not see my friendliness and my compassion as weaknesses anymore. In fact, I derived the greatest satisfaction and happiness from talking to juniors and becoming 'friends' with them. I had finally reconciled the House Captain with who I was.

OUR THOUGHTS ON KANISHKH'S ESSAY

Unwinding in his dorm room after a long day, we glimpse key aspects of Kanishkh's world. While we can envision him moving from role to role: student, editor, writer, director, performing roles through the day, here, however, he can hang up his many caps and just be himself. Reflecting on Henley and Whitman and taking stock of the day, Kanishkh's description of his room reads like an exhalation. This makes the interruption caused by a mysterious 'piece of paper... patiently waiting' all the more effective. Significantly, the shift in tone predicates the internal metamorphosis that the rest of the essay explores.

The gap between who Kanishkh is and who he becomes as House Captain is exposed by his junior's perceptions of his behavior. Through the course of the essay, his actions attempt to bridge this gap. He accepts the criticism openly and seriously, showing a readiness to revaluate his choices, displaying humility, and a strong sense of duty while demonstrating a commendable depth of self-awareness. Instead of pushing back against a member of his house for questioning him, Kanishkh lauds him for stepping up and holding him accountable.

The dilemma Kanishkh faces—choosing between who he is and who he thinks he should be is relatable across the board. All of us find ourselves wearing varied masks more often than we would admit, and yearn to peel them off. Kanishkh builds on this, connecting with the reader by being open and honest about this vulnerability. Consequently, the essay's ability to connect, and its depiction of Kanishkh as someone capable of connection (with predecessors, juniors, role models and the reader) augments its impact immensely.

Ultimately, Kanishkh's satisfaction in reconciling his captaincy with his instincts are emphatically felt. We are invested in Kanishkh's journey, despite not knowing him at all. Simultaneously, the essay aces in communicating the attributes he will bring to university: dedication, openness, and the propensity to make any experience uniquely his.

ARNAV AGRAWAL

Cornell, Class of 2025

Major: Environmental Engineering
School: The Doon School, Dehradun, India
Hometown: Nagpur, India

Science requires questioning. Questioning everything. So when my housemaster 'asked' me to pack up my rucksack for a five-day trip to the Yamunotri Glacier in the Himalayas, I (well) questioned it. God knows I did. He didn't give me an option. 'You have to go. Trust me, you will love the wild,' he said. Defenseless, I followed his instructions and ended up spending one of the best five days of my life. Disengaging from technology helped me appreciate the workings of Mother Nature. The seed had been sown.

After a few tree-walks, bird-watching sessions, and webinars, I had transformed into an ardent conservationist. My newfound passion turned into an inconvenience for my brother who liked to brush his teeth with the tap open and sleep with the air conditioning on. 'Closing one tap isn't going to save the world, Arnav!' He was right. To 'save the world', I had to take a more active stance. I approached my goal the same way I approached Math problems. I broke it down into smaller, more manageable pieces. With that, I conceived Climate Crew—a podcast where I interviewed (and was exposed to the thoughts of) the very best environmentalists who had a deep-rooted love for nature. The seed gave way to a sprout that rapidly spread its roots into deeper soil.

I found myself conflicted with the dual instincts of an environmentalist and an engineer. The fields seemed unrelated, but somehow, I felt that they were the perfect balancing act. Engineering was motivated by sound, but cold logic while my environmentalism was motivated by a burning passion inside me. So when my school's environment committee was looking at rewilding our residential campus, I was quick to suggest 'Amnis'—a stream development project that would provide me with the opportunity to experiment with, and combine both my passions. An environmental engineering project, 'Amnis' would facilitate higher biodiversity in the campus, while providing me with a formidable engineering challenge. As its shoot grew out of the soil, the plant encountered a board that blocked its sunlight. Instead of perishing, however, the plant wrapped itself around the board and grew taller than ever before.

The relatively small scale of our school's environment committee meant that there was a distinct lack of funds and support for the project. However, through countless speeches delivered locally in each dormitory, I was able to racket up a group of fellow environmentalists and would-be engineers who helped me in the project. 'Amnis' transformed my identity in school from the 'consulting mathematician and physicist' to an environmental activist, something I would have never thought I would be perceived as!

The plant withstood the test of time—instead of withering in the face of drought, it adapted to its surroundings. Nothing could stop its growth. With over 500 listeners, 'Climate Crew' served its purpose of enriching people's understanding of sustainability and the environment. 'Amnis' too achieved its goal of improving the biodiversity inside the school campus. A walk around the campus at six in the morning would usually lead to about five or six different bird sightings—after 'Amnis', the number grew to twelve. On an academic and practical level, both of these projects helped me understand sustainability and environmental concerns through both secondary and primary experience. Personally, they provided me with an amazing opportunity to build friendships with the people around me, who shared my passion for the environment.

The plant flowered and finally bore fruit.

As I packed my rucksack for yet another expedition, I moved to the 'box room' to retrieve my sleeping bag from my trunk. While searching, I overheard a younger student speaking to my housemaster. 'Why do we have to go to Yamunotri? I don't want to go!' I smiled. I knew what was about to happen. A new seed had been sown.

OUR THOUGHTS ON ARNAV'S ESSAY

The innate conviction that builds the ardent desire to 'save the world' is one of the many (sometimes derided) virtues of youth. Brimming with hope, idealism and his newly germinated passion for conservation, Arnav's essay provides a look into his origin or 'sowing' story, exploring the birth of his dedication to environmentalism, and consequent leadership in the domain. Nurtured by his scientific temper and fertilized by his engineering capabilities, the essay navigates the growth of his early, nascent interest in the field into a defining part of his identity.

Arnav is transformed by a trip to Yamunotri, the glacier at the source of north India's dying Yamuna river. Upon returning home and having to negotiate with a less-transformed world (brother), he conceives a podcast, 'Climate Crew', to make his views more accessible to people. Here, we get an insight into how Arnav deals with problems. Leveraging his methodical thinking, he identifies an actionable issue that will both increase his sprouting knowledge and strengthen his environmental activism. The confidence from the podcast bleeds into him taking initiative to create 'Amnis', a stream development project at school. As he delves further into conservation, he also begins to think of creative ways to harness his instinct for science, intuitively feeling a potential connection between the two. The resulting marriage between his lifelong commitment to science and burgeoning passion for environment helps sculpt a creative niche where Arnav comes into his own. Working on the mechanics of rewilding, educating himself on the realities of environmental degradation, working in his technical capabilities and confronting the realities of grassroots activism, he finds his métier as an 'environmental activist'. Significantly, beyond merely discovering a cause that he is passionate about, he has found the means to effect lasting change.

All through the essay Arnav employs the metaphor of a seed sown into fertile ground, sprouting and growing to 'bear fruit' against the odds. Transposing this with his own story of growth, he closes by expressing his belief that the movement will continue to grow and change, planting more seeds along the way.

DHRUV GOYAL

Harvard, Class of 2016

Major: Economics
School: Dhirubhai Ambani International School, Mumbai, India
Hometown: Mumbai, India

My tenure as House Captain was an enriching experience. Interacting with two hundred students across various age groups has been instrumental in my development as a human being. There were several challenges that I faced during this eventful journey as Captain. I worked with a core team and there were constant conflicts when decisions had to be taken. We made sure that nothing was done arbitrarily, and all opinions were fairly evaluated. This ensured that unbiased decisions were taken in the best interest of the House. As per the situation, I had to adopt different management styles taking bold decisions at times.

The Lion House started off on a disappointing note, losing several events at the beginning of the year. There was despondency among fellow members and motivation levels were low since our House had not won in six years. As their leader, I worked towards instilling that sense of belief that we could still win. It taught me how to continue fighting even in the face of adversity. A couple of events in the middle of the year went in our favor and there were positive vibes floating around our House once again. I continued to exchange ideas with my team members and motivate colleagues to work towards victory. After that we never looked back and made a wonderful comeback from being last in the points table to winning the House Cup.

One instance, in particular, comes to mind. In the final match of the inter-house chess competition, our opponent arrived late at the venue. She was a national level player and the clear favorite. As House Captain, I had to decide whether she should be allowed to play against us, as the delay on her part was a ground for disqualification. This event was crucial since it took place towards the end of the year and could potentially decide the House Cup. I could have disqualified her and won the points with ease. It was a difficult predicament. I decided to stand by the principle of healthy competition and allowed her to participate at the risk of losing the cup. She did win that event, but fortunately, in the end we still won the House Cup. Not only was this a great learning, but also, adopting an ethical approach gave me immense satisfaction.

At the end of the year, all captains had to address the school with concluding speeches. It was a very emotional moment for me as I summed up a whole year's experiences in just ten minutes. The cheers of a thousand students were well worth every moment spent during the year.

As part of the Student Government, I learnt how to delegate work and oversee the functioning of events. I can now appreciate the dynamics of responsibility-authority relationships better. It became clear to me that every student has different needs and motives and hence I had to be empathetic in order to help them realize their maximum potential. I recognized that I was more of a facilitator, encouraging my team to participate enthusiastically and put in their best effort, irrespective of the outcome. Now, I am able to manage my time better and balance extra-curricular activities without compromising on academic performance.

OUR THOUGHTS ON DHRUV'S ESSAY

The impact of this essay derives from its direct response to the 'significant experience' prompt. Dhruv, in describing his role of responsibility as House Captain in high school, structures his essay to take the reader through the challenges and ethical dilemmas he faced in conducting his prefectorial duties. He discusses how he addressed these, adopting 'different management styles' using his personal strengths and intuitive leadership skills, taking risks that finally result in transformation and achievement. Through his rather matter-of-fact telling of the process, Dhruv was also able to indirectly yet cogently convey various positive facets of his personality.

What is noteworthy is how Dhruv sets the tone with energy-loaded language right from the get-go—'enriching experience', 'instrumental in my development as a human being', 'eventful journey' while dealing with 'several challenges', 'constant conflict', 'decisions', with 'fairly evaluated', 'unbiased decisions', and 'different management styles', which were 'bold…at times'. He then goes on to outline the challenge, and his 'motivating leader and learner' strategy to work towards addressing it. He does not walk alone, but with 'fellow members'. Casual mentions like these and 'It taught me…' speak of Dhruv's solid character, strengths, and achievement in 'working towards victory'. The words serve as action points.

Next, Dhruv provides more specific detail to whet readers' curiosity, and describes his 'ethical dilemma' with an anecdote, where his spirit of sportsmanship supersedes the call of victory, even though the rules are in his favor. He does not shy away from allowing readers to see his emotions—his satisfaction and pride in his achievements. Instead, Dhruv continues to reflect, with humility, about what he has learnt in his role as a leader, appreciating 'the dynamics of responsibility-authority relationships', and the power of empathizing with the students he has led. He reveals himself as a compassionate, responsible, and constant learner, which is refreshing, considering his achievements.

Dhruv lets his authentic inner voice come through, showing us at the end, what became 'clear' to him as a leader. Thereby demonstrating through action and results, why he would be such a great addition to any university. This style goes down especially well with a school like Harvard.

ANONYMOUS

Columbia, Class of 2020

Major: Economics and Psychology
School: The Cathedral & John Connon School, Mumbai, India
Hometown: Mumbai, India

My knight reaching g5 marked the end of the Scotch Gambit—an opening in which both players make calculated moves to reach 'open position'. The central files are open and my pieces are flexibly placed to be maneuvered. My opponent advances his knight into my territory, signaling attack. This move is sufficient to devastate my situation.

15th March 2015. A day of reckoning. The pole position of The Cathedral & John Connon School, HEAD GIRL, would be conferred to me. My girlfriends had heard it—and the rumor spread like Chinese whispers. I was THE candidate of this post. I was ready for the year. As Head Girl. It meant more to me than the metallic glint of silver on navy. I had channeled efforts throughout high school into attaining this title. I had demonstrated electric versatility, auditioning for the school play as lead actor. Performing cartwheels at the gymnastics competition. Brick by brick, I constructed my future Palace of Happiness based on being Head Girl. I would take my school to fame in every realm, inspire by example.

The opponent is confident the game is his. He has the light of battle in his eyes. Just when I think nothing can get worse, I face a severe attack. The opponent signals his queen to attack and my king is left unguarded.

My stately principal, aglow in her sari, stood on the dais to announce the office-bearers to a knowing audience. Her words in the stone atrium of the heritage building had a familiar ring. I've heard them often in my mind: 'The Head Girl for the year 2015–2016 goes to…' I flexed to rise, hoping there would be no missteps en route to receiving the badge. Six hundred pairs of eyes on me. But temporary paralysis set in as I am announced the new

'Savage House Captain'.

That day I drowned in tears. Throughout, my parents and caregivers had played the role of my 'pawns' on the checkerboard of life, shielding me from reality. Now, they stood helpless as I ricocheted between feeling cheated and betrayed.

I transport my knight to f3 and bishop to f4. The next 45 minutes in the game are spent on thinking of a way out of this precarious situation.

Blinded to the proverbial silver lining, I was coaxed out of my delusory mindset by my ex-house captain who admonished me gently. This she said, was the great gift of opportunity: there was more than one route to taking my school to glory. I was forgetting the 150 'Savage-ites' who looked to me, their captain, for direction.

I re-think my battle plan. After much thought, I restore the balance on the battlefield. I begin to drive my opposition's pieces back to their defensive positions.

I rose for my school. For Savage. For myself. I found myself on a stairway to heaven and nothing could stop me. My Palace of Happiness in the distant future was illusory, it existed right here, and over the next six months, I gave it contour and shape.

I started restoring Savage's one-time glory. Under my leadership, my House *would* emerge victorious and lift the 'Cock House' trophy after fifteen years. I nurtured my House. Every junior was a treasure-trove: I ensured no-one was left on the backburner. I took initiative and the change was tangible. The 'Super Savage Register' I conceived was emulated by other Houses. On color-coded pages dedicated to each child, I tracked events, experiences, their unique talents. My record-keeping benefits over 150 students. In seeking avenues to ensure each of my charges shine—my despair morphed into strength. In instilling unity and resilience, I started embodying that change.

I learnt that adversity is a perception that conceals opportunity. Today I prime juniors facing setbacks to strive for greatness irrespective of hurdles.

I sign 1–0 on the score sheet and it is CHECKMATE!

OUR THOUGHTS ON THIS ESSAY

The student chose to style her Common App essay using a chess battle as a metaphor for a significant setback she faced—being passed over for the position of school head girl for the lesser post of Savage House Captain—and how she overcame her disappointment, excelled in her new post, and took the performance of Savage House to stellar heights.

She opens the essay with the exciting, rather aggressive moves of the Scotch Gambit in a particular chess game, clearly one of her stronger skills, where her opponent's attack move '*is sufficient to devastate my situation*'. Readers immediately draw a parallel with what comes thereafter.

She takes pains to describe in detail how she had prepared for 'the pole position', enhancing her multiple talents with hard work and harboring high hopes to 'take my school to fame in every realm, inspire by example', further fueled by the school rumor mill.

Yet, as they say, 'the best-laid plans…' crumble. The moves so carefully constructed, 'brick by brick' well in advance, that should have brought victory, tumble with one sharp battle call of her confident chess opponent's Queen, and one short announcement from her queen-like 'stately principal, aglow in her sari'. Her dream dissolves in a flood of tears, all her protective 'pawns' helpless, unable to buffer her emotional 'ricocheted between feeling cheated and betrayed'.

The action-packed vocabulary carries the reader with her as she propels her house to ascendency. She has layered the progress of the chess game, with reflections on her experiences and her responses to them, showing wonderful self-awareness, even if in retrospect. Her language changes with her acceptance of new positive perspectives—rising, building, shaping, moving upward.

She heeds her ex-house Captain's wise words, understanding that in life as in chess, strategies can be altered. She presents her ability to extend her focus beyond herself to 'the 150 "Savage-ites" who looked to me, their captain, for direction' and to '...restoring Savage's one-time glory'—her 'despair morphed into strength'.

Finally recognizing that 'adversity is a perception that conceals opportunity', she sees the importance of being the best at what she has been given and then, succeeds in taking the Queen in the end, and taking her House to summits unscaled for years.

KABIR WALIA

Cornell, Class of 2022

Major: Computer Science
School: Dhirubhai Ambani International School, Mumbai, India
Hometown: Mumbai, India

My senses heightened. The tension was palpable.

'Pre-stress in the struts won't support the prism. Swagam's calculations are wrong.' Pulkit's declaration, unequivocal.

'I experimented twice on the ice-cream stick model. I'm not wrong.' Swagam, equally indignant.

'Well, it looks like you are.' Pulkit's self-satisfied retort.

School-captaincy skilled me in conversing with even angry parents. I searched, but only managed a meek mumble, 'Reducing strut A might correct those calculations.'

Six eyes glared at my velvet-clad precocity.

Pulkit calmly, 'We could try that.'

At Team Indus' headquarters in Bangalore, the isolated conference room was a veritable teenage shack with scattered Pringles, MJ music and a tumult of papers and dialogue.

Being selected to join an aerospace start-up springboarding a rover to the moon, each day at Team Indus (the only Indian entrant in the Google Lunar XPRIZE) entranced me.

When I proffered my hand for a handshake with Indus' 'Fleet Commander' Rahul Narayan (Founder), he countered with a high-five.

Later, during my introductory tour, ribbons of conversation streamed, from the Pele–Maradona debate to spaghetti recipes.

And then that Ping-Pong competition in the canteen. I wondered: Aerospace start-up? Seriously?

Expecting hard-nosed scientists in lab-suits, I encountered instead robotic nods of iridescent polo-clad techies who animated instantly on hearing 'thrusters' and 'star-sensors'. Over lunchtime and in washrooms eschewing Bollywood and Hollywood they discussed *Hohmann transfers* and *honeycomb structures.* I kept pace.

Their relentless engagement with complex scientific problems inspired me and my three co-interns, tasked with creating a Tensegrity Tower, taller than Swastik, the tallest employee at Indus, standing at 6'2".

Using steel rods and metallic cables, we would build a unique Tensegrity tower which maintained its balance through interactions of compressional and tensional forces existent in rods (struts) and cables (tendons). Literally, 'Tensional Integrity'. This sturdy structure, paradoxically, required finely calibrated processes and intricate calculations.

I spent hours deciphering Mech. Engineering books provided by IIT engineers from Structures, and construing research publications by mathematicians. I derived the Pre-stress elements and vector analysis behind this twirling tower. Working out coordinate system calculations and formulating construction methodologies, I arrogantly thought, 'Cylindrical geometry and some vectors. Why give something so basic?'

I learnt why.

The same math, conflicting calculations.

Aditi: Keep each tendon at 80...

Kabir: 80's loooonnng... Listen, dimensions are crucial. Hole-drilling can be...

Pulkit: Can't be omitted! The math will fail.

The chasm in opinions on methodology and physical dimensions caused belligerence.

I was annoyed. Pulkit was horribly correct. And my foundational understanding of science and binary approach was shaken.

I found comfort in black and white, spoke science in the language of math. Subjectivity was antithetical to objective science.

However, I saw, through this, that even as the tension caused by conflicting opinions compressed, and shaped our ideas, the tension in the cables resurrected the tower.

My voice now rang true, 'Alright, stop! This argument's directionless. Let's scrutinize one thing at a time. The base prism, the strut lengths, the tendons. Done!?'

'Woah, Kabir. Chill,' said Swagam. '*Stay mellow,* buddy.'

Bangalore lingo.

However, as our conversations, through peaks and troughs, advanced in a continuum, the tower rose.

Aditi: Base radius?

Swagam: Fixed with 'D.sinx'. Struts 80 then?

Kabir: No, 90. Leave room for holes.

We smiled.

Piece by piece we assembled the structure using relevant calculations. As the tension in the tendons grew, the structure became stronger.

Inexorably, the tension in the room increased. This tension was constructive, bringing not chaos but order. And cohesiveness.

After eight hours of equation-scribing, critiquing, drilling and knotting, we completed level-1 of the Tensegrity Tower. And oh! It was beautiful. Standing...

Confident.

Strong.

Poised.

I then understood Mr Narayan's response to an earlier query. Witnessing aggravated arguments between the Structures and Thermal departments, I asked, 'How have these guys worked together and built the spacecraft amidst such conflict?'

He'd replied, 'It's this conflict that makes them so successful.'

Our Tensegrity Tower reflected this principle. Without the tension in those cables working in unison with the compressed rods, the structure wouldn't, well, *tower.*

Without that tension, the structure would have no integrity.

This experience changed my perspective on 'tension'.

OUR THOUGHTS ON KABIR'S ESSAY

Kabir's essay is a dazzling example of how a central motif—in this case 'Tension'—is carried right through, with sensory, physical, emotional, psychological, verbal, structural and educational (the list goes on) explorations of the concept at various stages.

Leading in with tension that is 'palpable', Kabir shows himself caught in a position where his leadership skills for conflict resolution are challenged. 'School-captaincy skilled me in conversing with even angry parents. I searched, but only managed a meek mumble...'

Kabir provides a physical backdrop and context to his story, contrasting his 'velvet-clad precocity' with the unexpected, unassuming intelligence of the aerospace start-up team. He also manages to establish a tension between the high levels of his team's and his own talent, skills and achievement that belie their youthfulness. He is surprised when his stereotypical expectations of 'hard-nosed scientists in lab-suits' are foiled by encountering, instead, the 'robotic nods of iridescent polo-clad techies'. It is a tempo he has to match.

And, so begins Kabir's journey from a mild arrogance to humility, discovering that he is not more important than his teammates, while also understanding through their successful teamwork that he is no less important than them. The 'Tensegrity Tower' becomes a metaphor for his own internal and their combined 'Tensional Integrity'.

Kabir continues generating the tension, where his hard work to prove his point is caught in 'conflicting calculations'. 'The chasm in opinions on methodology and physical dimensions caused belligerence.' He reflects on his own chagrin at finding that a team-mate is 'horribly correct'. He does not shy from telling us that his self-esteem is thrown into doubt, that he is outside his comfort zone. Reading, we see how humility dawns and he accepts his limitations, recognizing 'that even as the tension caused by conflicting opinions compressed, and shaped our ideas, the tension in the cables resurrected the tower'. This self-examination helps him suggest re-examining their work, with a renewed appreciation that 'the peaks and troughs' of everyone's input are equally valuable for progress. 'This tension was constructive, bringing not chaos but order. And cohesiveness.'

Kabir's use of the team's actual conversational speech patterns adds an animated, lifelike element. Readers become observers in the 'lab'—flies on the wall listening in to the chatter, as 'the tension in the room' mounts, and takes the team to new heights of discovery, and ultimate triumph.

Kabir marvels as he fully understands Mr Narayan's response—that 'It's this conflict that makes them so successful.' He concludes with a transformed perspective on the value of constructive 'tension', which he now embraces.

SAHIL RAI

Columbia, Class of 2019

Major: Applied Mathematics and Economics-Statistics
School: Singapore International School, Mumbai, India
Hometown: Mumbai, India

COMING OF AGE

Holding the school flag, I await the new Head Prefects to enter from the wings. It's an emotive moment and my year as Head of the Student Council flashes through my mind in slow dissolves.

'Our Head Boy, Sahil Rai,' Diploma Coordinator Mr Riad had announced at the 2013 Investiture ceremony only a year ago.

My climb onto the stage where my predecessor, Aryan, waited with the flag had been uncertain. He dipped the flagpole to the horizontal and held it out. I hoisted the flag. As 500 pairs of eyes watched me, I wondered if it was too heavy for me.

My moment of self-doubt—Was I ready? Would I cope? Why did the flag feel heavy?

It took a few experiences for these questions to dissipate.

My first major event 'Confluence' was baptism by fire. 300 students from over 20 schools arrived to hotly contest at the interschool debate, quiz, and art competitions. After days of preparation, we expected a flawless event, but on the final day, Murphy's law struck. Long, unwieldy lines formed impossible labyrinths near registration counters. Chaos reigned. How do you make 300 enthusiastic teenagers wait patiently in well-formed lines? The answer came from something as simple as traffic lights: I gathered the Prefects; we sorted the students in batches, held the batches in separate areas, and completed the registration batch-wise. This eliminated the long queues and saved us the embarrassment of an ill-prepared event.

Thanks to Confluence, the crowd control at SIS Model United Nations (SISMUN) was as smooth as butter. But I still had plenty to learn, as the lead up to SISMUN had its own incongruities. While we prepared for a debate, a debate raged internally. We'd planned a party to give the delegates a chance to connect in an environment away from the heat of argument and glibness of diplomacy. But it seemed that my peers organizing the 'Delegate Fest' and Mr Mukesh, faculty in-charge, had diverging definitions of 'party'. Having lived and partied in Mumbai, my peers wanted expensive professional lighting and an 11 p.m. closure. But Mr Mukesh disagreed: 'It's a school, not a club! No professional lights and the fest should be over by 8:30 p.m. sharp!' The controversy intensified as time passed. As the Deputy Secretary General I then stepped in to mediate a slowly conflagrating argument. As Dumbledore said, 'It takes a great deal of bravery to stand up to our enemies, but just as much to stand up to our friends.' After great convincing and persuasion, I eventually got both sides to compromise: a few professional lights and an extended deadline of 9:30 p.m. This experience taught me to not succumb to the popular vote, work as a team with peers and faculty and communicate effectively.

Along the way, my challenges stopped feeling onerous, but more like exciting puzzles. We introduced new programs, made changes to existing ones and left an irreplaceable imprint on our school's culture. During SISMUN I noticed that seasoned debaters from SIS performed poorly. To refine their debating and MUNing skills and kindle the interest of other students, I co-founded the 'MUN Peer Mentoring Program'. We conceived the 'Intra-MUN' to ready them for inter-school MUNs.

Being Head Boy has been intensely transformative. I have learnt to identify critical issues, delegate tasks, manage an enthusiastic team, pay heed to their suggestions and ideas, and demonstrate my responsibility to my co-council while making tough decisions. Characterized with both highs and lows, this experience has given me a valuable insight into myself and helped me recognize my strengths and capabilities and contributed immensely to my all-round growth.

I smile, I've run my lap. I will now pass the baton to the new Head Boy. I wait with the school flag and dip it to horizontal as he walks up.

The flag is no longer heavy—in fact, it fits my hands perfectly.

OUR THOUGHTS ON SAHIL'S ESSAY

Shakespeare gave us the enduring phrase, 'Uneasy lies the head that wears a crown' four centuries ago. Even as 'uneasy' has now been replaced by the more commonly used 'heavy', the expectations, self-doubt and anxiety attached to positions of power, as the phrase suggests, are universally experienced and understood. Through his essay, Sahil leverages this understanding with great effect, delivering the story of how he came into his own through his role as his school's Head Boy.

The deliberate use of the school flag as a metaphor for leadership underscores Sahil's essay. The flag embodies responsibility, but it also represents the school and its values that a leader must exemplify. Sahil's initial description of the flag's 'heaviness' communicates his internal narrative, doubts and apprehensions without needing much elaboration. As he guides the reader through his experiences; organizing school events, liaising between administration and the student body, and mentoring students, we see him learning from each occurrence, growing in confidence. He evolves from reacting to chaos at 'Confluence' to taking initiative, and proactively addressing the lack of MUN training at school. Throughout the essay, Sahil adds dialogue (his grumbling teacher at the MUN), descriptive details ('Long, unwieldy lines formed impossible labyrinths') and quotes (Dumbledore) that inspire him, infusing the narrative with his personality.

Consequently, the admissions committee gains implicit insights into Sahil's personal brand of resourcefulness, problem-solving, teamwork and communication skills. While his election to the position of Head Boy might have been stated elsewhere, it is the depth and dimension added by a personalized process of learning and growing that the essay offers.

As Sahil closes the essay, he comes full circle from the moment of his appointment. Repeating the actions of his predecessor, he performs the rituals associated with bequeathing his responsibilities to the incoming Head Boy. As the flag makes a reappearance, he references the absence of its previous heaviness. Having witnessed Sahil's growth, we bear witness to this change. The crown is no longer heavy, it fits perfectly.

7

THE MELDERS

'I have put duality away,
I have seen that the two worlds are one;
One I seek, One I know, One I see, One I call.'

—Rumi

Funambulism is the art of walking a tightrope between precariously placed ends. Even attempting it safely requires tremendous skill and patience. However, the key to mastery lies in what is perhaps one of the rarest qualities: balance.

Addressing famous dichotomies like modernity-tradition, past-present, organic-man-made and urban-rural, the melders in this section symbolize sensitivity, awareness and, above all, balance. Negotiating space between warring, contradictory and incongruent worlds, they bargain, merge, meld and blend, using tea, letters and history to eventually carve out their own path.

AANYA BHANDARI

Cornell, Class of 2024 *Major*: Government
School: Mayo College Girls' School, Ajmer, India
Hometown: Udaipur, India

We Indians are a tea-loving nation. I realized this on visiting Churu Village, Rajasthan, during winter 2018, accompanying my grandfather as he campaigned for the Legislative Assembly elections. Wherever we went, we were surrounded by angry, disgruntled villagers looking to vent their grievances. I was apprehensive. My grandfather, in contrast, calmly sat them down, patiently hearing them out while serving steaming cups of fragrant tea. As the cinnamon-scented warmth seeped into their circulatory systems, the mood shifted. That is when I understood that a nice, hot cup of tea could build bridges.

I started researching an awareness program: *'Chai par Charcha'* (Talk over Tea) aimed at breaking communication barriers over chai, a British legacy, yet ubiquitous in government corridors, apartment blocks and villages. Over eight weeks, I visited homes in Churu Village of Sardarshahar to gather perspectives on issues such as education, healthcare, and caste-based politics. While Grandfather bonded with the villagers, I was an object of derision, an urban teenager, ergo naive, privileged, and conceited. To forge any kind of bond, I would have to take the first step.

The villagers were less than receptive, and I wondered if my efforts were in vain. Just then a young voice asked tremulously, 'Don't you miss your parents?' 'Oh, I do indeed!' I answered. I told her about how I've grown from a weak eighth grader who'd cry on every phone call home, into a formidable twelfth grader who thrives outside her comfort zone. 'I too will go to the city and make my parents proud,' she replied, then offered me hot cardamom-flavored tea that, paradoxically, broke the ice!

Soon enough, this tête-à-tête became a group discussion of twenty. The villagers' anger bated, their thoughts crystallized, their emotions quelled. Guards down, they dwelled on caste, corruption and all that concerned them. As they narrated their grievances and experiences, I was one amongst them.

One frosty evening, communicating with villagers beneath a peepal tree, chai pungent with black pepper, I noticed the men dominating the conversation, while the women remained silent. I initiated a conversation about sanitation and hygiene, only to realize that the women kept their counsel, cowed by patriarchal dominance and misogyny so deeply woven into their social fabric. Later, many privately confessed they were embarrassed to speak up before the men. 'Does this happen in the big city too? Do you speak with men?' a middle-aged woman queried. 'Does it?' I asked myself. Yes, the degree differed, but the problem remained. I could read the tea leaves in the earthen cup.

Soon after, I participated in a national debate competition where the motion being argued was 'This House Apologizes to Savitri Bai Phule'. Savitri Bai was an Indian educationist who championed the education of every girl child. The opposition was an all-boys team who outrageously claimed that our side, an all-girls debate team, was rather privileged to be even sitting for this debate. This incendiary statement triggered wild cheering from some in the audience, as I sat there, red-faced, and livid.

When I ascended the podium to deliver my reply, I intended to speak up for every woman who had sat silent beneath the village peepal tree, voice silenced by patriarchy. My mouth felt like sandpaper, but I knew I would one day hold forth in other forums to deliver a message with greater meaning and import, beyond the national competition. As I spoke, the narrow domestic walls of patriarchy seemed to dissipate with the hissing steam from the boiling teakettle, purposefully deconstructed and disposed.

The eight weeks of Chai Par Charcha left me resolved to break through persistent social and political barriers and engage the world in reality conversations. Back at the village, an old man confided, 'Chai is just an excuse, a warm-up, for what we really need… to talk.' *If there be tough conversations, bring forth the tea.*

OUR THOUGHTS ON AANYA'S ESSAY

Aanya's essay is an unexpected, evocative exposition of her interests and upbringing, circumscribed by the explosions of taste brought forth by cups of tea!

Take, for example, the first paragraph: She begins with a rather banal sentence, 'We Indians are a tea-loving nation', a surprising opener into her life in Rajasthan and obvious interest in social issues and, perhaps, politics, as she shadows her grandfather during his campaigns in rural India. This essay is not about tea, it is about a girl learning how social battles can be won through dialogue and by finding common ground.

Tea is the facilitator.

We love how chai both drives and defines the narrative, a rhetorical device that might run the risk of being ineffective in a short piece, but here, it unifies the prose. Chai becomes the force of communion between the villagers and Aanya's grandfather—two people on opposite ends of the socio-economic spectrum. In the shadow of an Imperial hangover, chai exposes the chasm between Aanya and the villages she visits. And just as easily and paradoxically, chai is the insinuator that narrows that chasm, creating opportunities for Aanya to realize that vulnerability crosses economic divides. Each cup of chai is flavored distinctively—with cinnamon, cardamom, and black pepper. Each flavorful cup is a bullet point, supporting Aanya's narrative on how her understanding of social issues evolved.

The first half of the essay foregrounds the second half, which reveals Aanya's interest in women's issues and equality, a revelation over aromatic chai, of course. As before, common ground is found. She makes the powerful point about women asserting themselves in front of men—something that happens infrequently, and everywhere, with the differences lying only in degree. This is a smooth transition into a debate on girls' education, where she imagines her words dissolving the patriarchy, like steam rising from the kettle.

This essay is a great example of one that tells a powerful story without having a climactic moment. Instead, it is a series of events that have shaped Aanya's thinking—none of them, on their own, are earth-shattering, but they come together to communicate Aanya's view of the world and passion for social justice. It is a view into the inner workings of Aanya's mind as a reflective individual who builds bridges between people, even as she readies for her future. As she concludes, *'If there be tough conversations, bring forth the tea'.*

VATSAL SAHANI

UPenn, Class of 2022

Major: Economics (Wharton)
School: Mayo College, Ajmer, India
Hometown: Surat, India

The bus ground to a halt, ending my reverie. I had reached Lahore in Pakistan, now a foreign country; this though was only discernible through the hoardings scripted in Urdu. It could well have been Chandni Chowk, New Delhi. Admittedly, I had arrived with, right or wrong, preconceived notions even though I disembarked into what might have been an urban precinct in any large city in India.

Five colleagues and I had crossed the border from Amritsar, India, a bare fifty kilometers away, to participate in the French International Competition at Aitchison College, Lahore. French, common to neither India nor Pakistan, had me view the world through another prism and has been an enduring passion for years.

It was surreal: Pakistan was the land of my antecedents, where my grandfather had schooled. I'd arrived with my luggage and the emotional baggage bequeathed to citizens on both sides of the border by our shared history of recent years. India-Pakistan relations, after the bitter 1947 Partition and three wars have historically been less than cordial—animosity has been a constant, be it border disputes or cricket. Understandably, I was suffused with mixed emotions: this was purportedly 'hostile' territory, but strangely, it felt like home.

I spent the next few days with Pakistani students shopping in their bazaars, visiting their homes. Comparing cultures and lives was redundant; theirs mirrored ours in language, clothes, music and cuisine… not kebabs though, theirs were better! The hostility was a veneer, a product of political expediency. The border that divided geographies was a function of the Radcliffe Line drawn on a map by the reluctant Cyril Radcliffe; it separated territory but could not dislodge emotion.

Strangely enough, French became a catalyst for understanding ground realities. Visiting Pakistan for a French competition, I shed entrenched prejudices in this city of my forefathers. I understood the aphorism that 'all men are created equal' and determined to bridge the historical divide through education. 'Why not through French?' I thought. This idea crystallized into an international level French competition, 'Les Concours de la Francophonie', which had me express my passion for the language and culture, while providing a platform for bringing students from Pakistan, Bangladesh and Indonesia to Mayo, my boarding school in Ajmer. Playing cricket and hi-fiving with my Pakistani friends, it was hard to believe that the wounds of Partition yet festered.

This was reinforced when I explored the subject further as Ambassador of Harvard University this summer. I worked on their project 'Looking Back, Informing the Future: 1947 Partition of British India' and conducted interdisciplinary research interviewing people who lived through the traumatic days and witnessed the atrocities that sadly, still punctuate our past and present. Over a fortnight, after 15 extensive interviews, 900 minutes of conversations across Delhi, I learned of Partition events, actions and individual stories that so distorted perspectives. Interviewing them, I felt I'd opened a Pandora's box; suppressed emotions, bitterness and tears surfaced. Often, my interviewees, overwhelmed by memory, could not complete the interview. I always returned.

Sohindernath Chopra, then a teenager recounted visiting his closest friend Arman's home on Eid, and the next day, leaving abruptly—no au revoir, no goodbyes. Researching the Enemy Property Act, I met the Superintendent, Office of the Council of the Enemy Property Act, who revealed that estranged properties were recompensed. But there is no recompense for families and friends divided. Borders cannot erase centuries-old shared history, yet can cause seismic dislocations of the heart.

I learned the travails of uprooting and starting again in a 'new' country. Completing the interviews, I had boarded refugee trains with migrants, lived in refugee camps and, like them, walked the same hard road to build another life.

I now know the power of an arbitrary line drawn to tear communities apart, to overturn centuries-old societal mores. I look forward to fostering change for the coming generations through my education.

OUR THOUGHTS ON VATSAL'S ESSAY

Vatsal's essay explores the shedding of 'entrenched prejudices' born of an enforced migration, and his transition from youthful prejudgment to mature understanding through a slew of events. These events made him view those prejudices through a contemporary lens and significantly accented his development. It starts with his (and his school team) arriving in Lahore, Pakistan, with mixed emotions stemming from a 'preconceived notion, …and the emotional baggage bequeathed to citizens on both sides of the border by our shared history….'

He admits that paradoxically, given the commonality of spoken languages in India and Pakistan, it took learning French, a longstanding passion, to upend his deep-seated notions and get an overview of 'ground realities'. By experiencing life in Lahore, albeit briefly, he acquired a whole new perspective to the common thread binding the citizens of what might have been just another 'large city in India'. So what was so different? 'Pakistan was the land of my antecedents,' he writes and makes clear that every aspect of this supposed 'hostile' territory, language, customs, music, et al, made it familiar ground and feel 'like home'.

Vatsal's comparisons of both cultures had him discover so many commonalities, that he realizes that the hostility was a veneer, limited to political dispensations on both sides. He is clearly knowledgeable about the history of the 1947 Partition, India-Pakistan relations, their history of warring, and bent on exorcising the demons of the past.

Vatsal offers deep insights for someone in his mid-teens. He is aware that the border that divided a people was an accident of history, a function of the Radcliffe Line hastily drawn on a map by a reluctant British lawyer. Vatsal sets out to blur the emotional lines then drawn, through French and his education which catalyzes his own 'shift', and ability to 'bridge the historical divide', at least among his peers.

Vatsal's continued 'interdisciplinary research… opened a Pandora's box' of bitterness, emotional baggage and, yes, nostalgia for another era. He found that although borders cannot erase a shared history… [they] 'can cause seismic dislocations of the heart'. This is what Vatsal set out to understand and heal by daring to walk 'the same hard road to build another life.'

Through describing his experiences, his responses to them, his transformed perceptions, and his affirmative actions, Vatsal smoothly sculpts a personality profile that has us marveling. Character strengths that particularly stand out above all others, however, are his sensitivity to everything around him, his innate empathy and immense capacity for compassion. Significantly, as readers, we too come away viscerally feeling change beginning to catalyze from Vatsal's cross-border crusades.

AVANTI DIVAN

Princeton, Class of 2020

Major: History
School: Vasant Valley School, New Delhi, India
Hometown: New Delhi, India

Mumbai: The roar of thunder echoing across turbulent skies. The sight of commuters crowding through train stations. The touch of a cool Arabian breeze on a muggy monsoon day. The lingering smell of salt and sea in the air I inhale.

Delhi: The clamor of beeping rickshaws on tree-lined boulevards. The view of medieval monuments set in stretches of green. A brush of crisp winter air seeps through my sweater. The aroma of spiced street food rises from vendor stalls.

Mine is a tale of two cities.

Mumbai, the city of my birth, is where I spent the first eight years of my life. I retain my connection with the city, returning to my old home every summer. It is a city to which millions flock, compelled by adversity and propelled by aspiration. It is a city of dreams and of survival, of indomitable energy and a thriving spirit. It is a city of great diversity, where differences of class, language, ethnicity and religion melt away on trains packed with daily commuters. It is also a city of resilience—successive terror attacks have failed to crush its invincible soul and spirit.

My family relocated to Delhi in 2006 when my parents, both lawyers, moved their practice to the Supreme Court of India. My new home promised open spaces unlike the clutter and chaos of Mumbai. Here, both Hindi and English were spoken in different accents and a mélange of cultures bubbled together in a melting pot. I adjusted to a new school, made new friends and struggled to improve my Hindi. Steeped in a history of 5000 years, Delhi is one of the great cities of the world. It has survived many upheavals, the last being the partition of India in 1947 that caused mass killings and forced the largest human displacement in history. Many of my friends in Delhi belong to families that suffered this displacement.

While I missed Mumbai, I was soon drawn to the charms of Delhi. As my family traveled between the two cities, I began enjoying the best of both my worlds. My roots in these very cosmopolitan cities with distinct cultures have helped me understand the social fabric of my country. What a great challenge it was to stitch together different kingdoms and peoples into a united India. The greatness of my country lies in her diversity. Nothing excites me more than exploring and interacting with different communities, studying their origins, their beliefs and practices. The cultural exchange programs and public-speaking competitions where I have represented my school, both at home and abroad, have strengthened my belief in the value of multicultural societies.

Observing people from different economic and social backgrounds makes me deeply conscious of my relatively privileged status. I belong to a slice of India with access to an education in the English language and a window to the world. This opens up opportunities not available to most—including aspiring for an education at the world's best universities. While I too aspire for the best education the world has to offer, I want to use it to enhance, not limit my engagement with the rest of India. Life for the privileged in my country is too often lived in a social bubble; the massive disparities between those who live in the luxury of high mansions and those in the wretchedness of the shanties below are so easily filtered out of existence. As my nation strives to lift its people towards a better economic future, a great social transformation is underway. In the coming years, I most look forward to participating and contributing to this churning after garnering a global perspective through a liberal American education. I want to use my education to stay grounded, connected to people and to explore the difference I can make in public life.

OUR THOUGHTS ON AVANTI'S ESSAY

Avanti's story is about a heart divided between India's two largest cities, even as it wholly pledges fealty to the country's diversity, development, and progress.

Mumbai and Delhi leave their unique indelible marks on Avanti and her essay.

Wrapping her biography around her movement between the two cities, she explores her connection with both. Her words sing paeans to Mumbai's soul, bringing it to life on paper as 'a city of dreams and of survival, of indomitable energy and a thriving spirit'. Avanti also invokes Delhi's antiquity, the city's ability to retain souvenirs from its complex mosaic of inhabitants to display a 'mélange of cultures bubbled together in a melting pot'. These observations and references may not perhaps be original or unique, but their descriptions are alive with Avanti's connection to each of them. She invites us to witness how the resilience of both these cities and their inhabitants in the face of terror attacks, displacement, and irreversible change prompts Avanti's investment in all that they represent: diversity, multiculturalism and the spirit of acceptance. They validate and strengthen her investment in India.

The essay is remarkably honest about Avanti's awareness of her economic and social privilege. Poignantly presented as her 'access to an education in the English language and a window to the world', this cognizance sensitively grounds the essay and reveals more about her than her relocation history and sense of belonging. Importantly, her love for Mumbai, Delhi and their diversity awakens her genuine desire to leverage her position of privilege to give back to her home country. This is her abiding motivation behind seeking a world-class education outside the country; the desire to contribute as best she can to India's progress. The depth this revelation adds to Avanti as a person is immense. The case she is making goes beyond the purpose of her education; rather, it encompasses the *value* her education will add to her future endeavors in social transformation.

Avanti's essay is as much about the impact her two homes have had on shaping her, as it is about her commitment to public life. Encoded in her understanding of herself, and the cities that cradled her, is a promise to her country's future.

MEHEK PUNATAR

Princeton, Class of 2012

Major: Chemical and Biological Engineering
School: Dhirubhai Ambani International School, Mumbai, India
Hometown: Mumbai, India

Peace between India and Pakistan. A stereotypical idea.
A week-long Indo-Pak peace conference for the youth. An unusual approach.

◆

'Pakistanis not allowed'—the headlines of the *Mumbai Mirror* summed up the bloody rivalry that India and Pakistan have been subjected to for six decades. If the sportsmen of these two nations can indulge in healthy competition, if our movies can encourage fraternity, then why can't the two nations come together as one? The answer is complicated and lies in the psychology of the people, in the prejudices and stereotypes that gradually penetrate our minds through media, education, and upbringing.

A dove glittered in the distance.

◆

Along with some friends, I decided to organize '*Paigaam—Aman ka Farishta*', *Urdu for: A message—the angel of peace*, a unique Indo-Pak conference, comprising twenty-six passionate youth from the two nations, dedicated to a more peaceful future. Paigaam went beyond the notions of a conventional peace conference. It aspired to promote teamwork, encourage trust-building and stimulate an exchange of opinions through various activities. The true essence of Paigaam was to bring together people who thought similarly; it was a chance to break the biased notions we had grown up with, and to get to know the people who lay behind the dark masks so often portrayed by the media.

Slowly, cautiously, I approached the dove,
aware that the slightest movement would drive it away.

◆

I made calls to almost every school in Pakistan, inviting them to Paigaam and hoping for a positive response. But none came my way. Exams, other commitments, lack of financial aid—were the excuses that were meted out.

To resolve the financial difficulties of our participants, we requested that our school finance the accommodation of all our guests. However, the school authorities were hesitant. After all, this was the first time that such a conference was being initiated by the students and they were unsure of its success.

We met with the Head of Seeds of Peace for India for her advice and guidance, and it was then that we learnt that six months were not enough to procure visas for the Pakistanis. The process was long, cumbersome, intricate and most likely to yield failure.

With each setback, I was more determined to realize this dream called 'Paigaam', to prove that the power of today's youth cannot be underestimated.

I reached out for the dove, but my fingers had barely grazed past
its soft feathers when the dove flew further away.

◆

It had been six long months. The process of procuring visas for the Pakistanis was filled with obstacles. I had drafted numerous letters to the Indian ministries. A friend in Delhi decided to help us by visiting the ministries daily, convincing them to grant the Pakistanis entry into our country. But to no avail. On the other side of the border, our eight Pakistani participants were furiously trying to procure visas too. Then one day, unexpectedly, one of the Pakistani participants called me. She informed me that Mr N.K. Pal, an executive of the Indian High Commission at Islamabad, had contacted her and promised that they would have the visas within a week. I felt exhilarated.

The approval for the visas hadn't come from India; it had come from Pakistan. Somewhere inside me, the small monster of prejudice was calming down. And a pride in being the youth of today, who could realize something which seemed so impossible, roared.

The dove was calm, no longer in a hurry to fly away.

I extended my arm and it perched itself beautifully on my palm.

OUR THOUGHTS ON MEHEK'S ESSAY

Mehek's essay is an example of external action setting up internal transformations. '*Unusual*' is somewhat of an understatement for the long, complex and often acrimonious relationship that has existed between India and Pakistan. Despite periods of tenuous peace between the two neighbors, Mehek's wish for enduring unity seems innocent and child-like at first. However, Mehek shows her awareness of the deep-rooted reasons for prolonged conflict—'the prejudices and stereotypes that gradually penetrate our minds through media, education and upbringing' that keep the two countries apart.

And still '*A dove glittered in the distance*'. The dove is no chimera, especially in the face of Mehek's resolve. Her essay dexterously describes a brave initiative she embarked upon: A week-long Indo-Pak peace conference for the youth. Energized by her youthful convictions, the essay picks up pace as she accelerates action. Her plan involves gathering like-minded youth from both sides of the border and celebrating similarities and differences beyond those sensationalized by media organizations. Her ability to look beyond her own biases and encourage others to do similarly is remarkable, especially as someone who is entrenched in a society with the same biases she tries to overcome.

'With each setback, I was more determined to realize this dream called "Paigaam", to prove that the power of today's youth cannot be underestimated.' The institutional blocks and prejudices that stand between Mehek and this goal demonstrate the untenable situation she is trying to navigate. She 'cautiously' approaches the 'dove', recognizing it can get away. Battling close to seventy years of mutual miscommunication, mistrust and anger, the scope of Mehek's victory does not do justice to her effort. Still, she perseveres, intent upon proving that 'today's youth cannot be underestimated'.

If anything, the Mehek we see through the essay is patient, persuasive and persistent, sending letters to government officials, convincing diplomatic channels, and scholastic institutions, corresponding with her peer participants and forging a cross-border community even before 'Paigaam'. The resolution comes unexpectedly, but symbolically—an approval of Indian visas for her Pakistani youth delegation, granted by the Indian High Commission in Islamabad, no less!

Earnest as ever, Mehek admits that a 'small monster of prejudice' had reared its head on encountering obstacles but is quickly replaced with roaring pride. Lion-hearted Mehek had reached out and made peace with the dove, which '*perched itself beautifully on my palm*'.

Writing about an issue of national and international concern, her sights fixed on 'the other side of the border', it is overarchingly important to Mehek that the Pakistani participants obtain their visas. This foreshadows how Mehek will use her education—to proactively build a better, more peaceful world.

AVANTIKA SHAH

Stanford, Class of 2025

Major: Art History/ Economics
School: The Cathedral & John Connon School, Mumbai, India
Hometown: Mumbai, India

The biting wind gnawed at my face; dust-clouds smothered me; the smell of rotting flesh activated my olfactory receptors. The breaking dawn lifted the cloak of darkness. Vigilant for the slightest signs of movement and alert to the alarm call of peacocks, I scanned the muddy tracks for discernible pugmarks. My observation skills and deductive prowess honed by Agatha Christie novels were instantly roused as I traversed Ranthambore National Park, aching for a glimpse of India's most celebrated tigress. I was six when I first heard the story of the fearless tigress Machali and her triumphant encounter with a fourteen-foot crocodile. I have been smitten, ever since, by the lore of the jungle and the enigmatic tales of this remarkable animal.

On wildlife safaris my family bonds together, as in a Confucian ritual devised to unite disparate people, changing them for the better. Work commitments keep my father away four days each week, which makes huddling together in a jeep, eight hours a day, precious indeed. Being a night owl helps me navigate the pressures and pulls of student life, rendering a 4:45 a.m. wake-up inconceivable. But not on a safari! Here, the trusty snooze button is relieved of duty. Earphones playing Adele on repeat give way to the orchestra of the cicadas. My subsistence on Wi-Fi abates and I nonchalantly tolerate dirt, moss and, otherwise disconcerting, arthropods.

The impact of a jungle expedition on me, however, goes beyond transient changes. It recalibrates my internal compass. The long, suspenseful waits for Machali become more than lessons in patience; they serve as periods of reflection. As an Art History student, I wax lyrical about Monet's mastery of light and color, but I am spellbound by the myriad hues of the sunlit sky and the mesmerizing beauty of nature's canvas, a masterpiece I feel obligated to help conserve. Observing the *baya* weaverbird patiently create its intricate nest reminds me of the rigors and rewards of my classical dance training, reinforcing my belief in the Japanese philosophy of *kodawari*—the relentless pursuit of perfection. The determined dung beetle rolling an enormous ball of dung ten times its weight puts my seemingly large high-school problems into perspective. Every time I forget my lines or go off-key on stage, I try not to lose heart and instead keep on 'rolling'. The symbiotic relationship between the *chital* deer and *langur* monkey, who warn each other of predators from their distinct vantage points, underlines not only the value of collaboration in my undertakings but also the merit of different perspectives that my diverse band of friends brings to my life. Nature's classroom teaches me to immerse myself in each moment, the benefits of which, as my 104-year old great-grandmother affirms, are greater than longevity. The true rewards of the safari are in these meaningful connections between my life and the natural world.

On that cold winter's day in January 2016, luck did not abandon me. Machali emerged fleetingly at dusk, feeble and gaunt, a shadow of her former self. A few months later she breathed her last, leaving behind an extraordinary legacy. In a life fraught with challenges, Machali shaped her destiny—surviving perilous confrontations with territorial males, evading deadly poachers, successfully raising four litters and living longer, at twenty years, than any known tiger in the wild. Inspired to push my boundaries, I discover the value of courage over comfort whether in finishing my first marathon or attempting a scuba dive despite a fear of the open sea. I continue my adventure off the beaten path as I explore a realm of limitless possibilities, where diverse species like Art History and Calculus happily coexist with Indian classical dance and Western musical theater. Looking forward, I know I will seek opportunity in every obstacle, find meaning in the mundane and infuse my life with passion and purpose—all while eagerly navigating the wilderness of my concrete jungle.

OUR THOUGHTS ON AVANTIKA'S ESSAY

A tigress in the wild can seem like an enigmatic choice for a role model, but not Avantika's Machali, who is widely identified as the face (or paw) behind the revival of tiger conservation in India and beyond. Avantika's essay adds such a personal touch to Machali's legacy that the imprint left behind is at least as evocative as pugmarks on the forest floor.

Filled with sensory cues from the regular safari trips she takes with her family, Avantika's account juxtaposes her experiences in nature's arboreal thicket with the life she leads beyond it. While recognizing the differences between the two, she resists the temptation to adjudge one as better than the other; rather, she chooses to showcase these trips as her way to take a step back, zoom out of everyday life to gain perspective and phoenix-like, come back anew. She appreciates the time she gets with her family, the invaluable lessons imparted by the jungle ecosystem and the different aspects of her persona that the forest teases out. Painting a stunning picture of the mirroring parallels between the wild and the 'concrete wilderness', the jungle serves as her muse. She articulates this eloquently. From the industriously toiling dung beetle to the patience of the weaverbird, to the teamwork of animals at the risk of falling prey, Avantika is inspired by the forest. But even as she details the mature, hardy, adaptable, jungle-ready person she becomes, there is a sense of the Avantika away from this—that of the Agatha Christie-reading, Adele-listening, classical dance-performing, Monet-critiquing version of her that we are more likely to glean from other parts of her application. It is the permeable tightrope-connection between these two disparate but connected worlds where we get a complete sense of who Avantika is.

Significantly, the essay does not stop there. Avantika does not just want us to know who she is—she wants us to understand the whys, know the motivations behind all that she hopes to become. And this is where Machali emerges, beating the odds as she always has, embodying everything Avantika admires about the forest, its nurturing aspect and more. Evolving from a childhood love borne from forest lore, Avantika's identification with Machali gives us a powerful glimpse into the strength, courage and freedom that equally define both.

SAHIR DOSHI

UPenn, Class of 2015

Major: Political Science and African Studies
School: The Cathedral & John Connon School, Mumbai, India
Hometown: Mumbai, India

RIZE

I fell in love with hip-hop music about five years ago. It's not just a music genre to me, but an integral part of who I am. It's an outlet for all my strongest thoughts and emotions. It's my voice, and it's a voice I am grateful to have got from Africa.

Over summers with my aunt's family in Uganda, I studied Swahili and developed a deep appreciation of African cultures, history, and people. Uganda is where I first experienced the true power of hip-hop. It felt realer than anything I had heard before: more honest, more heartfelt, and more hardcore. African rappers are not embarrassed to talk about the world as it is. Across Africa, listening to hip-hop can be like listening to the news.

In 2007, I tried to write a song in Swahili that would have a socially relevant message. My first attempt was a disaster—a boring, inauthentic song about the 'hard-knock life' in Kampala's ghettoes. The lyrics were bland and depressing and lacked the clever wordplay and use of metaphors that is so characteristic of Swahili rap verse.

I restarted from scratch, and decided to reinvent the message of the song. Channeling all that I had learned through my personal observations, experiences and friendships in the streets, slums and schools of Uganda, I wrote something different: an energetic anthem of upliftment for the Global South. I called it 'RIZE'.

The message came to me naturally, but I did not want to deliver it in English. To be true to the culture that had educated me in hip-hop, I wanted to write the song in Swahili. I'm conversationally fluent but learning the art of Swahili poetry was a challenge. Swahili might have the richest collection of proverbs, phrases and idioms of any language on earth. I spent days chatting with friends from neighboring Tanzania and Kenya, listening for those brilliant turns of phrases that Swahili banter so casually creates. Once I had sufficiently grounded the song in its cultural roots, I added an English verse and threw in a few lines from other languages to reflect the international appeal of its core message. It was finally all coming together. RIZE was ready to record.

But the real test was still to come. How would Uganda react? How would Africa react? Would RIZE be taken seriously, or would I be seen as an Asian trying too hard to fit in? I spent hours sitting around local radio stations trying to get RIZE on the air. Every once in a while, I would catch a break—an Indian rapping in Swahili was a novelty to most Black Ugandans, with racial tensions still high in the country that once saw the expulsion of all Asians under General Idi Amin. People appreciated the universality of the song's message, but also the specificity of the circumstances in which it was forged.

The ultimate validation, however, came from Roger, the janitor at the recording studio. He was listening to the second verse of my song, in which I had strung together fisherfolk sayings to comment on economic exploitation, when he burst out laughing and shook his head as if to say that's so true. I knew then that RIZE had struck the right chords.

Later, my producer felt we should make a music video. We both agreed that it could only be filmed live in the misunderstood mega-slums of

Kamwokya, whose hustle, energy and survivalist spirit most resonate with RIZE. I storyboarded every detail, from footage of the 'boda' motorcycle-taxis to shots of the shanties against the city's modern skyline, only for all planning to be discarded when we arrived at the slum. A local dance crew was putting together a makeshift stage for an upcoming event, and invited me to test it out for a shot. Crowds gathered at the sound of the music, and asked to be in the film. Kids jumped into every frame. On the spot, my producer and I decided to include all these people in the video. I performed and danced with this organically assembled entourage on tin roofs, in muddy alleyways, and over open sewers. I even got to do an impromptu 'ghetto concert' on the dance stage.

That moment of exhilaration was the culmination of one of the greatest experiences and proudest achievements of my life. I have since taken the song to many schools across both Uganda and India to motivate young people with its message. I might modify the verses to suit the local language, but that one word in the chorus always remains the same, in all its misspelled glory: RIZE.

OUR THOUGHTS ON SAHIR'S ESSAY

Usually, counselors advice students writing their Common App essay to avoid esoteric topics as they might be outside Admission Commissioners' 'familiarity zone', and not always resonate—topics like an Indian boy's love for hip-hop would rank high on the list. Sahir's 'Rize' had us raising eyebrows to proclaim, 'That's bold!' 'Such blatant defiance has to be purposeful surely?' We're curious!

So we move on past the passionate declarations of hip-hop being more than 'just a music genre..., but an integral part of who I am... outlet for my strongest thoughts and emotions... my voice... grateful to have got from Africa'. Oh wait! Africa? We were expecting... Now Sahir has us really listening!

From this point on, though, Sahir follows every golden rule of Common App writing. He is determined to tell this 'story' to showcase his identity. He writes it in, what is, genuinely his voice, true to how he would talk in everyday life—no verbal gymnastics, no clichés, but 'more honest, more heartfelt, and more hardcore' like the 'Swahili poetry' he so admires, where 'African rappers are not embarrassed to talk about the world as it is'.

What enchants most, though, is Sahir's emphasis on the specific human elements of his central story. He keeps his writing style simple and speedy, focusing on recounting the events as they happened, almost as if in real time. The structure flows from unpretentious detailing to intense deliberation to energetic action, then gathers even more momentum as 'Kids jumped into every frame'. And he 'even got to do an impromptu "ghetto concert" on the dance stage.' We want to have been right there participating in that wild street celebration of life, dancing 'with this organically assembled entourage on tin roofs, in muddy alleyways, and over open sewers'!

Sahir has set himself apart by managing, through the unaffected history of his one song, to clearly frame many aspects of his personality: his capacity for persistent effort, his keen ear for multi-linguistic analysis, his clear awareness and understanding of the culture, the people and the politics around him and, most admirably, his humility, positive attitude and natural empathy. So, Sahir, RIZE! We rise with you!

ANONYMOUS

Princeton, Class of 2013

Major: Anthropology
School: Dhirubhai Ambani International School, Mumbai, India
Hometown: Mumbai, India

Like many young girls, my early childhood was spent watching Disney movies like *Cinderella* and *Sleeping Beauty*. I have seen each of these 'Princess movies' many times. While I imagine that many little girls watching may want to be one of these heroines, I never did. Perhaps this was because I knew I never could be one of them. The romances, ball dancing and Prince Charmings that characterized these movies could never exist in my life. I come from a traditional Indian family, where romance and ball dances happen only after one had an arranged marriage. I'd resigned myself to the idea that I would never be able to feel like a fairy-tale princess.

Freud would probably say that it was this suppressed childhood desire that fueled my fascination for the Mughal empire when I first learnt about it, on a visit to the Taj Mahal, the mausoleum that Mughal Emperor Shah Jahan had constructed for his wife Mumtaz. The romance of this building seemed to represent more than all of the Prince Charmings and every single waltz combined. It was then that I fell in love for the first time.

This love affair with the Mughals prompted me to read about them widely, introducing me to Jahanara, Shah Jahan's most loved daughter on whom he bestowed the title 'Princess of Princesses'. Initially, I was intrigued by her because of superficial similarities we shared, but as I discovered other Indian princesses including Gayatri Devi and Rani Laxmibai, I still felt the deepest connection with Jahanara. Since I connected with her on an ideological and emotional level, her life did not appear antiquated to me despite the centuries between us.

Jahanara's life was bound by the rigid Mughal customs; mine is dictated by tradition. My childhood was as protected as hers; and I echoed her shock and felt her vulnerability when we discovered the real world. Perhaps because I felt I knew her, I tried to imagine her in modern-day situations and tried to react to them as she would have done. The regional conflicts that had plagued her life influenced my perception of wars and terrorism. I learnt from her to find a refuge for these thoughts and fears in writing, although she wrote poetry while I write short stories. As a Mughal princess, she was forbidden many of the things she could see her friends enjoy. While she was conscious of her loss, she learned at an early age to accept what was expected of her. Instead, she lived out her dreams in her poems. As a girl from a conservative Indian family, I could empathize with her disappointment, and because of her, I learnt to put my own challenges in perspective.

As I matured, I better understood and respected the profound challenges she faced. After losing her mother during adolescence, she inherited tremendous responsibility balancing the role of 'ghost queen' and mother to her younger siblings. Her unprecedented popularity within the court grew as she displayed an insight and intuition uncommon for women of that time. Unfortunately, she lost much of her power following the bloody battles for succession, during which her father was dethroned by his own son. Her stoic silence and courage of conviction as she watched her brother Aurangzeb dethrone and imprison their father made the most profound impact on me.

The compromises I make due to my family's strict traditions pale in comparison to the struggles she faced. However, her resolve and determination resonate with me, spurring me on when answers and solutions seem to elude me. From her life I have learned that there is nothing that is not worth fighting for, because even if we cannot obtain it in our lifetime, we can become timeless leaders for forthcoming generations. It was this durable spirit that touched me and prompted me to try and reconcile tradition with modernity, to try and find a balance without unnecessary rebellion. It is through these attempts, that I've been able to develop as a more holistic individual, understanding my grandparents as well as I understand my friends, accepting what is expected of me, but daring to venture into unexpected realms as well.

One of the defining experiences of my life occurred when I took on the role of organizing and facilitating Paigaam, an Indo-Pak-Bangla peace initiative. As I spent the better part of the year working to organize this conference, I often found myself remembering an account I had read about Jahanara, who also believed in secularism, wherein I leant that Jahanara had been deeply inspired by her great grandfather, Akbar, who practiced the same religious tolerance that he preached. The chance I got at Paigaam to interact with people from different nationalities and religions, as well as to play an important role in forging friendships with people from across the border made me understand how rewarding it was to live a life of compassion and tolerance. I had learnt from Jahanara the importance of trying to make a change, but Paigaam was one of the instances where I could apply this belief and see how significant even these small attempts could be in changing the mindsets and views of others, paving the way for peace and hope. Acceptance, I learnt, was an essential accomplice in hoping to live a fulfilled life.

As an adult, Jahanara no longer existed for herself, but for others. She spent her life tending to her ailing father and supervising the building of the Taj. An intrinsic part of Shah Jahan's kingdom, she left a subtle yet indelible mark in Indian history. Her life has guided me and molded my personality as I have grown trying to imbibe the qualities of diplomacy, courage, conviction and loyalty which epitomized her life. In searching for a princess to emulate, I found the Princess of Princesses in the truest sense of the words.

OUR THOUGHTS ON THE ESSAY

Rarely do the idols that accompany us through childhood and adolescence remain intact and untarnished. The perspectives and knowledge that confront us as we grow all too often have us re-contextualize and critically question their relevance in our space. The essay speaks of the exception—centering the enduring legacy of a girlhood fascination that gave the author a sense of self through representation.

The longing at the core of the narrator's search for a princess who she can identify with is all too familiar for millennials born growing up in communities entrenched in tradition and orthodoxy. The description of her feelings of alienation and resignation upon being excluded poignantly convey her struggle to find an entity and story she can connect with. Her eventual discovery of and bridge with Princess Jahanara, the daughter of Mughal Emperor Shah Jahan, is a forceful expression of identity. Through the stories of Jahanara, both recorded and imagined, the writer places herself in history, feeling understood in that created space. As she puts it, 'her (Jahanara's) life did not seem antiquated, despite the centuries between us'.

The writer's connection with Jahanara is not just the story of a young girl finding the familiar in history, but a source of confidence that imbues her with a sense of self and makes her feel accepted at an age when belonging somewhere feels important. This confidence, in turn allows her to step sure-footed on the dichotomous tightrope of tradition and modernity. She navigates this as a teenager in a conservative household, while growing up in a cosmopolitan city. She contextualizes her struggles, acknowledging the sometimes-impossible choices she must make, but also accepting that it's a choice *she* gets to make. Showing considerable maturity, she does not condemn either one of the worlds she is a part of or choose one over the other; instead, she confidently carves out her own space between the two.

The essay shows the narrator's growth into a composed, intelligent, and sensitive young woman with gumption. For a girl whose search for an empowered life that mirrored hers took her to history's annals, she now holds the power to be just that: for herself and so many like her.

VARUN GUPTA

UPenn, Class of 2016

Major: International Studies and Business (Huntsman Program)
School: The Doon School, Dehradun, India
Hometown: New Delhi, India

As an eight-year-old, the only thing I wanted to do was wear a business suit and carry a briefcase. At twelve, that naïve aspiration manifested itself in the desire to become a successful entrepreneur. Soon, however, my experiences in working with the underprivileged, coupled with my reading of the *Bhagavad Gita* made me realize that true fulfilment can only be achieved through selfless action and that money alone is inadequate. More importantly, I started to wonder if this dichotomy was necessary: couldn't I build a business that would not only be profitable, but would also provide sustainable social welfare?

When I was sixteen, I got a chance to try my hand at one such social enterprise during an internship at our family's steel factory in Ghaziabad. Although watching molten metal flowing at dangerously high temperatures sent my adrenaline rushing, the presence of huge piles of slag (steel waste) was perplexing. Both, the space they consumed as well as the expenditure for their removal seemed to be unnecessary. Moreover, the sight of children playing on these piles was highly unnerving. Motivated to find a solution, I researched and inquired until I learned about a method to transform this slag into low-cost commercially viable bricks. A few days and many dirty clothes later, we had built our first prototypes.

With the support of a Doon School (my high school) alumnus social worker, I was able to schedule meetings with some local politicians, business leaders, and the sarpanch (head) of Rajokri Village. I developed a business plan on the merits of a slag brick manufacturing business and presented it to thirty-five villagers and the panchayat (village governing body). They agreed to provide me with a seed capital of Rupees One Lakh ($2000 USD) for my venture and, in return, I promised employment to twenty-five villagers as well as cost-effective bricks to the entire village. Moreover, I projected that I could pay back the panchayat within a year from initiating the project.

Today, this pilot plant is producing five hundred bricks a day at three-quarters of the cost of traditional bricks. A large number of new houses built in Rajokri are made of our slag bricks that have proven to be very durable. The success of this small venture has made me realize that with just a little bit of inspiration and creativity, it truly is possible to serve others and do so profitably. Moreover, this success has strengthened my confidence and has solidified my mission of social entrepreneurship. Today, not only have I realized that social entrepreneurship is not an idealistic concept, but also that I have the ability to make it a reality. As I look back upon my childhood visions, it is satiating to know that I can do social good... in a suit!

OUR THOUGHTS ON VARUN'S ESSAY

Varun's essay is an analytical exercise in identity construction, negotiation, and realization. Transforming drastically from the briefcase-dreams-toting-eight-year-old he begins the essay as, Varun employs the age-distance to create a nuanced and compelling account of settling into his purpose.

Setting the agenda in his first paragraph, Varun's early realization of the apparent conflict between his dreams and the requirements for fulfilment lead to a question that predicates his actions through adolescence; 'Couldn't I build a business that would not only be profitable, but would also provide sustainable social welfare?' His exploration of this question is validated by his choice to layer detailed descriptions of the places he acts in with the larger ethical dilemma he negotiates. Details about visits to his family's steel factory (molten metal flowing, children playing on mountains of slag deposits) offset his internal dialogue about creating opportunities to do good.

The little nuggets of insight the essay provides into Varun's process of doing better effectively rounds out his personality, making it easy to imagine who he would be in a campus setting. From his proactive attempts at finding a solution ('a few dirty clothes later'), to his ability to leverage his alumnus network and convince local officials by presenting a detail-oriented action plan, we see Varun's ability to navigate difficult circumstances while remaining cognizant of his larger goal of social entrepreneurship.

The dilemma Varun chooses to expound on is a big part of why his essay works. The conversations around profitability and social good contextual to businesses often present a binary of choosing one or the other. Varun's essay balances these seemingly disparate goals and provides an optimistic outlook on a third way forward. The success of his pilot plant, included at the essay's end convinces him of this and energizes him for the future, showcasing him as a lucrative prospect for any college.

However, even without its context-specific details, the tone and structure of the essay make it an exemplary account of bridging the gap between being and becoming.

VENKATESH JINDAL

Yale, Class of 2018

Major: Economics
School: Vasant Valley School, New Delhi, India
Hometown: New Delhi, India

Since I was eight, my father would wake me at dawn to hoist the Tricolor, our national flag. It was one of the special ways I would spend time with my father. Not understanding its significance, I'd often ask him, 'Why?' He would reply, 'That's for you to discover.'

My father had fought for the right of every citizen to display the Indian flag. Previously, only those holding high government offices were permitted to display it. When my father hoisted the flag at his office, the authorities asked him to take it down. He decided to file a case and after a decade-long struggle from 1996–2004, the Supreme Court of India ruled in his favor, declaring the right to fly the Tricolor as a fundamental right. As I've grown older, my relationship with the Tricolor has evolved into a feeling of duty and responsibility for my nation. Hoisting the flag was no longer just a ritual, but a reminder to get involved.

Indian youth do want to get involved and have been galvanized by social causes such as fighting corruption, increasing transparency in government, and responding to violence against women. After participating in one such movement where people were protesting against lack of accountability, my own perspective about using social activism to mobilize civic consciousness changed. I felt that while protests did serve a purpose, we needed to invest in the ability of democratic institutions to seek social change. There is a need to empower people through the electoral process so they can choose representatives who stand up for the right causes. It was through this inspiration that I founded 'Voice Your Choice', my vision to transform India's youth from political cynicism to democratic engagement. 'Voice Your Choice' is a nine-member electoral voting awareness initiative aimed at motivating the youth to cast their vote in the 2014 Indian elections. We reached out to students in universities, presenting the importance of voting, followed by question-answer sessions that encouraged debate. Further, we are recruiting students for leadership roles on campuses nationwide, hoping to stimulate further enthusiasm among the youth. In order to expand our impact across India, we have extended 'Voice Your Choice' into an online campaign, aggressively leveraging social networking sites such as Facebook to spread our message.

While interacting with the students of a university in the state of Haryana, Sahil expressed how little faith he has in change. He asked, 'What is the point of this? One party or the other will win the elections but poor quality of governance remains unchanged!' Disappointed in his skepticism, I articulated my views to him in which I underlined the role of people in a democracy, which is to assert their rights and ensure that the elected representatives fulfil the aspirations of the people and are made accountable to them.

I want to see an India whose youth is not alienated from its politics but engaged in it; who is not waiting for change to happen but is driving it; who doesn't accept mediocrity as the norm but takes the initiative to excel beyond expectations.

Today when I help my father hoist the flag, I realize that I have discovered its true meaning: it represents not just nationality, but humanity. The flag stands for the shared ideals, beliefs, and aspirations of a society. Unfurling the flag, I reflected on how the meaning of the flag to me has changed with time, exposure, and perspectives. As a child, the flag was something that linked me to my father. As I grew older, it taught me to question my place in the world and my desires for the future. Today, the flag provides equanimity to my life. As my father hands me the rope, I feel a quiver and a spark igniting. Watching the sunrise, I raise the flag higher, and I salute this symbol that has defined both my country and me.

OUR THOUGHTS ON VENKATESH'S ESSAY

Pertinent, to the point, and rich in timeless symbolism, Venkatesh's essay is a mission statement that neatly summarizes his journey thus far and emphatically states where he wants to go in the future.

Venkatesh begins the essay by proudly recalling days begun by hoisting India's national flag with his father, whose decade-long legal efforts led to the precedent which allowed the flag to be displayed by all citizens, effectively democratizing ownership. However, instead of feeding him this answer when asked about the significance of these dawn-tinted hoistings, Venkatesh's father encourages him to explore his own relationship with the flag, and the country it represents. As the fountainhead of Venkatesh's political awakening, this memory implants a firm commitment to democratizing power and an abiding faith in India's democratic institutions, values that guide his actions, as discussed in the remainder of the essay.

Had Venkatesh's father been dismissive, or unaware of his own ability to make a change, access to the Indian flag would have remained limited to institutions and a few powerful people. By sharing these origins for his first political act, we can better understand Venkatesh's uncompromising emphasis on each citizen performing their political duty by holding elected officials accountable. Even as he comes to the realization that protests are not the space where he can add lasting value, Venkatesh looks to create avenues for making a difference.

The inclusion of his youth-focused electoral advocacy organization, 'Voice Your Choice', showcases him as an effective leader and canvasser who can inspire others. When seen in the context of his response to a student's skeptical views on voting, and his early movement away from protests, Venkatesh's commitment to and advocacy of electoral politics as the best avenue for change ably communicates his view on politics and policy to the admissions committee. His firm belief that substantive change can come from institutions within the system, showcases his ability to think critically, and constitutes a unique detail that makes his essay, and profile, memorable.

Venkatesh ends the essay with a sentimentality that resembles its opening. He retains his pride in his father's legacy and his commitment to the flag, but this time, he has found his purpose.

RIA MIRCHANDANI

Brown, Class of 2015

Major: Computer Science and Human Migration Studies
School: The Cathedral & John Connon School, Mumbai, India
Hometown: Mumbai, India

He did not want to leave. Karachi, with its ornate arches, multihued alleyways; and his palatial bungalow in Clifton, was all he had known for seventeen years of his life. Now his childhood friends were urging him to leave. 'Go to Hindustan, Bhau. This is now Pakistan, a Muslim state.' Denied the euphoria of independence, Gulab Mirchandani and his family spent 15th August 1947, fleeing their ancestral homeland for lands unknown. My grandfather's story is just one amongst those of the twelve million refugees who crossed the border during the partition of India. These stories, of hope and courage, fear and loss, were what I had grown up listening to. Our Sindhi community, they had told me, had lost everything; from our property to even a state we could call our own. But resilience and hard work helped my grandparents' generation slowly regain it all. Listening to their heroic struggles fascinated me as a child, but biased my opinions as I grew older. I developed an underlying hatred for Pakistan. My grandmother's face would often crumple up with disgust when she heard the word 'Pakistani'. She had seen trainloads of Hindus, butchered at the hands of the enemy, enter bloodstained platforms; she had reason. But I wondered, why should I react the same way?

Sixty years of animosity should not be followed by sixty more. Partition was a historical event that was disappearing into oblivion, depriving my generation of the chance to learn from the mistakes made. I wanted to form my own opinion on Partition, but I also wanted my grandparents' stories to be remembered. And so I embarked on a year-long exploration of my history. Remembering Partition was an event that my team and I conceived. Its goal was to create an unbiased perspective of Partition, while honoring those who survived it. On 24th October 2010, seventeen-year-olds and seventy-year-olds, Indians and Pakistanis, came together in Mumbai to discuss, debate and try to heal the scars from Partition.

I had started with a vision to open a museum on the partition of India, akin to the Yad Vashem Holocaust Memorial Museum in Jerusalem, which I had visited recently. It was another one of my grand plans, one that I normally would not have had the confidence to follow through. My low self-confidence while growing up had prevented me from even participating in any kind of public-speaking competitions—leave alone daring to try anything new. But this was different. I was going to make this happen, with the Remembering Partition event as a first step.

Despite the risk of failure at each step, whether signing up keynote speakers, raising funds, or lobbying the government for visas for our Pakistani participants, I persevered with a determination I did not know I possessed. It was not a new-found confidence that kept me going; it was passion. I was archiving the Partition stories I had grown up listening to, I was trying to neutralize the way my generation looked at our national history, and I was engaging youth from both sides of the border in constructive dialogue—I was doing something I loved.

Confidence, or its lack, did not matter anymore.

I had never considered myself to be a leader. My voice lacked authority and my words lacked weight. Through this journey, I discovered that leadership was about the power of ideas, not just words. My idea captivated five busy high school students enough to drive themselves to work relentlessly towards making it a reality. Leadership was also about making tough calls. When a teammate's indolence hindered our progress, at the risk of losing our friendship, I asked him to leave. Indecision used to be my best friend; so much so that it would exhaust me to even choose an ice cream flavor. But leading the Remembering Partition team forced me to take quick calls, however difficult some may have been.

Perhaps the most profound impact of Remembering Partition was the opportunity it gave me to redefine Pakistan for myself, rather than to inherit my grandparents' tainted views. The stories my Pakistani friends and I shared about our lives across the border, across coffee tables, made us realize that we were still one people, divided by politics. There were more similarities than differences; we were both excited by Linkin Park's new album, stressed by the SATs and eager to build a better future.

If you visit Mumbai today, you will not find a museum on the partition of India, yet. But you will find a greater appreciation amongst the seventy students who attended the event, for their country's history and for their neighbor's views. You will find gratitude in the eyes of Partition survivors, who now know that their sacrifices will not go in vain, and their stories will not go unheard. I saw these emotions in my audience, as I stood on stage (the fear of public speaking a distant memory) and brought the Remembering Partition event to a close. Remembering Partition, while it was a stepping stone to realize my dream of a museum, helped me to realize so much more.

OUR THOUGHTS ON RIA'S ESSAY

A growing body of scientific research devotes itself to establishing the existence and implications of trans-generational trauma. The idea that traumatic events in one lifetime can be encoded in genetic material and passed on to future generations is mindboggling. But, in a way, it is the biological parallel to the oral histories we inherit, like memories that aren't quite our own but become a part of our subconscious selves, nonetheless. Ria shows this through her essay, even as she takes ownership of her encoded memories. Woven into her narrative, somewhere between her desire to preserve her grandparents' fading memories and her own quest for self-discovery lies the question: what do we do with the traumatic legacies we inherit?

The essay begins in 1947, sixty-four years before Ria applies to university. Recounting her grandfather's painful experience of forced displacement from his home in Karachi, she contextualizes and humanizes the story of twelve million refugees who survived the violent, bloody journeys, only to face an uncertain future. Ria captures the memories evocatively. And then, she encrypts them, making us see that enveloped in them are messages of hope, courage and hard work but equally, prejudice, bias and hate. The stories become hers through her ability to distinguish between these messages. This, despite her keen sensitivity to her grandparents' experiences. Evident also, in the action Ria takes is her desire to archive these memories and move past the trauma. Much like Holocaust survivors, Ria's grandparents are the last generation of Indians and Pakistanis with first-hand recollections of Partition. Their stories, as Ria concludes, deserve to be preserved in a way that correctly contextualizes them and provides her generation a 'chance to learn from the mistakes made' instead of inheriting anger and loss.

'Remembering Partition' gives Ria a purpose, and the resulting confidence transforms her. As the conservator of her grandparents' memories, she connects with other stories, storytellers and audiences of these memories. We see in the course of the essay, Ria expanding her network and her worldview; and we laud her developing instinct to look beyond the bias she inherited. Amid all the plans that follow, Ria emerges as someone she had hitherto never seen herself as—a leader. Making tough decisions, collecting funds, planning for the future, and inspiring people to join her, Ria sets course for a future her grandparents were once unsure of: forging her own destiny as a leader, with certitude.

8

THE HEAVY-LIFTERS

'Life doesn't give us purpose.
We give life purpose.'
—The Flash

Most of us spend time looking for opportunities to do good and act on the values we hold the closest. Certain people, however, create opportunity through the sheer weight and force of their will and effort. The heavy-lifters in this section belong to this domain.

Essays that focus on giving back to society and changing the world are frequent. However, the accounts in these essays convey the sentiment and emotion motivating the action so well that the impact of each essay is intensified. The writers' earnestness and authenticity suggest that in changing contexts and settings (like a college environment), the seminal values of equality, fraternity and dignity for all will continue to define their purpose.

PULKIT AGARWAL

Harvard, Class of 2019

Major: Economics
School: The Doon School, Dehradun, India
Hometown: Pilibhit, India

GESELLSCHAFT—A SOCIETY BASED ON IMPERSONAL TIES

One winter evening, as I mounted my saffron-colored bicycle to visit a friend's place, my grandfather grabbed me by the wrist and dragged me indoors. Agitatedly pointing to the color of my bicycle, he said that if I were to visit that neighborhood on this bicycle, 'even a stray dog would understand I didn't belong there.' I didn't challenge him then, for having grown up in a society where communal divides are omnipresent, I had learned to accept them as established conventions.

In the spring of 2013, however, I had a revelatory experience that not only made me question these divides, but also taught me that I could do something to debunk them. I participated in a program called 'Big Brothers Big Sisters' at Deerfield Academy in Massachusetts. At its heart, I felt, lay a concept that Indian society was crying out for: the idea of a collective transcendence of conventional cultural divides. When I saw students from markedly different backgrounds eating buffalo wings off the same plate while fondly sharing their differing exploits,

I understood that perhaps the divides that our society had grown to accept didn't have to be taken for granted after all.

On returning to India, I interested myself more in understanding what causes communal divides. I walked the crowded backstreets of Pilibhit, my home city, and came across more small pockets of minority-concentrated areas than I had previously known. It was virtually impossible to locate a mixed neighborhood. Since Pilibhit had also been an outpost of the contentious Mughal Emperor Aurangzeb, Hindu-Muslim interactions here were seldom congenial. One day, as I got into an auto-rickshaw, the driver asked me whether I wanted him to take the 'Hindu-route' or the 'Muslim-route'. Taken aback as I was on hearing this, he clarified that there had been recent clashes between the two communities, and he wanted to take the safer route. My grandfather's concern suddenly made sense to me: the very real fear that the association of the saffron color with Hindu fundamentalism risked inciting disharmony.

I began to understand, then, how social barriers based on religion, caste, and social status are built through both active and passive experiences. I decided to bring 'Big Brothers Big Sisters' to India, which presented a massive challenge: to implore children to shed some part of their established identities. While the program was intended to give students from my school (Bigs) the chance to mentor young children from local slums (Littles), its initial results were far from promising. I would split students into pairs, only to see them return to their original company within minutes. Numerous unsuccessful interactions later, the supervising teacher insisted that I give up, for 'a few hours now will in no way compensate for the differences in their lives to date.'

I internalized her remark as motivation; my sole intention was simply to take a small step to soften these ubiquitous barriers.

On Independence Day this year, I got the opportunity to do just that. I had the Bigs and Littles prepare short skits and dress as freedom fighters. I paired them matching the roles they played, cheerily watching 'Big Gandhi' lead 'Little Gandhi' on his salt march in protest against the colonial government, while 'Big Nehru' and 'Little Nehru' delivered their lyrical speeches waking India up to its freedom. For the first time, I saw everyone commune together just as I had seen last spring. I felt as though I had found the central pivot around which this program could revolve and be replicated: a common regard for the nation.

Even today, the Bigs visit the same Littles I paired them with months ago, wearing the same 'Gandhi caps' as before. By making them embody nationalist icons, I have helped them in successfully transcending their established identities and morphing into a new community.

Gemeinschaft—a community based on personal ties.

OUR THOUGHTS ON PULKIT'S ESSAY

Sociologists have long debated the true meaning of *Gemeinschaft*, often agreeing that it represents something that is more experienced than seen. A hall of movie-goers sitting in rapt attention, spellbound listeners at a concert, stadiums filled with chanting legions of fans. *Gemeinschaft* is a collective or a common intent, greater than the sum of its constituents. Pulkit's story draws on these elusive, universal desires for finding belonging beyond ascriptive identities assigned at birth, using details embedded in the socio-religious conditions of his hometown, Pilibhit.

Pulkit opens the essay with the inheritance of belief. A seemingly innocuous detail, the saffron color of his bicycle, takes on a whole new meaning as a symbol of group identity. Even without knowing specific details about Pilibhit's religious demographics and history, the panicked concern shown by Pulkit's grandfather effectively communicates the charged atmosphere of a city where the color saffron (considered sacred by many Hindu communities and flaunted by fundamentalist groups) can seem like religious incitement. As Pulkit explains later in the essay, this is a 'passive experience' that quietly but effectively strengthens his understanding of who he is (Hindu) based on who he is not (Muslim), thereby erecting the barrier of identity. Pulkit's essay delivers impact through similar, relevant lived experiences, keeping the reader engaged through complex sociological concepts without getting entangled in dense and weighty academic language. His experience of Pilibhit's contours as being divided into distinct Hindu and Muslim neighborhoods, backstreets and corresponding routes echoes his opening inheritance of learning that saffron is a 'Hindu' color.

The essay conveys Pulkit's sensitivity to religious differences and his high regard for Pilibhit. Even a continent and a few oceans away in Massachusetts, he relates the cultural transcendence embodied in the 'Big/Little' program to his hometown. His consequent efforts to provide positive and intentional active and passive experiences to a new generation are an effort to replace the differences he imbibed as 'natural' in his childhood years with memories of unity and togetherness. Pulkit's love for his hometown is overtly agnostic of religion, class and creed. Significantly, his successful 'Big/Little' program born of his intent and efforts to bridge communal divides aptly exemplifies *Gemeinschaft*—an ideology that will drive his future.

DHRUV KEDIA

Stanford, Class of 2019

Major: Computer Science
School: Dhirubhai Ambani International School, Mumbai, India
Hometown: Mumbai, India

6 a.m., Sunday morning, I wake up apprehensive yet excited to accompany Jal Jyoti, a social initiative that provides innovative lighting solutions to slums in Mumbai at just Rs 300 ($3.33) for five years. Week after week, for the past one year, I have been avidly accompanying Jal Jyoti and have helped light up close to fifty-seven homes.

Slum dwellers in Mumbai rely on harmful kerosene lamps or steal power due to the unaffordable cost of energy. Jal Jyoti's solution requires cementing a 1.25-litre plastic bottle containing a mixture of clear water and 10 ml bleach into the roof. As light passes through the bottle it refracts and lights up the dark windowless houses. I vividly remember the moment when I first walked through the four-feet wide, unevenly paved lanes of the Koliwada shoreline slums with over 200 densely packed shanties, women in nightgowns expeditiously doing their daily chores, scantily clad kids playing with broken toys and the stench from open drains and garbage making us feel nauseous.

At the slums, we split into groups of three to visit shanties and convince the wary families to install the bottles. It was hard just getting them to give us a hearing. They doubted everything we said. They questioned us about the technology, sustainability and, more importantly, our motive. Only after lots of convincing did one of the house owners finally allow us to start the installation. His contract with us was oral and based on trust.

On entering the 100 square-feet windowless house, I was moved by the sight of a small boy crouched in a tiny space gazing at his book under a minuscule lamp. I was ashamed at my demands for branded spectacles, a bigger room and a cozier bed, while a boy 10 miles away was straining his eyes and making do with little. It was a Zen moment for me that brought me closer to my soul and made me reflect on the privileged and the underprivileged.

After analyzing which point to drill the hole in, we climbed on to the roof and carefully began drilling a four-inch hole. The ramshackle rooftop was made of corrugated rusted metal sheets, plastic tarpaulin and broken slate blocks. This simple task had become challenging because of the precarious roof and the expectations and trust the family deposed in us. A force so great had fallen upon my shoulders and I understood what it means to own responsibility. I knew there was no passing of blame and not once did I move to wipe the sweat off my face or itch my arm.

After drilling we slowly started to cement the bottle with the top half exposed to the sun. As I worked on the roof, the Mumbai heat slapped against my face putting me out of my comfort zone. Usually, I would have zoomed off to find a juice vendor but this time I was fully consumed by the mission of making a difference to someone who trusted me. On completing the installation, we stepped down from the roof and went inside the house. My reward that I treasure to date was the smile on their faces, and glitter of delight in their eyes as they saw the sunlight pass through the bottle and light up the room. The extreme gratitude they displayed was unbelievable. We then went on and lit up the lives of two more households. Each installation was challenging yet different and wonderful in its own way.

This experience changed my life mission to commit to innovating impactful solutions and made me realize that real success is measured by how much you have done for others and contributed in making the world a better place. Today, I feel extremely content that my journey in solar energy from my 'Engineering Design' course at Columbia University to the designing of a solar kit has paid off and I am able to give back to society.

OUR THOUGHTS ON DHRUV'S ESSAY

Dhruv's story sensitively channels the conditions of the world outside his privileged milieu to communicate his expanding worldview and growing understanding of responsibility, success, and purpose. Centered solidly in the socio-physical context of Mumbai, his essay demonstrates how still-shifting identities can be effectively conveyed.

We live in times with record levels of global inequality, a dichotomy visible perhaps more than anywhere else in Dhruv's home city Mumbai, where the physical proximity between skyscrapers and slums does not diminish the starkness of their divide. His work with Jal Jyoti serves as a portal into a city experience that his privilege would, in the normal course, insulate him from.

Dhruv's description of his first visit to Koliwada and the wariness of the local community communicates the palpable distance between the Mumbai he has stepped into and the utopian one he usually inhabits. Refraining from exploiting or detailing the existential realities of urban poverty, Dhruv shifts focus to the impact the visit has had on him. This is a particularly remarkable quality of the essay. Despite the narrative being overtly externally focused (the slum, the unrelenting heat, the physically taxing process of attaching the refracting light to a precariously patched roof), we get a visceral sense of Dhruv: his reactions, emotions, and internal changes are focal and woven around the action. His experience of being 'trusted' is a good example of this. The physical act of holding up the roof is used to convey the weight of responsibility that he feels to succor the family whose home he could effectively (and metaphorically) make or break. The essay also stands out for the well-incorporated moments of empathy, like his observation of a child making do with minimal lighting. While it is impossible for Dhruv, or anyone with privilege, to fully experience the life of Koliwada residents, the nature of Dhruv's work makes the resulting reflection on privilege credible.

The technical nature of the lighting and the mention of an 'Engineering Design' course at the end do offer allusions to Dhruv's academic background, but the diffused focus has a more revealing message. His skills find purpose in helping others.

HARSH MESWANI

UPenn, Class of 2021

Major: Mechanical Engineering and Finance (M&T Program)
School: Dhirubhai Ambani International School, Mumbai, India
Hometown: Mumbai, India

REPLANTING MUSICAL ROOTS

I have grown up watching, listening to and interacting with some of the most iconic Indian classical musicians. I remember nights in Mumbai concert halls, when Ustad Zakir Hussain's tabla blew my mind, and car-rides spent listening to U Srinivas's mandolin melodies. Experiences like these have made me appreciate this unique art form and revere its practitioners. My self-produced original music album 'Trail of Thought', though played on keyboards, contains distinct Indian influences.

As a musician, I recognize the 400 hours of practice required to produce four minutes of classical music. It seems unfortunate that the majority of today's Indian youth are either unaware of their inherited cultural treasures, or too 'cool' to appreciate them. Indian classical music is not getting the recognition it deserves, and not enough is being done to preserve its legacy. In fact, most classical concerts I attend are characterized by a scattered crowd devoid of young people. When I see a born genius on stage struggling to succeed, I feel pain. I feel a burning desire to preserve the art form I love. This inner restlessness inspired me to act.

I began writing a book, *The Torchbearers,* featuring my articles about and interviews with twenty-five classical musicians. Young but established, these musicians are the future leaders of a generation of Indian classical music. I therefore found it appropriate to document their compelling stories. Writing the book was an arduous and complex creative process for me, an inexperienced writer. The tasks of formulating interview questions and formatting a book were completely new. Travelling to meet artists, adapting to their speaking styles and editing every word challenged me. I decided to frame the interviews based on artist-specific questions about the challenges facing the genre of Indian classical music. I hope this framework brings out the artists' passion and inspires youth to recognize the cause.

After the first few interviews, I still felt a bit directionless. But then the most unexpected thing happened. My favorite musician U Srinivas, whom I had fortunately already interviewed, tragically died. The sense of loss motivated me to work with passion and commitment and dedicate the book to his legacy. Eventually, I started enjoying the book-writing experience so much that it subconsciously became part of my daily routine for over two years. The book now took me even deeper into the classical music world, and had me appreciate the struggles that these artists endure to reach their level of expertise. It did eat time away from my schedule, but I do not regret a single minute!

Now complete, *The Torchbearers* is a compilation of musicians' inner voices coupled with my own spontaneous flow of emotions. I hope the book convinces readers to appreciate the art form, and kick-starts a youth-awakening process. Part two of the preservation process of this art form was the creation of a sustainable, thriving community of musicians and audiences. For this, I found creative use of technology to be the answer. I conceptualized the Indian Concert Guide, a website and weekly newsletter solely dedicated to informing people about classical music concerts, events and artists. In addition to show information, the website has links to book tickets. It is a free, convenient and user-friendly platform for Mumbai audiences to gain exposure to Indian classical music through blogs, articles and media.

My website has received an overwhelming response! Within a few months, over 3000 subscribers signed up to relish the joys of Indian classical music. However, what pleases me most is the fact that more than half the subscribers are under thirty. It reassures me that the youth have the potential to keep the ship of Indian classical music sailing.

I hope my endeavors play a role in filling those empty concert seats that caused me to begin these initiatives. My dream will be fulfilled when tomorrow's children think, 'Yeah, Indian classical music is cool!'

OUR THOUGHTS ON HARSH'S ESSAY

Not all Indian classical music lovers would look at empty seats at concerts and resolve to proactively enact change as Harsh did. His essay maintains focus on process over product wherein, he describes the journey emanating from his passion for an old, treasured art form that was fast losing patrons. The result is a testament to his passion, perseverance and will to act rather than remain passive.

The essay points to the schism between the dedication, art and finesse behind the music and the lukewarm reception that belie the efforts underpinning the performance. Harsh keenly feels this dissonance on behalf of musicians and fans, or, in his words, the 'restlessness inspired me to act'. This became the fuel to leverage his knowledge of Indian classical music to write a book titled *The Torchbearers*. He conveys his meticulousness in tailoring questions for each interview to the background of selected musicians; thereby demonstrating his investment in the project, knowledge of the genre and, importantly, his commitment to popularizing classical music across generations.

In being honest about the trials of book writing, Harsh includes his struggle with motivation. However, following the death of one of his favorite musicians, he channels his resulting grief into further immersion in the musical world: he strengthens his resolve to be the one to make lasting change. His demonstrated ability to overcome challenges and remain devoted to his cause for two years is vindicated by the completion and publishing of his book.

At this point, Harsh shows us, through a precise descriptive narrative, how he is unstoppable. He soldiers on, creating a newsletter-styled website that contemporizes the information and booking process for classical music events. That he manages this alongside school, his own music endeavors and the commitments that come with teenage life is truly impressive, especially in the context of university, where students are expected to balance multiple spheres of life.

However, ultimately it isn't the 3000 subscribers his website attracts, nor the published book that sets the essay, or Harsh apart. While these contributions are significant towards the revival of Indian classical music, they are not the heart of this essay. It's that upon seeing an empty concert hall, Harsh sets aside and ignores what is 'cool' and, follows his heart—this distinguishes him.

JUHEE GOYAL

Harvard, Class of 2022

Major: Engineering Sciences: Biomedical Sciences and Engineering and Integrative Biology
School: Shishukunj International School, Indore, India
Hometown: Indore, India

Filthy, packed living quarters, no space to wiggle, occasional rotting food fed at their captor's whim, malodorous unswept excreta of weeks, piercing screams, and above all, isolation from any form of love.

This scene I saw established a fundamental part of me. It was in 2015, on my first visit to the local avian pet shop in Indore.

Growing up in a home that has traditionally never kept companion animals made convincing my family that I had to adopt one, a herculean endeavor. For eight years I tried to convince them to adopt a dog, cat, hamster, even a bird, arguing passionately for my cause. I identified, dissected and countered the weak links in my parents' arguments and presented compelling evidence of my sense of responsibility. After their acquiescence, I weathered weeks of wait until finally told, 'Today's Diwali. We'll go and choose a pair of birds.' I was the happiest girl in the world.

An hour later, I was anything but happy, I had seen avian hell. Thirty parakeets were cramped into a small 80cm x 35cm x 40cm cage, some birds had blue feet indicative of pneumonia, and droppings encrusted the cage floor and flecked their birdseed and water bowls.

I was torn: get a pair of birds, and tacitly support such conditions, or not, and lose the chance of finally getting what I had strived for over several years?

That's when it struck me. This was a problem that I needed to solve. A problem whose solution could potentially transform the lives of budgies, finches, cockatiels, conures, indeed, of all caged birds.

I decided on a pair of cockatiels, *Nymphicus hollandicus.* I would learn to take care of them, and then apply that learning to derive solutions for this problem I had found. And I did.

And so it began. Endless sessions of trying to teach Hedwig to whistle and the treatment of his initial eye infection, the frantic scrambling to deter Niboo from eating droppings, the initially futile attempts to get Hedwig in the water bowl for bathing, the now equally futile attempts to get him to cease bathing. I kept them warm with hot water bottles changed every two hours on cold nights, chose toys to replace those they'd ripped apart and enjoyed the learning curve hugely. I did indeed discover, as anticipated, most of what I needed to know to make a difference to the birds in the pet shop. I learned all I could of cockatiels and the other avian species there. I learned through experience the constituents of a happy environment for birds.

Every visit to the shop was punctuated with tears at seeing those unfortunate birds. Yet, I shared what I learned with the shop's owner after buying birdseed.

'Blue feet indicate illness,' I would say.

'No, no, color of the feet doesn't matter,' said Ravi the shopkeeper. Shrugging off their obvious hostility, I choked back my anger as I provided them the resources to learn about bird care. My overarching intent was to foster change. Their problem was mine, I would find a solution. I leveraged my learning from those two years to write a booklet on the care of cockatiels in the Indian context.

The change was gradual, month by month. Cleaner water trays. Better seeds. Fewer droppings in their cages. I hoped that though their lives had not changed completely, they suffered less. I am gratified that I could make a small difference. Armed with my booklet and persistence, inflicting even more sessions on even more irate pet-shop owners, I will reach the goal that remains entrenched in my mind: happy, vocalizing budgies with healthy pink feet, finches frolicking in bigger, cleaner cages, cockatiels with crests indicating contentment, and conures with gleaming feathers and shining eyes.

That day back in 2015 instilled within me the need to work for the happiness of all living beings.

OUR THOUGHTS ON JUHEE'S ESSAY

Persistence. That is what rings out loud and clear in this precious essay, one that is also about kindness, empathy, and a recognition that larger goals are worth fighting for, however pocked the road.

As with other great essays, the first line grabs our attention, and begs the question: *what on earth is she talking about?* And then it unfolds—we learn of Juhee's tireless eight-year negotiation with her parents on the imperatives of acquiring a pet, an argument she finally wins. Persistence.

In exploring the mental calculus behind purchasing a pair of birds, Juhee reveals a maturity in thinking through the choices she had; she could walk away, but the harder and right choice was to help make a difference in the living conditions of the 'unfortunate birds'. Choosing the harder option is indicative of persistence, too.

Juhee treads the learning curve, and takes us with her—we learn that birds are the happiest when they're warm and clean (who isn't?). In caring for the birds, Juhee reveals how she learns the uncomfortable truth of meaningful progress—that it comes in fits and starts, and sometimes reverses course, but slowly, and sometimes painfully, things creep forward. This is evident when she teaches her birds to bathe (and then stop), and not to eat their own excrement. Here, as before, persistence paid off, and the lessons of what it takes to keep birds healthy took shape. Here, too, is kindness. As anyone who has had a pet with questionable behavior patterns would know, it can be a harrowing experience. We see a problem-solver at work—tinkering with ideas and documenting progress. And above all, persisting.

The final test, of course, is Juhee's tackling of the shopkeepers. While much is left unsaid here about the class and, possibly, gender politics, we have a sense of the challenges Juhee faced when one shopkeeper brushed aside her concern for the pneumonia-ridden birds in cavalier fashion. That Juhee reached out to the shopkeepers at all provides a telling insight about her ability to connect with people different from her. She stepped out of her comfort zone in service of a higher goal. While progress was slow, it was measurable, and Juhee, in a moment of grace, hopes the birds suffer less than they had before.

We like this essay because it reads like a short story, and the writer's personality traits are revealed in a gentle, engaging narrative. Aside from persistent, Juhee is kind, community-focused and analytical—all traits an admissions officer would want in the student body!

SHREYAS DUTT

Brown, Class of 2024

Major: Computer Science
School: Delhi Public School R.K. Puram, New Delhi, India
Hometown: Dhanbad, India

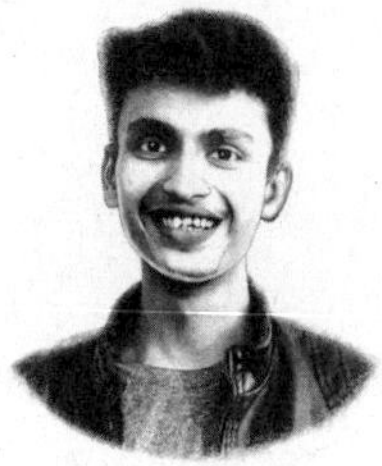

SNAKES-VENOM-HARMLESS-PASSION

These words connect the main story of my life. Being brought up in the coal-mining town of Dhanbad, in the state of Jharkhand, India, snakes were a part of my daily walk to school. It was not uncommon to spot different species of snakes harmlessly moving along the rural paths of the town. Watching the Steve Irwin and Brady Barr shows on Nat Geo exposed me to the way in which animals were caught, tested for their bite strengths and toxicity levels, and then released. I always wished to explore snakes at a deeper level especially because my neighborhood boasted of species like the Indian rat snake, Russel viper, monocled cobra, banded krait, Indian rock python and the sand boa. I was alternately fascinated and frightened of these snakes but soon developed an interest in saving them when I observed people killing them needlessly. A memorable incident that reinforced my belief was getting too close to a snake in my playground but standing still in fear made it slither away.

This incident brought a paradigm shift in my attitude. I began to research the behavior of snakes and discovered that most of them were harmless if left alone. They did not have the memory of a dog or cat and struck out only when they sensed danger. No one was a friend or an enemy because they were cold-blooded. Snakes were vital for our ecosystem because they killed rats and other rodents. I passionately wished to create an environment of sustainability so that both snakes and humans could co-exist. The desire to do so made me connect with an NGO that focused on saving snakes. An expert taught me to handle snakes using snake tongs and snake hooks. The first time I picked up a snake holding the back of its head, I was terrified beyond words. Every successive handling made me realize how harmless they were. They seemed more frightened of me than the other way around. I accompanied the experts from the snake rescue NGO on various distress calls.

The next step was to visit neighboring villages where the maximum killing of snakes took place. Unsurprisingly, the number of killings coincided with the number of human deaths despite the availability of antivenom and medical services. I sensed that a vital link was missing. I interacted with different people and realized that they looked at snakes as bad omens. Exorcists created another issue. People blindly believed in their abilities to cure snake bites. The fake doctors chanted rubbish and pretended to cure people of bites that were not fatal to begin with. Most were false bites where the venom was not injected. Seventy-five percent of the victims died because of the delay in taking them to hospitals. I recollect an incident where an elderly man died of a fear-induced heart attack and not the actual bite.

To counter all these myths, I held meetings with villagers, counseled them about avoiding snakes and getting timely medical help instead of fake exorcists. It was challenging to communicate with them since they spoke different languages like Bengali, Santhali, Bhojpuri and Oraon depending on the region in which they lived. I learned the basics of each language to communicate effectively with them. It was intriguing how working for snake protection transformed me into a linguist!

Additionally, we conducted regular patrols around snake-infested areas, particularly in sunlight, when the snakes came out. The journey is long but making a beginning in understanding both snake and human behavior will hopefully make a difference to saving snake and human lives. My personal learning was in the form of developing unusual animal-handling skills, leadership talents and helping the villagers demarcate their land to develop a sustainable environment, in which each creature played its part in contributing towards a healthy ecosystem.

OUR THOUGHTS ON SHREYAS'S ESSAY

Unique circumstances make for compelling stories. And this one provides a glimpse into Shreyas's environment and the lessons he took from it. It is said that nature is a great teacher—and that certainly rings true here. Instead of being jaded by frequent encounters with snakes (we tend to ignore things that become commonplace), Shreyas used them as a starting point to learn more, do more, and connect with the wider community. Through snakes, Shreyas shows us how he is able to amplify his life and sensitivities.

Shreyas provides us with rough, barely contoured sketches (again, showing, not telling) to imagine his walk to school—a daily occurrence punctuated with serpentine companions. Here, he tells us of his first lesson—that snakes would rather escape humans than attack—and simultaneously (perhaps unintentionally?), of his kindness. Shreyas is proactive in turning this teachable moment into a clarion call for acting on civic duty. His research into snake behavior, work with a snake rescue organization, and learning to handle and rescue snakes, provide a portrait of an intellectually curious student who pushes the boundaries of his comfort zone.

In doing so, he is exposed to rural India, a world likely vastly different from the one he knew, and he makes a point of understanding local and indigenous perspectives on snakes. To counter the false local impressions on the reptiles, Shreyas makes a concerted effort to connect with the local communities on their terms, by learning their local language. This attempt to understand a variety of perspectives demonstrates that Shreyas will thrive in a diverse environment. He also does not hold back his views on faith healers who foster entrenched fears, and he uses these encounters as a springboard to counter myths.

All told, this essay clearly tells the reader who Shreyas is—observant, curious, up for a challenge, and willing and able to reach across social and cultural divides and build consensus over seemingly contentious issues.

JAI THIRANI

UPenn, Class of 2021

Major: Computer Science and Finance
School: Nath Valley School, Aurangabad, India
Hometown: Aurangabad, India

I have always been fascinated by the ability of code to transform into work; the infinite potential energy of 1s and 0s to convert into meaningful action. Throughout school, nothing excited me as much as pressing 'Run' in the command window and watching my creation unfold. A line of code is absolute. It is my enabler.

However, computer technology was far from my mind as I walked down the narrow, murky streets of Satara village, a mile away from my home. The heat was debilitating, and the garbage-lined streets encapsulated the squalor of my surroundings. The newly elected Indian government had recently initiated the 'Swachh Bharat Abhiyan' (Clean India Mission) envisioning a clean India. However, execution was complacent.

The juxtaposition of the old world and the technologically advanced one was conflicting. Having lived seventeen years in the historic city of Aurangabad, I proudly call it home. Seeing portions of my city, once a bastion of ascetic monks and valiant Mughals, degraded was unacceptable. I needed to be the change to pro-actively work towards reversing this apathy.

My plan was simple: There were irregularities in the collection of garbage in the vicinity; and I would capture this. I was sure the City

Corporation would welcome the intervention, and we could harmonize our efforts to eradicate the bottlenecks in the current garbage-collection system. When faced with the question of how I would monitor garbage collection of various locations with regularity, I instantly resorted to my opium—coding.

I knew I had to code my way to finding a solution. The only question that remained was, 'Code what?' Having been an aero-modeling buff since I can remember, I envisioned an aerial vehicle would be my facilitator; a quad copter—my eye in the sky.

The summer I spent in Calcutta this April was fortuitous. In a by lane off Park Street, on the third floor of a rundown building, I spent my time designing, building and coding my quad copter with Mr Irshad Anwar, an expert aero-modeler. Although I was clueless initially, with his expertise to guide me, I kick-started my execution.

The integration of all the concepts and code, to form logical algorithms that performed perfectly, gave me satisfaction like no other. The first time I saw the rotor blades spin, I knew it was real. In his small room filled with aero modeling paraphernalia, we constantly made minor tweaks, tried them out on the field, and eventually ameliorated. I faced impediments. From debugging code to watching my quad fall from the sky, each incident was a significant part to my quad's evolution. After a number of prototypes, each more stable and powerful than the last, we made it work.

On my return to Aurangabad, I deployed my creation. I equipped it to take aerial videos and photos of my vicinity, through a live video feed. This gave me a hawk's eye view of the environment. It empowered me to speak out. I was determined for a 'Swachh Bharat' (Clean India).

Over the next few weeks, while perfecting my flying, I began surveying garbage sites. If garbage was left unattended, I knew first and, subsequently, so did everyone else. After the initial incredulity at my creation, the officials were inspired to work towards cleaning the city.

I had not brought about a revolution, but simply taken a small step. I had provided the spark needed to ignite the minds of the people to work towards a clean Aurangabad.

From drawing boards to open skies—the significance of the experience is not lost on me. I have learnt that the technology around me has been built by normal people. To know that I am capable of doing it, too, is my revelation.

'Productivity is never an accident. It is always the result of a commitment to excellence, intelligent planning, and focused effort.'

In my case, a commitment to a cause.

OUR THOUGHT'S ON JAI'S ESSAY

Through this essay, Jai's growing confidence in his power as a citizen, transforms him into an advocate for a universal, involved and intentional approach to our future. Arrived at by design, instead of by accident. His own story, with clear motivations, struggles and lessons, tells us how he sought resolve in small, yet substantial ways.

Jai starts his narration with two seemingly disparate interests. His love for coding, and the sense of control it gives him as 'his enabler'. And his move to civic action, motivated by the gap between the government initiative, 'Swachh Bharat', and the reality of garbage-strewn streets near his Aurangabad home. Setting the scene for the two interests to engage with one another early on, Jai shifts the focus of the essay from his realization about using coding to assist in his cleanliness drive to the process by which it is enacted ('I knew I had to code my way to finding a solution. The only question that remained was, "Code what?"'). His main focus now moves beyond the world of coding and technology's power to help enforce policy. Instead, Jai hones in on his struggle to chisel *his* approach of contributing as a citizen of his hometown. While Jai's coding prowess is a vital component in the essay, he implies that his capabilities truly take optimal shape when channeled towards a cause.

Further, Jai pays attention to two sets of details that help ground his essay and highlight the qualities he hopes to hero. First, his pride in his historic hometown, Aurangabad. This is envisaging and fuels his motivations as he begins the project. Second, his efforts in the direction of building a functioning prototype for monitoring efficiency. This inclusion, which emphasizes the process of trial and error over the moment of eventual success, helps highlight Jai's tenacity and ability to remain wedded to the cause. Evidently, he works for the long haul and sees his project through to fruition.

Through the essay, Jai demonstrates his belief in his talents and abilities, his acceptance of his capacity, his commitment to the larger community, and responsibility to catalyze change.

SHUBHAM PODDAR

UPenn, Class of 2018

Major: International Studies and Business – Finance and Operations Information Decisions (Huntsman Program)
School: Modern School Vasant Vihar, New Delhi, India
Hometown: New Delhi, India

We're shaped by our narratives. My community—the Marwaris, known for their ability to transform the environment, come from the arid desert state of Rajasthan, India. From here they fled to domains where they acculturated, establishing glistening steel and textile empires. And if they did not succeed, they moved again. And struck gold. Leaving home was commonplace. Perhaps it's genetically programmed—today, I'm about to move to a country thousands of miles away. Like my ancestors, I will flourish in diversity and go that extra distance to actualize my dreams. My gold? I'll challenge myself intellectually and equip myself to catalyze positive change.

Ingenuity runs in the blood. The Hundi System Marwaris innovated was a first. This cashless remittance facility moved money through traders across India, thereby facilitating commerce. I felt handicapped when appointed Head Boy as there were no formal guidelines on duties and protocol. I brainstormed with past leaders, drew from their experiences, and created a book of Standard Operating Procedures including council responsibilities; interspersed with guidelines on ethical leadership. This was unprecedented and necessary. I'm delighted that I'll hand over to a leadership that can hit the ground running.

Patriarchs of Marwari families created master plans for townships they'd build.

But there were challenges: vines to be cut, forests cleared, panthers chased to the jungle's edges to accommodate cities. They overcame every impediment to make it happen. With a spring in my step, I escorted Mr Salman Khurshid, Foreign Minister, to the podium. I couldn't believe The Young Leaders Conclave was happening. As he commended the idea, I reflected on the innumerable hurdles we overcame to bring the event to life.

Realizing the dearth of 'thought leadership' in my domain, I wanted to strengthen leaders of today for tomorrow. I conceived this three-day event, drawing participation from a hundred head boys and head girls of schools in India, the US and Singapore, and current leaders in their fields. The exceptional scale required fund-raising, bargain hotel-hunting, sponsorships. The run-up was obstacle-ridden. Our main sponsor backed out ten days before the event. We raised almost the entire budget again. Our guests' dates changed daily—we strenuously juggled travel and hospitality bookings. Persuading eminent personalities such as the Foreign Minister, Opposition Leader and social activists was a coup. The President of India, Mr Pranab Mukherjee, accepted an invite to discuss social responsibility and attunement. A day before the launch, he cancelled due to a national emergency. I learnt to think on my feet; resourcefully amended the schedule without compromising purpose, thereby creating an enduring legacy for my school.

In the mid-twentieth century, my great-grandfather helped found an industrial township in Bihar. Marwaris played an integral role in holistic development, creating productive ecosystems—including hospitals and schools from scratch. Studying German opened new worlds. The Goethe Institut offered opportunities to advance this. I created an ecosystem in school that includes the Deutsch Klub of which I am Founder–President. We organize language-based competitions and field trips. I've incepted an exchange program with a school in Germany. Our magazine *Vasant Parag* includes the German section that I edit; and the Institut commended our 'Oktoberfest' as I marveled at the shared affinities between distinct cultures!

'Businessmen are trustees of wealth which belong to the community.' Marwaris

espouse inclusive growth. Seeing that the women slum-dwellers of Yamuna Pushta, Delhi, weren't allowed to work outside their homes, I devised that work be brought to them. I aligned with a non-profit and evolved financial and marketing plans for a wool knits enterprise. Today, skeins of wool are delivered to them, each morning. I learnt to ally the interests of four stakeholders' (slum-dwellers, non-profit, corporation, raw-material supplier), and ensure they work in unison. The project is sustaining, and we will replicate it elsewhere.

Thus, influenced by my backdrop and the remarkable community I belong to, I will take my unique ethos to university and beyond, to help forge a better future for our planet!

OUR THOUGHTS ON SHUBHAM'S ESSAY

Almost fifty years ago, Bob Marley memorialized the importance of knowing where we come from, paying tribute to our longing for lost and erased connections in his song, 'Buffalo Soldier'. While occurring in an entirely different era and context, Shubham's essay is rife with this sense of history and home, a homage to his Marwari community.

Much like most communities that migrate, or are displaced from their homeland, Shubham's artefacts are oral renditions of movement, value-laden stories passed down through generations. He shows us how he is part of this fabric, this rich community-bonding that takes pride in renewing traditions. Stylistically, he distinguishes the narratives by italicizing them at the start of each paragraph. This helps in distinguishing between community truths which he assimilates, and their impact on his life. Such formatting and structural choices increase the readability of this unconventional essay. The use of stories, quotes and history also help create a broader picture and context from which Shubham emerges. While conventional wisdom might suggest that applicants focus on themselves in the Common App essay, Shubham has created room for reflection on his background—his personal, family and community history. He maximizes this opportunity by outlining a legacy that he draws inspiration and commitment from, personalizing these universal themes with great effect.

Shubham is successful in choosing a diverse set of evidence to showcase his achievements. Cutting across leadership and initiative (Head Boy, Leader's Conclave), organizational skills and creativity (learning German, negotiating an event) and his desire to use his abilities to help others (women of Yamuna Pushta), he does not shy away from presenting a rounded profile. Importantly, he does this while taking care to emote and display inspiration in each example, ensuring the essay remains highly personal.

Shubham uses his cultural background intriguingly—to contextualize his work and communicate who he is. He then concretizes his claims with examples. For example, his work with women living in the Yamuna Pushta slum is framed by his preceding reiteration of the Marwari community's commitment to inclusive growth. His balanced descriptions combine a genuine concern for the beneficiaries with the practicality of a sustainable business model. Throughout, a stream of wisdom, received as a legacy from his forefathers, runs through—a back story of his community which lends vibrancy to Shubham's distinctive profile. As also, measure and gravitas.

ANJALI DUGAR

Dartmouth, Class of 2021

Major: Philosophy
School: Cheltenham Ladies' College, London, UK
Hometown: Mumbai, India

'*Do you think refusing Sam-I-Am's* Green Eggs and Ham *was fair, given that he hadn't tried it? Are judgements based on reason better than those based on experience?*'

The cramped circle of thoughtful minds sits cross-legged on the dusty floor of the classroom; the electricity flickers. Ruthless sunshine streams in through the window, but their scintillating energy never subsides. Their passionate discussion consumes me. Three years ago, few would have believed that twelve-year-olds from Mumbai's harshest neighborhoods would be discussing the epistemological dichotomy between a priori and a posteriori reasoning.

I spent most of my childhood in Akanksha and Teach for India (TFI), tagging along with my mother to schools or home visits. I sat at the back of classrooms on my bamboo *chatai*, absorbed with curiosity in the older kids' lessons despite understanding little. I ventured into the heart of Mumbai's slums to help Seema decorate her house for the Ganesh festival, or to share rice pudding with Tabassum's family during Eid-ul-Fitr. Countless happy hours were spent painting, singing, discussing favorite Harry Potter characters—not as a volunteer or teacher, just a friend.

At ten, I began volunteering at both NGOs. Given this upbringing, I had no heart-breaking or eye-opening turning point that made me appreciate my fortunate life and want to get involved. Inequity is something I have always been acutely aware of, with almost a sense of duty to contribute to change. An uncomfortable desire for parity convinced me that apart from having more, I was no different. My sense of injustice heightened when, at thirteen, my parents sent me to school halfway across the world for the best possible education; it felt grossly unfair that while I was being given extraordinary opportunities, my friends at Akanksha were being further left behind.

I first encountered Philosophy at boarding school. By pushing me to think deeper, questioning what I know, how things are and how they ought to be, Philosophy made my life more meaningful. It taught me to think critically and creatively, analyze information, and reason logically—vital skills not being taught in classrooms in India. I believe they should be.

I read extensively, corresponded with experts of the Philosophy-For-Children movement, and created a contextualized curriculum. Taking this to the classroom was hard. I was grilled by the Akanksha Education Head: What really is critical thinking? How will I measure progress? I had to convince skeptical school principals, TFI Fellows and others that Philosophy is as important as English or Maths.

In July 2013, I entered my first classroom—terrified, barely three years older than my students, without training or assistance. However, I had a clear vision: of every child having an education that empowered them to think for themselves. The class was initially reticent; the girls close to silent. After weeks of planning, reflecting, pushing the class hard—we underwent an extraordinary transformation. Puzzling our way from metaphysics to morality, our reluctant class began constructing coherent arguments and having noisy, impassioned debates.

This journey taught me persistence, commitment, how to execute an idea, to overcome challenges and fears. Most importantly, I learnt that if a fifteen-year-old teacher can create a small impact that has begun to ricochet (through sessions for interested teachers who now use my curated curriculum), the possibilities are endless. Running Philosophy Clubs at my school, I noticed uncanny similarities between ideas put forward at Cheltenham and at TFI—confirming that the difference is merely that of opportunity.

Last month, I presented academic research validating the importance of including Philosophy in mainstream curricula to the TFI executive committee. If this proposal is accepted, it can touch the lives of thousands.

'Surely he reasoned he wouldn't like it because of what he imagined it to taste like—but doesn't imagination come from experience?' asks twelve-year-old Suraj. I feel my heart leap with a little more hope, and a touch of pride. It always will, every time.

OUR THOUGHTS ON ANJALI'S ESSAY

Anjali's essay is a statement of purpose in the truest sense. Its flow of background, histories, emotions, stories, technical details, and future plans wonderfully amalgamate to reflect a self-aware, driven and deeply conscientious young woman with a defining commitment to equality for all.

Her choice and description for the opening anecdote tempts us in. Using a much-loved children's story (*Green Eggs and Ham*) as reference enables us to focus on the feel of an engaged student audience impervious to its surroundings and potential physical discomfort ('Ruthless sunshine streams in through the window, but their scintillating energy never subsides'). She then casually knits Kantian logic into the folds of this scenery, not pausing to explain its implications because the logic itself is not half as important as the classroom, alive with discussion.

The movement from this scene to her story is seamless in its timing and connecting trigger. Leveraging the interest generated by the opening paragraph, Anjali flashes back to days spent in similarly ill-equipped classrooms shadowing her mother, where her desire to teach was born.

Keeping her awareness of her privileged position present through her recollection of her unique childhood, she continues to weave purpose into her story. The effect is a cohesive patchwork that balances Anjali's early awareness and tackling of inequality with the starker reality that the opportunities and privilege she had far exceeded those of the people she interacted with. ('An uncomfortable desire for parity convinced me that apart from having more, I was no different.')

As Philosophy makes a reappearance in Anjali's essay, we are transported to another classroom, this time, at her boarding school in London. Again, she does not focus on the content or center her expertise in the subject; instead, she creates room for exploring how the discipline enriches her life and holds the potential to help others. We experience Anjali's anticipation before her first class, her push for comprehension through initial reticence, and her visceral happiness when she succeeds.

Few essays can claim to be both eloquently written so as to impress, and impactful, in that readers feel entirely invested in the story. Anjali's counts amongst the few.

ANIRUDH REDDY

Stanford, Class of 2015

Major: Civil and Environmental Engineering
School: Chirec Public School, Hyderabad, India
Hometown: Hyderabad, India

From 40,000 at the start of the 20th century to 1,411 today. Shockingly, that is how much the tiger population has dwindled in India. The tiger is India's pride, a symbol of bravery and magnificence. But illegal hunting and rampant poaching have led to a startling decline in the tiger population.

Besides being India's national animal, the tiger occupies a deeply revered and meaningful place in my heart. I will always associate the tiger with the stuffed toy that magically came to life as 'Hobbes' and the one animal that would light up my face and mesmerize me as a child. *Kanha, Kaziranga, Bandipur, Nagarjinasagar-Srisailam, Ranthambore*... I feel privileged to have visited all these tiger reserves over the years.

Shortly after my visit to the last tiger reserve, *Ranthambore*, I found out that there were only 1,411 tigers left in the wild, and I was truly devastated. In an effort to contribute to saving this majestic beast, I decided to take a few initiatives. After some research, I realized that the tiger is battling extinction due to loss of habitat and poaching. The only way to help the tiger in its battle for survival is to ensure safe habitat, as well as curb trade of illegal tiger organs and bones.

I realized that both measures required tremendous funding, something that could not easily be acquired. I thus decided to campaign for the cause by spreading awareness and generating funds at the same time. I first contacted eYantra, a corporate gifting company to produce T-shirts. I also hired a designer who came up with amazing designs. The Future Group, a large retailer, gave me permission to set up stalls in the popular retail outlets. I presented my campaign to local newspapers and a city-based magazine *WOW! Hyderabad*. They promised to give my endeavor publicity, a great boon for a campaign that depended solely on the public's awareness and perception.

My next crucial step was to contact the local branch of WWF. They received the proposal with much appreciation and were willing to cooperate with me on the cause. So I planned a statewide campaign to sell tiger-themed T-Shirts produced by eYantra, and offered to have my father make the first purchase of T-Shirts to kick-start the campaign. But when I least expected it, I got a call from a WWF employee saying that they could not participate.

I was devastated. Without the WWF logo on my T-shirts, I lacked the credibility to make sales. Moreover, all the commitments made by the designer, retailer and press were based on the fact that WWF was involved in the campaign.

I failed to understand why WWF would walk away from a campaign that had the potential of generating tons of funds for them with zero investment from their side. I tried e-mailing WWF and made several phone calls to persuade them to change their mind. But my efforts were in vain. Just when I was about to give up, I got a call from WWF informing me that it was against their policy to be involved in a campaign that had large-scale sale of items.

Despite the disappointment, I was undeterred. A few months later I was elected Co-Head Boy of the school and I found the perfect opportunity to plan and execute a 'Save the Tiger' Campaign. It involved all the students making 'Save the Tiger'-themed posters, T-shirts and stationery and selling them to parents on the day of the sale. The sale was an inter-house competition and the house that collected maximum funds through the sale would be declared the winner. The campaign was a runaway success and we generated close to Rs 200,000. Moreover, I had succeeded in spreading passion for the cause.

Martin Luther King once said, 'The silence of good men is more dangerous than the brutality of bad men.' The disappointment with the failed WWF campaign had almost tempted me to surrender. However, I realized how much the tiger meant to me, my country and the world, motivating me to persevere.

While I was organizing the 'Save the Tiger' campaign in my school, I heard that a tigress had given birth to a cub in one of the tiger reserves. I was heartened to know that this had increased the number of tigers in the Indian wild to 1,412. I would like to think that I played a small role in increasing that number.

OUR THOUGHTS ON ANIRUDH'S ESSAY

Anirudh's story, involving his deepest concerns, actions, and efforts in the realm of wildlife conservation, is what makes this essay stand out. He excitedly describes specific experiences and achievements related to a cause he is passionate about—while revealing insights into who he is as an individual in fascinating ways.

Anirudh's narrative structure starts with a 'shocking' situation that causes him concern—'the startling decline in the tiger population' in India due to 'illegal hunting and rampant poaching....' He guides us through the context of his deep feelings for the tiger, which is, to him, the epitome of majesty and courage. All of this is rooted in a childhood of family sojourns to wildlife sanctuaries and tiger reserves—'I feel privileged to have visited... over the years'.

Anirudh uses the thematic thread of the plight of the Indian Tiger, and his efforts to ensure its survival to tie together the strands of some of his core values and beliefs—his determination, his tenacity, his resilience in the face of adversity. He aligns thought and effort to put together an incredible campaign plan to further his 'cause by spreading awareness and generating funds at the same time'. He is devastated—but only momentarily—when the main ally whose support he had counted on, the World Wildlife Fund, is unable to join him. He refuses to give up. He makes the most of an opportunity when it presents itself 'a few months later [when] I was elected Co-Head Boy of my school' and is rewarded with resounding success in his T-shirt sale campaign. His sense of pride in his achievements is softened by the hint of humility, evident in his simple, informal style.

At conclusion, we come face to face with three strong attributes, hallmarks of Anirudh's persona. One is his strong belief, reflected in a Martin Luther King quote: 'The silence of the good people is more dangerous than the brutality of bad people.' The second is the depth of his feelings about the value of the tiger to himself, his country and the world 'motivating me to persevere'. And finally, his positivity and joy at the addition of one new little tiger, in whose birth he feels he has 'played a small role'.

9

THE CHRONICLERS

'Storytelling is the most powerful way of getting ideas into the world.'

–Robert Mckee

To write someone else's story is a responsibility not many people are willing to undertake. To tell our own story through our interactions, experiences and learnings with someone else, while being respectful of their person requires a level of care, respect and compassion only a few can live up to.

Using dialogue and imagery, the essayists in this section write compellingly and share their space generously with the stories they chronicle, discussing universally relevant themes of poverty, inequality, and connection. Through telling the stories of others, they tell their own. The effect is a lasting sense of the person being written about and a distinct impression of the narrator's life-purpose.

AMAAN KULATUNGA

Brown, Class of 2023

Major: Economics
School: Elizabeth Moir School, Colombo, Sri Lanka
Hometown: Colombo, Sri Lanka

'I wish I could bowl as fast,' I said.

'Come, let me show you my trick,' he said.

I spent my summers at my family's mountainside cottage, nestled in the remote heart of Sri Lanka's Knuckles Conservation Forest, overlooking a grassy field where shoeless boys play cricket. It was a scorching evening in November 2011 when I plucked up the courage to join them. That was the first time I met Sanduru. Confident, gregarious, and somewhat mischievous, he seemed a bit like me. I did not know then that subsequent interactions with Sanduru would profoundly impact and shape the rest of my childhood.

After the game, I handed out fingers of KitKat to the players, who devoured them in excited frenzy. But not Sanduru. He had one bite, then wrapped the rest in a used serviette.

'You don't like it?' I asked.

He smiled. 'I love it. But I want to share it with my little sister.'

In the following years Sanduru and I grew close, taking long walks through the village paddy fields, chasing his father's buffalo and swimming in mountain streams. We had no secrets: he asked me about girls, shocked as he was that I had a girlfriend. I asked him about his mother, who he had not seen for years as she worked as a housemaid in Saudi Arabia. He invited me to his family home, where his father and sister, grinning proudly, offered me ribbon cake, which they could ill-afford. I noticed that their home did not have electricity but said nothing.

I never returned the invitation, reluctant as I was to show them what they did not have.

Rather, I wanted to help. So, with introductions from my parents, I cajoled Colombo's elite and affluent into funding a charity for Sanduru's local school, my primary focus being revision classes for the students.

Three years in, I was proud of what I had accomplished, through hard work and perseverance, and so I was hurt when Sanduru kept missing classes. Each time I told him off, he smiled inanely, bobbed his head, and said 'sorry'.

Yet it kept happening and one day I lost patience. 'You absolutely have to go to the classes or you'll make me look terrible in the eyes of the people funding my charity!'

'I don't have to do anything,' he said, raising his voice at me for the first time ever. 'I never asked for these classes. You just decided for us what we wanted and needed.' He pointed around. 'Why do you think we're not happy with our simple life here? Why do you think we must become *you*?'

'I just...'

'Do you know, for every hour I'm in class, I cannot work in the fields?'

And there, with homespun wisdom and no education, Sanduru had contextualized opportunity cost better than I ever could. I had never felt so hollow in my life, knowing that my childhood friend no longer saw me as a peer and ally. Did he resent the unspoken label of 'patron', I wondered, a subtlety I had overlooked?

Despite best intentions, or because of them, I'd taken away Sanduru's autonomy and become that thing I would complain about in Economics class—a benefactor with conditions, like a rich country which loans poorer nations money; then tells them how to live their life, as though they're incapable of self-governance. In that moment of realization, I understood that service, governance and diplomacy are too often about back-scratching, optics and advanced economics when it should be about empathy and heart.

This summer, I saw Sanduru again. He called over at our family cottage to proudly tell me he had been offered a job at a bottling plant. He picked up the document on the table before me, but I knew he could not read it.

'My geography research paper,' I said.

'I wish I could write these things,' he said. 'What's it about?'

OUR THOUGHTS ON AMAAN'S ESSAY

Amaan's essay is a wonderful combination of storytelling, narration and personal growth.

We often tell students to 'show, not tell'. That's what Amaan does here—we can picture the verdant green of his summer home, the sweltering South Asian weather, and a friendship born from a mutual love of cricket. The first few paragraphs provide a glimpse into Amaan's life and context, and the background of a friendship that would change his perspective on 'social good'. He shows us illustratively how his social conscience is activated by Sanduru's cautious reactions to the KitKat he magnanimously and perhaps mistakenly distributes after a cricket game in which he joins, followed by a visit to Sanduru's home.

Once he sets up his philanthropic venture by way of revision classes, Amaan deftly describes the moment of hubris where his self-involvement ('you'll make me look terrible') blinded him to Sanduru's reality. Amaan's realization is nuanced and points to a recognition of his own privilege and the 'savior complex' many philanthropists fall victim to, despite best intentions. Importantly, Amaan realizes the value of understanding context in the often-confusing space of development economics, class politics, philanthropy, and friendship. Aman conveys both the complexity and gravity of the situation by incorporating silence and conversation: 'I just…'—being stunned to silence often conveys more than a soliloquy. Amaan's essay shows humility, an eagerness to learn, and an ability to critically consider the implications of his actions in a larger context. It is obvious in this essay that his academic interests lie in economics, without it being explicit.

Structurally, this essay reads like a story that is far from over: a circle, not a line.

The essay began with Amaan learning from Sanduru and concluded with Sanduru wanting to learn from Amaan. The conversation will continue, both at university, and whenever Sanduru and Amaan encounter each other next. That being said, Amaan did take a risk in this essay, when recounting the subsequent meeting with Sanduru. A less forgiving reader may have viewed it as an 'I told you so' moment—one where Amaan gets the last word, because had Sanduru attended the extra revision sessions that Amaan's efforts had funded, he might have been able to read the geography paper.

AMISHA SRIVASTAVA

Princeton, Class of 2023

Major: Mechanical and Aerospace Engineering
School: Amity International School, Noida, India
Hometown: Faridabad, India

We're here to participate in the Asian Regional Space Settlement Design Competition January 2018, at Manesar in Northern India. I am all set to win and take home the *Campo del Cielo* meteorite trophy.

It's past midnight. The winter wind howls outside. Inside a bright, musty hall, there's a constant shuffling of feet, some stumbling over people sitting on the floor intensely peering into their laptops. The *designers* huddle around a table filled with empty coffee mugs. In a corner, *ideators* crowd around the white board and across that, on makeshift tables strewn with papers, *writers* brainstorm. *Drafters* sit in another corner, with a laptop plugged and an assortment of pen drives scattered around. I jog from one lot to another, getting ideas across or collecting work done by the one of four departments I head. Then, I find a corner with the *polishers*, stitching the paragraphs together. The tension is palpable.

It's 4 a.m. and our company of sixty-four students from India, Pakistan and China has now worked for over twenty hours. We have three hours left for deadline. The countdown has started, but we haven't even finalized our draft proposal yet. The humongous task seems impossible to finish on time. Stress mounts, as does the realization that our six months of hard work may not bear fruit. Nevertheless, we continue relentlessly.

There's no time to waste.

It's 5:30 a.m. My department is reduced from fourteen team members to just three. Most are resting before the final presentations while others, exhausted, are tucked into sleeping bags right here on the floor. We rush through the work—the feverish clicks of keyboards, the only sound echoing in this dingy hall, bear testimony!

At 6, I feel a tinge of happiness as I do final touch-ups to my department's work. The file is ready for transmission. But I celebrated too soon. Our main proposal document crashed and, with it, all the efforts of the last twenty-two hours had vanished. A stunned silence was followed by hysterical panic. In a frenzy, everyone recollected individual paragraphs, images and pages from each laptop, pen drive and hard disk in methodical madness and effort is made from the last saved point.

Every clock now reads 6:55 a.m. and the tension multiplies manifold with each passing second. The file is being saved to a pen drive, and everyone has their fingers crossed. The moment the progress bar reaches 100%, a kid bolts with the little plastic stick, and everyone intently watches him disappear as though he is carrying our fragile new-born brainchild that has now matured into the real world. A huge wave of relief washes over us, and people trickle out to breathe in the fresh air, quite literally. While packing up, I notice some teammates talking. In the next fleeting moment, I'm hurrying in search of my camera. It is a scene that will remain ingrained in my mind forever!

The photograph shows a trio of tired and disheveled students hugging each other, against the chaotic background of empty chairs, scattered papers and strewn belongings. It is a trophy better than any other.

The moment records the deep friendship between three teenagers from different worlds who have known each other for only three days. Their countries, cultures and languages may separate them, but the will to work towards a common goal brought and kept them together. Each of them brought a different skill and perspective to the task, and together they created a unique team that nurtured every idea, solved every problem and tackled every challenge.

What I witnessed in that moment was the possibility that, even in times of upheaval, against the background of a chaotic world, we can come together and work towards achieving our goals, because what unites us as creators will always be greater than what divides us as individuals.

OUR THOUGHTS ON AMISHA'S ESSAY

Amisha establishes clearly even in her first two sentences—that she is talented, skilled, and competent enough to have reached the Asian Regional levels. Also confident, and, competitive and ambitious. Moreover, she is ready for the challenge.

Amisha takes the time to intricately paint in the intensely focused backdrop and tensely 'creative' ambience of the event—and it is time well spent. In doing so, she establishes herself as being extremely observant, detail-oriented, and a leader, clearly in charge of bringing together the efforts of not just one, but four departments that she heads.

Having cogently outlined her personality, readers can now sit back and enjoy the story.

She shows herself involving hands-on and pulling her weight—'I jog from one lot to another, getting ideas across or collecting work....'—giving movement and energy to the deceptively quiet yet nervously buzzing atmosphere of busy young competitors scattered around the 'bright, musty hall', working through the night. She has built the tension to a 'palpable' level of urgency and stress so well, that readers may find themselves standing in the room, holding their breath as the clock ticks—another strategic element she uses to intensify the pressure in the countdown from midnight to the 7 a.m. deadline.

There is the oh-so-familiar 'main proposal document' crash. We have all been there, seen that. We feel her tension. However, it does not get any easier. By this point, readers have completely identified with the 'stunned silence... followed by hysterical panic...' and the frenzied efforts of 'methodical madness' that ensues.

And as if there was not enough anxiety around, the suspense mounts, '*Every* clock now reads 6:55 am....' until 'the progress bar reaches 100%, a kid bolts with the little plastic stick, and everyone intently watches him disappear as though he is carrying our fragile new-born brainchild....' Finally, '...relief washes over us, and people trickle out to breathe in the fresh air....'—readers included.

But wait! Amisha's story has a corollary. She noticed something more—a 'fleeting moment' that formed a deeper and dearer memory, of 'a trio of tired and disheveled students hugging each other, against the chaotic background'. She beautifully and wisely sums up her personal growth and a new understanding in her conclusion, declaring: 'what unites us as creators will always be greater than what divides us as individuals.'

ISHAAN JAJODIA

Dartmouth, Class of 2020

Major: Art History
School: Dhirubhai Ambani International School, Mumbai, India
Hometown: Mumbai, India

My first visit to the storage space in central Mumbai led me to a football-field-sized room lined with teak shelving and filled with medieval terracotta figurines, canvases, drawings, pottery and porcelain. They belonged to another era.

Enameled Satsuma from Japan, blueberry-colored Sparrow Bowls from China, Royal Dalton Bone China, Yuan dynasty porcelain with swatches of cobalt blue; Medici Soft Paste Porcelain, and a curious collection of porcelain dogs. The diversity was artistic and geographic. It was an art and history lover's paradise, the collection of an erstwhile Indian royal, a Maharaja. A relative knew this veteran collector and knew my passion for history and art. The Maharaja's collection needed curation and documentation and I needed a summer job.

And so I spent the summer of 2015 working with the erstwhile Maharaja, cataloguing his art pieces, some dating to the Indus Valley Civilization, circa 3300 BCE.

I first curated a team. I scoured the internet and visited city art dealers. I spoke to restorers from a prominent national museum, who later joined us to get the collection up to scratch. A friend, an art major attending college nearby, offered to help. Five of the Maharaja's retainers who were used to handling the collection became integral to our team.

We began by organizing artifacts by era. Armed with gloves and passion, we learned as we catalogued. The porcelain and pottery presented an artistic conundrum. Munnabhai (we affectionately call the King this), innocent about the value and significance of the collection, had, naively catalogued the porcelain through color-coding. Intensive research across Mumbai and Prague, to shed light on the blue porcelain, followed. I researched in libraries including at the Asiatic, Mumbai's oldest, and not content, accessed the Prague Central Library through my exchange friends. They scanned and mailed pages from almost two century old art books. We then organized the porcelain period—paste, kiln and country-wise. Seeing history come alive, we determined that other pieces in the collection too would be methodically catalogued.

Munnabhai's naiveté was manifest in the fact that our ritual afternoon tea was sipped from Satsuma teacups from the Meiji Era, Japan. These gold-lacquered, enamel painted cups were museum pieces and drinking from them was nerve-racking. They will soon rest on velvet cushions in a museum to be started by him. Here, Munnabhai's favorite item, a carriage exclusively crafted by the Faberge Work Masters, will hold pride of place. Its bejeweled extravagance is presently hidden under musty bed sheets, albeit on close inspection, the carriage is well signed by the Work Masters.

Once, over tea, Munnabhai reminisced about his childhood years at his father's palace—'Sukh Bhavan' or Happy Home; his move to Ķolkata, and their atrophied position and wealth. I contemplated history's vicissitudes. I learnt to take pride in work well done. I was seventeen, trying to curate an irreplaceable collection. I learnt research methodology, and to work with diverse team members. I learnt to delegate and accept authority myself. I learnt that a team functions best with a unity of purpose. I learnt the importance of relationships, the necessity of decisive action. This being a time-bound project, I learnt how to handle my time, and encouraged people to do their best and develop new skills.

Once, Suresh, my colleague, and I, hands safely encased in gloves, were picking up panels from unbound frames, when his eyes lit up. He had spotted an inscription in minuscule lettering on the base of the panel. Although I knew German, I let Suresh translate it, giving him the thrill of discovery. His success motivated him to work even harder.

Laying the building blocks to Munnabhai's gallery, and proximity to some of history's milestones, had me in parallel, lay the foundation to my own future, of which both History, and the History of Art will be major components.

OUR THOUGHTS ON ISHAAN'S ESSAY

Ishaan's essay reads like a series of discoveries—first, of the location that housed precious artifacts, then, the artifacts themselves, and finally, of the vital lessons of teamwork. Along the way, we learn about Ishaan's personality.

Ishaan makes explicit his interest in Art History in the essay, his excitement about the field apparent in his enumeration of the inventory of priceless objects he is expected to catalogue. We learn how, at seventeen, Ishaan sought advice from art professionals and built a team of colleagues more experienced than him to organize the Maharaja's art collection. His friend from a nearby college is studying art, and the Maharaja's retainers were already handling the artwork. Working with this group became an opportunity for Ishaan to learn. That he actively sought out these mentors speaks for Ishaan's thirst to learn.

The description of the research process, in deciding how best to catalogue the artifacts, reveals Ishaan to be methodical. He is also resourceful, and perhaps persuasive, as we are given to understand that he enlisted the help of friends in Prague to research, scan and send the historical details of a cache of perplexing blue porcelain. It also merits mention that Ishaan's evocative descriptions imbue the story with authenticity—'swatches of cobalt blue; Medici Soft Paste Porcelain, and a curious collection of porcelain dogs'. He clearly loves what he is doing.

The vignette describing the team's tea break with the Maharaja is less about adding information about what we already know is a vast art collection, and more about the respect Ishaan has for century-old crockery. Old cups from Imperial Japan should be encased in velvet and glass, he ponders, not used for serving tea.

Ishaan's inclination to work with diverse team members would translate well in a university environment. As would managing time efficiently (a sometimes hard lesson learned in Freshman year) and motivating a team. The latter is evidenced by a particularly kind moment when Ishaan stepped back to give his colleague Suresh the opportunity to translate an inscription from the original German.

Ishaan's passion for learning and thoughtfulness are further revealed in the universal lessons he gleans from this summer project; these give us the sense that he will continue to draw richly from, and contribute to eclectic group efforts.

ANANYA GOENKA

Cornell, Class of 2025

Major: Economics
School: Dhirubhai Ambani International School, Mumbai, India
Hometown: Mumbai, India

It was midsummer two years ago, torrid and dusty.

The India sun shone hot, indomitable and unrelenting. After practising my jump shot for over an hour, I took two lefts from the basketball court, and a right from the pharmacy to Brijesh's gola stand.

He offered rose, orange, mango and strawberry golas, even chocolate golas—but, as I'd ordered for eight years straight, I instinctively said, 'Brijesh, one Kala Khatta, please!' He nodded and chipped at a stubborn block of ice, crushing which, he regaled me with tales of his mischievous sisters Seema and Bhargava, and the goings-on in the neighborhood. Then he splashed copious amounts of tangy, dark purple syrup into the cup over the gola, squeezed in lime juice and finished it with dashes of a piquant spice mix.

The gola was refreshing (and delicious), but something seemed amiss that day. Even as the vibrant syrup diffused through the gola, I noticed the color drain from Brijesh's face. This usually jovial ice candy vendor was dejected because, yet another bank had denied his loan request. Twenty-six-year-old Brijesh had always dreamed of expanding his family's gola business and for three years had unsuccessfully approached multiple banks and a few predatory loan sharks, but was always either outright denied a loan or quoted criminally usurious interest rates.

There it was, another example of a young entrepreneur's aspirations falling prey to India's societal inequities. Why is it that to get funding, paradoxically, one actually needs to be well-funded? I could not wrap my head around this skewed access to financial institutions in India. In a country where our youth is our greatest strength, it seems counterintuitive for ambitious entrepreneurs like Brijesh to be denied financial assistance.

I wanted to help him.

Yet, little of what I studied in Economics about the Gini coefficient or the poverty trap prepared me for the piercing reality I faced when I visited Brijesh's ram-shackled, one-room tenement and saw his family's home-bank, where his parents and grandparents had stored and saved money for years. That was when epiphany struck! I would find a way for Brijesh, and people like him, to gain access to financial institutions.

Interning with Sindhuja Microcredit, a micro-finance institution, I worked on a credit evaluation algorithm to determine the creditworthiness of a microcredit loan seeker. The algorithm considered parameters like age, number of earning family members and even the number of cattle! Although the firm did not use my program (remember I was a sixteen-year-old intern), this experience revealed that the real issue was financial literacy or lack thereof. Brijesh, for example, knew nothing of his creditworthiness and instead saved his money in his cupboard.

I evolved my work on the algorithm into a smartphone app, *Paise to Rupee,* for the use of loan seekers. Brijesh was my first user. When he entered his data into the application, he realized that he possessed a sizable amount of assets (beyond the conventional): one cow, one buffalo and two goats. Later that month, I helped Brijesh connect with a local financial institution.

It took time to traverse the learning curve. But, in the end, Brijesh got his loan—as did many others. With the help of Sindhuja Microcredit, my smartphone app was distributed among over 300 micro-loan seekers in rural parts of Uttar Pradesh, and it aided fifty-three applicants in receiving loans.

Financial illiteracy and the inequitable access to credit is a complex issue, so complex that for much of my journey I was unsure of the problem I was trying to solve. This problem cannot be solved by a single algorithm, but leveraging machine learning for resolve is indeed a good beginning. I will continue working on this.

After basketball practice today, I visited Brijesh's glistening *new* shop with iridescent and flavorful golas on display and thirstily requested, 'Brijesh, one Kala Khatta, please!' He complied. This time he was smiling.

OUR THOUGHTS ON ANANYA'S ESSAY

Ananya chooses to tell her story through that of Brijesh, a street vendor who serves as her connection to a world that is unfair and much harder than the one she occupies. The essay, a lucid tribute to Ananya's willpower, analytical skills and ability to see projects through, tracks her growth over two years.

We begin the essay accompanying Ananya as she goes about her day. Travelling a familiar route through her neighborhood, seeking the relief of a tangy kala khatta icicle after practising her jump shot in the scorching heat, we get a sense that this is a long-established routine punctuated by Brijesh's street kiosk. In devoting space to this ritual, Ananya communicates the importance Brijesh holds, making her subsequent concern for his well-being and investment in his dreams seem organic, rather than patronizing. Witnessing the full impact of his impoverishment through a visit to his home, Ananya seizes the opportunity to effectively come to terms with the stakes for Brijesh and others similarly disadvantaged. This investment grounds her motivations and anticipates her efforts through the rest of the essay. For Ananya, Brijesh symbolizes the cost of India's skewed financial system and the decaying demographic dividend, but it is her awareness of him as a three-dimensional person that puts a face to the societal malaise. Even as she identifies and acknowledges the lack of access to suitable financial institutions as an issue, it is Brijesh's dream of expanding his 'gola' stand that gives Ananya an opening into addressing this complex and one-sided structural matter.

The rest of the essay follows Ananya through her work with micro-finance institutions. Determined, she is neither overwhelmed by the complexity of systemic financial exclusion nor is she discouraged or deterred by frustrations along the way. Taking small deviations in her stride, she learns from the rejection of her first algorithm and goes on to develop *'Paisa to Rupee'* to thereby effect tangible, positive change for others. Similarly, she measures her expectations in the face of success, acknowledging the enormity of the task ahead while expressing her desire to work towards financial inclusion in the future.

Coming full circle, Ananya ends with the kala khatta that began her journey even as we share in her amplified satisfaction this time around.

ADHYA MENDA

Yale, Class of 2024

Major: Economics and Global Affairs
School: Mallya Aditi International School, Bengaluru, India
Hometown: Bengaluru, India

I take the sun for granted. Except when it shines through the perfect square that is my living room window behind whose Euclidian precision I grew up. I yearned to exit its safe confines—not in 'glissade' and 'etendre' perfected in ballet training, but feisty like sunbeams dancing through. Like them, I imagined exploring the frontiers of light and shadow. I was twelve. At thirteen, I met my camera and began a serious relationship—capturing images, freezing moments forever. Gradually, understanding dawned: arresting a life-moment does not capture its dynamic energy or potential. But it was a step towards finding my place in the sun.

In a village abutting Bengalaru, I encapsulated the purposeful energy of Navyatha monitoring cow-dung cakes drying on the compound wall. 'How can she, and others like her, have a stake in our shared futures?' I pondered. Drawing her ecological sensibilities from her parched Krisnagiri environment, Navyatha nurtures lemongrass around her shanty-home to repel mosquitoes—instinctive or considered? I capture her perusing Malcolm Gladwell's *Blink*, a book that captivated me. Attending a government school, she dreams of supporting her family while following her chosen profession. Gladwell tells us our dreams, despite disparate lives, converge.

Interactions with Navyatha sparked cascading reactions—frustration... anger... action. Given her receptivity, Navyatha must know she is part of something larger. For these next-gen change-makers, I launched IGNITE, a global virtual forum that garners insights around social issues young women face. Conversation snowballed.

Daily, I saw young women transcend boundaries, through discourses on education access, leadership and pay-parity. Navyatha was my first influencer. IGNITE is steadily gaining traction, empowering Navyatha and her peers to harness their potential and demand their rights.

My camera, now almost an appendage, led the way to other apprehensive yet resolved STEM aspirants denied what I take for granted—equal opportunity, education, housing. Through it, I immersed into lived realities, like Smita's whose soft gaze and tranquil stoicism belies the travails of her migration to a metropolis and her frustration of articulating her techinterests to her father. Tech? The concept eluded him despite her careful explanation in her vernacular, Kannada. I attempted, with my phone: I explained how orbiting satellites facilitated video calls across continents. 'Will this fill our bellies?' he retorted. Understandable—I'd cited an un-relatable example. It was a recurring challenge—convincing families that dividends from investment in education are manifold.

Kofi Annan said, 'Knowledge is power. Information is liberating but education is the premise of progress in every society, in every family.'

Eschewing safe choices that predicate complacency, I now ventured into uncharted waters. Could they too venture while priming for careers? Were the two mutually exclusive? Camera in tow, I moved to 'reshuffle', seeding my equal-opportunity initiative 'Women of Tomorrow'. That year, I traversed the inescapable protocols of team and awareness-building, application processes, interviews and unbiased selections.

To choose tomorrow's new-age women I conducted interviews in their spaces, away from the institutional sterility of meeting rooms and whiteboards. I yet remember eighteen-year-old Anusha's gentle song much like the koel's on the frangipani outside her one-room hut. She was a natural candidate. A district-level highjump champion, she chuckled: 'I try to ensure balance before running in to jump. Life is like that. Balance helps you aim and leap high.'

Her statement encapsulates my ambitions and the aspirations of the women of tomorrow who are now poised, balanced and sure, to open the door to opportunities hitherto denied to them. My camera too, taught balance and the value of perspective, of conceiving alternatives outside the limited geometric space the lens affords. Leveraging visual language, it helped me shatter a glass ceiling for those who needed a springboard to execute that high leap. I now look forward to joining them in traversing new paths and imagining new worlds, confident that these intrepid women of tomorrow will, like me, explore the square's limitlessness by reshaping its contours.

OUR THOUGHTS ON ADHYA'S ESSAY

Adhya's powerful first sentence—'I take the sun for granted.'—is like a solar flare, setting off an entire network of synaptic impulses firing across the reader's brain. First thought—don't we all! Readers are now engaged in this global concern, and open to hearing why Adhya thinks so. Only, she does not always take it for granted.

Adhya then paints a vision of being trapped behind the 'perfect square' of her window, longing to 'exit [the] safe confines of her home', 'feisty like sunbeams dancing through', to explore 'the frontiers of light and shadow'. Her ballet training is casually brought in adding movement to this visual. At thirteen, however, she begins her tryst with the camera—through which she learns photography techniques, and gradually an understanding of what is involved in capturing life's 'dynamic energy' in a picture frame. The juxtaposition of still photography (is it really still?), balletic movements, dancing sunbeams sets the stage for this compelling essay, where she breaks out of structured constructs.

The narrative flows in a series of snapshots and frozen cinematic frames with every portrait an action point. Adhya talks about young women whose 'life-moments' she could influence and be influenced by. She understands shared objectives, Navyatha's 'purposeful energy' and dreams converging with her own—except, Navyatha's dreams might so easily truncate. Adhya describes how this 'sparked cascading reactions—frustration... anger... action'—inspiring the activist in her to form a global virtual forum that garners insights around social issues young women face. Through IGNITE she facilitates empowering, boundary-transcending conversations on 'education access, leadership and pay-parity'. The imagery is in place, we can see the square's contours stretch for her, stretch for Navyatha.

Adhya's camera lens now points her 'to other apprehensive yet resolved STEM aspirants denied what she takes for granted—equal opportunity, education, housing'. Moving beyond the picture, entering other 'lived realities', she describes her learning curve—explaining satellite communication technology to a father in rural India, whose overriding concern is to feed his family illuminates both her naiveté and her willingness to go the distance.

To convince him and others like him that investment in education pays dividends, is a recurring challenge, causing Adhya to 'reshuffle', seed an equal opportunities initiative 'Women of Tomorrow', where she helps make 'unbiased selections' of deserving young female candidates for education sponsorship. It is not lost on the reader that Adhya, while thinking of her own further education, is encouraging a slew of young women to dream, and actualize their dreams. 'Shared futures' is the term that etches, it speaks for who Adhya is, and hints at what she will do with her education.

At the essay's end, Adhya cleverly returns to the start, and we see how 'the perfect square' has extended and recontoured. We are left with the feeling that with her education, Adhya will continue challenging boundaries and dancing her feisty dance, while 'conceiving alternatives' outside of the box.

PALASH SHAH

UPenn, Class of 2015

Major: Biochemistry and Economics (Roy and Diana Vagelos Program)
School: Dhirubhai Ambani International School, Mumbai, India
Hometown: Mumbai, India

'Move your legs!' I heard a blurring shadow-like figure cry out to me amidst the sound of my very own screams (after ten seconds) of agony and confusion (that were the longest ten seconds of my life). An accident? A catastrophe? A discovery? A miracle? As I was woken up in the middle of my spinal surgery to check my spinal cord function, the anesthesia faded and pain surged through my body like never before. T-12 and T-11 were replaced with a VBR-Cage of titanium. It was not just a congenital thoracolumbar kyphosis that was corrected that day; or two inches of height that I had immediately gained—it was the reconstruction of a life itself. I was born on 26 September 1992 in Mumbai, India. I was reborn on 2 May 2006 in Neustadt, Germany.

En route to an elusive recovery, came another unforgettable moment. I was taking off my patient gown for my first post-surgery shower, when the sight of a straight back on my body, in the mirror, evoked emotions in me that no form of human communication can ever convey. All the memories of hiding the shape of my back by wearing long t-shirts, fearing paralysis of my legs due to a damaged spinal cord, staying home while my friends went swimming, feeling alien and different from everyone else, and staring at my curved spine in melancholic perplexity flashed by in a minute montage. Now there would be no more looking back. I had overcome one of the greatest adversities of my life. I was liberated from some of the greatest adversities of my life. A whole new life path lay ahead of me. I was more motivated than ever to make the best of it.

Growing up with a deformity had always been the greatest test of not just character but also self-belief and willpower for me. Lacking self-confidence was something I tried combating through elocution which I continued until achieving grade 3 under the Trinity College examinations but I think it was the path to black belt in Goju-kai karate and representing my country with success that really armed me with the self-belief and self-confidence that were crucial in carrying me through probably the most difficult days of my life. But as I grew, so did my deformity. Nearing adolescence, the angle of my spine's curvature was increasing as disproportionately as my dejection at being so different. After years of opinion-seeking from numerous doctors, it was decided that surgical correction was the best option.

However, what was meant to be one surgery ended up being four. The initial two surgeries took two weeks, but felt like two years. I was then made aware of a spinal leak that was filling up my left lung with cerebrospinal fluid. One more surgery was needed to plug it. Mustering whatever courage I could, I went into surgery three. Two more exhausting weeks of slow recovery drew to a close, only for a dazed me to hear a barely perceivable murmur of yet another surgery, this time at Lübeck, due to an anaphylactic reaction to a dye used to detect the spinal leak. I felt as though I was stuck in an endless maze of hospital corridors, and optimism slowly changed to despondency. Fortunately, it was right on that day that my karate teacher text-messaged me, asking how her 'tiger' was doing. Suddenly I felt an energetic burst of strength and willpower run through my veins. I convinced myself that this time, this one last surgery would be a cakewalk, after having gone through three—immeasurably catalyzing my recuperation. I emerged a new person, convinced that when determination, willpower and self-belief are weapons in your armory, there are no battles in life that cannot be won.

A little later down the road, the once timid and confidence-lacking introvert was elected to the Cathedral student council by his very own peers as the leader and representative of the entire batch of Grade X. Not only did he return to Cathedral's inter-school football team, he also represented DAIS at district-level football. An aspiring musician was now rocking the stage as lead singer of the DAIS Band. He attained even greater academic excellence by achieving his first-ever four different Subject Awards. This was his story. My story.

I was once told that my days in Neustadt would seem like drops of water in the ocean of life, once I could swim with confidence. Yet, it was those drops that changed the direction of my life's current.

OUR THOUGHTS ON PALASH'S ESSAY

What stands out in Palash's essay is his honesty and candor. Palash's life-experiences with a congenital spinal condition—his prior experiences of being unable to participate in the cavorting and frolicking of childhood and early teenage years; the four grueling surgeries he went through, but most importantly, the new lease on life these surgeries gave him—are such strong motifs, that, at first glance, purposefully structuring or styling his essay seems redundant. He just has to talk about his experiences to make an impression on readers. Easy, right?

No, not quite so. Imagine reliving every second of the agonizing pain, confusion and disorientation when the anesthesia wears off, not once but four times! Imagine dredging up the past where the shape you were born with causes you shame and makes you want to hide it in embarrassment. Imagine thinking of yourself as deformed and yet, mustering up enough willpower and self-belief to step out the front door, working to build self-confidence through elocution and martial arts—and succeeding. It must have taken an incredible amount of resolve to not take refuge in self-pity, not give in to the pain and not give up—far more than most could cogently put into words. And yet, Palash rises and does it, describing the process in an essay that many strangers will read. That certainly takes immense courage, especially from a teenager.

Palash holds nothing back. He tells it like it is. He acknowledges his emotions, accepts his vulnerabilities, admits to needing support, and celebrates his triumphs. Palash is so buoyed by his new life-path that nothing can stop him from claiming his place in the sun and on the stage. He concludes his essay recognizing that adversities have taught him the value of life. Palash candidly tells of his most traumatic moments '...my days in Neustadt would seem like drops of water in the ocean of life....,' 'those (tear) drops that changed the direction of my life's current.' And other moments that both he and readers will long remember. Truly a memorable essay well rewarded!

KAIYA PANDIT

Brown, Class of 2025

Major: Music
School: American School of Bombay, Mumbai, India
Hometown: Mumbai, India

BUILDING BRIDGES

8.20.2019
Savita's smile widens as she begins to sing along with me, for the first time in her twelve years. Her weak limbs, once listless, dance with life. Her eyes no longer distant, her defeated gaze dissolves. Tones and rhythms reveal a secret bridge, connecting us. The anxiety so stark in all my prior visits fades, excitement reigns.

7.2.2018
I traverse the dimly lit Jai Vakeel School for the first time, alone. I am amidst chaos, much like Bombay traffic; the unfamiliar noises of autistic and Down Syndrome children echo as I navigate narrow halls. My eyes are drawn to an obviously frustrated teacher, with tired eyes. Her carefully enunciated words weren't reaching her students, whose manner oscillates between defeated indifference and a struggle for engagement. My gaze meets the eyes of a disinterested child in the corner; we connect momentarily. I can see beyond her hollow expression and disinterest. Savita is twelve. She cannot speak. She has a 'moderate intellectual disability'. The supervisor's wooden clarification: 'This

means she has an IQ between 45 and 60—like a parrot or chimpanzee only,' makes me want to connect with her, to pull her to a place of understanding and engagement.

I gather a team and begin building my bridge, not of brick and mortar, but of the building blocks familiar to me—measures and notes. I dabble restlessly with solutions, eventually committing to research music therapy. I compose melodies, rhythms, and harmonies, transforming them into the foundation, wood-planks, and handrails of new bridges. I design a series of songs, each with different frequencies, speeds, and keys, to evoke responses from each child. Nights after piano practice I sit on the piano stool contemplating: *Is this lullaby too disconnected? Should the key be minor? This melody energizes me; will it energize Savita? What sound frequencies invoke energy in a child with severe intellectual disabilities?* Each composition reaches a different child, traverses a different path to social awareness and joyful engagement. The journey is frenetic, anguished, and hopeful. It was brimming with purpose.

I sought to help Savita cross over, and then, countless others. I recall several moments where I sang and danced around Savita. I'd successfully have her lie down or stand but couldn't dispel her hollow expression. After weeks of composing, experimentation, and interactions with Savita, I found the song that sparked connection: '*Subhahua*'. And every long night spent composing and tweaking melodies seemed worth it. Even the slightest response gave me hope. I persevered.

Empathy is often defined as the ability to see through the eyes of another and walk in their shoes. But does seeing and walking build connection? Developing Thera Tunes was a journey of building bridges. It gave my music direction, our team a path, and teachers a course. I composed and produced a music therapy collection to reach students, made accessible to teachers. Importantly, we can now reach Savita. Her day, once a misty trail, now starts with music that connects her to her emotions, teachers, and environment. That dimly lit school is now a bright enabling space where music enriches the children's lives.

On 20 August 2019, Savita crossed the bridge. She traversed from indifference to engagement, withdrawal to joy. Yet, no note can stand alone to make a symphony, and Savita was the first note. As other children in Savita's class crossed over, Savita's smile widened. It paved the path to a more ambitious plan with a deeper purpose. How could this symphony be heard beyond Savita's school? My offering wasn't to only build a bridge but to gift teachers with the tools to build them. The Thera Tunes team was my orchestra: a writer, singer, illustrator, and communicator. They too built bridges of their own, to teachers, administrators, and parents across the country.

Savita has brought me closer to understanding the transformative power of connections. My own purpose is now clear. I can use my talent and passion to build bridges across anything and anywhere: connect to anyone, regardless of language, background, or ability. I now believe everything I learn can always be used to create connections and build bridges.

OUR THOUGHTS ON KAIYA'S ESSAY

Kaiya's essay is a clear and effective coming-of-age account, tracking her evolution from a well-meaning but reticent girl to a fierce advocate for 'connection' as a tool for change. Sharing space in the essay with Kaiya is Savita, a student at a school for children with developmental disorders. Kaiya charts her own journey through interactions with Savita, with whom she instantly connected at their very first meeting. Kaiya's subsequent purpose, fostering connections through music, is fundamentally shaped and directed by her relationship with Savita.

Kaiya's essay is unique in that it veers from the usual narrative and descriptive devices of most college essays. There is no grand revelation or moment of drama that punctuates her discovery; she knows from day one that her goal is to connect with the children at Jai Vakeel beyond their apparent capabilities. Even her self-admittedly restless process of leveraging music therapy to reach out is delivered in an even and measured tone that underplays the painstaking arduousness and anxiety underpinning this nearly two-year-long process (February 2018–August 2019). As Kaiya's musical skills find new meaning and purpose, she, as the essay conveys, focuses her efforts and genuine passion to improve lives where she can.

A particularly powerful passage further down sees Kaiya's interactions with Savita transform her—her joy at seeing Savita move from disengagement to engagement is unfussy but palpable. Universities often look for ways to ascertain the values that define students and guide their actions. By explicitly connecting her chosen metaphor of 'building bridges' to her idea of empathy, even titling the essay so, Kaiya channels her epiphany about 'connections' into a touchstone. It is through the linking of music with therapy that Kaiya finds the correct frequency for her skills.

While Kaiya chooses to hero empathy, many of her other attributes come through in the essay—significantly, her musical talent, which is an understated but embedded component. In her role as a musician, the admissions committee experiences Kaiya as a leader, an organizer, and a communicator, as she unifies and directs an ensemble of talent to common purpose: 'The Thera Tunes team was my orchestra: a writer, singer, illustrator, and communicator'. By the end of the essay, as Kaiya acknowledges forging connections as an approach to realizing focused goals, her qualities as a candidate for admission are as impressive as they are clear.

NINYA HINDUJA

Brown, Class of 2020

Major: Cognitive Neuroscience
School: International School of Geneva, Switzerland
Hometown: Geneva, Switzerland

ADAM

It's over 100° and I have been on my feet with the kids all day. As drained as I am, the feeling of accomplishment is pre-eminent. As I leave the All Special Kids (ASK) Summer Camp, I give an audience to the exclamation, 'Bye, Ninya!' I freeze at the sound of the voice I recognize instinctively. Turning around disbelievingly, I see the familiar little boy waving at me from his car seat. There is a flicker of recognition in his eyes before they return to passivity. My heart melts. 'Bye, Adam!' I yell back.

That moment.

Adam, five and diagnosed with Autism Spectrum Disorder. He has repetitive behavior and shows little interest in interactions. Adam dislikes eye contact, loves to eat glue, and for attention, he screams, throws tantrums, and bites his wrist until it bleeds. Most notably, Adam finds it difficult to express himself. His vocabulary is limited, he becomes frustrated when he speaks, and he has difficulty remembering even simple words. I had been mentoring Adam for the past three years and he had never once acknowledged me. Every time we met I felt as though we were starting from square one.

Although working with children with special needs is wearying both mentally and physically, while at ASK, I embraced a sense of achievement. Every night I'd reflect on the events of the day – on whether or not I'd handled a specific situation in the best way possible: should I have unplugged the hand dryer in the bathroom because Adam was terrified of the sound? Should I have taught him to face his fears, and how? My thoughts consumed me. The faces of those incredible children camped in my mind.

Children are my passion, and in particular, children with special needs evoke a strong emotion in me. I felt rapturous delight the day that Adam called out, 'Bye, Ninya!' It made me conceive that, while it might seem imperceptible, I really was able to access a deep recess in Adam and make some humble difference in his life. Children with autism tend to live in their own worlds. This seemingly insignificant interaction was a moment in time when Adam stepped outside his own head. As Lao Tau once said, 'The journey of a thousand miles begins with a single step.'

Working at ASK had unveiled the tangible circumstances that are beyond a person's control. Being exposed to children with special needs kindled an enthralment in me. I stumbled into a world of questions—questions about the disorder, questions about the brain, questions about life itself, and my place in it. Why are some people perfectly healthy while others are missing a leg, their vision, or have a mental disability? Why do some of us get the chance to apply to top-rated universities while others don't even get the possibility to attend primary school? Confronting these questions brought me to a new place within myself—a place where I am more cognizant of stark reality. The clock struck adulthood. Consequently, I feel as though it is my unmistakable duty to use my leg-up to benefit others who are less fortunate.

These realizations drove me to do everything in my power to obtain an internship with a top-rated pediatrician in Geneva, Daniel Halperin, and to spend as much time as possible learning from a renowned pediatric psychologist and autism specialist, Dimitri Gisin. Questions monopolized my everyday thoughts. They compelled me to ransack for answers. Curiosity is said to come in waves and, at that point, I was drowning. The dissatisfaction I felt by the accessible information charged me to write a children's book for the siblings, classmates, and friends of those affected by the disorder. My book *Aw-Tiz-Um* gives the perspectives of a pair of twins, one neuro-typical and one autistic, and aims to show a fragment of what an autistic child perceives.

Adam never addressed me after that first time, but I have not given up hope. In fact, that moment crystallized my goal of catalyzing the lives of children like Adam.

OUR THOUGHTS ON NINYA'S ESSAY

Ninya's essay is an exercise in clarity, determination, and compassion. Her interests are immediately clear to the reader, and she reveals herself to be reflective and to have derived a wisdom beyond her years from working with autistic children.

Ninya creates suspense in the first two paragraphs of her essay by giving importance to an otherwise mundane greeting by a little boy. It is not until later that we learn that the simple goodbye was a breakthrough, and Ninya conveys her reaction to it beautifully. She is transfixed, and awash in a sea of emotions – gratitude, humility, relief, and, undoubtedly, an acknowledgement of a larger calling. The experience with Adam drives her to do more, learn more, understand and question. This is telling—it is rare to encounter people who are motivated by the spirit of the work they do, making a 'humble difference', as Ninya put it, when the pay-off is seemingly small, and not at all assured.

The experience with Adam anchors this essay, and through it Ninya conveys her values and philosophies. There is existential angst, creativity, scientific inquiry, and frustration. The thoughts are overwhelming ('I was drowning'); but in this admission of susceptibility, we see Ninya's strength and her comfort with uncertainty, a trait that is indispensable in a field that is so fraught with scientific, social and cultural implications for those at the center of it—the children with special needs.

Our favorite (and perhaps most important) thing about this essay is that it does not provide answers—there is no 'eureka' moment of a problem solved. It is quiet and reflective; its pace evokes the slow drag inherent to working with children with special needs. It speaks of work that has been done, of how much more there is to do. And it conveys that she is absolutely up for the challenge.

DHAWAL KOTAK

Yale, Class of 2014

Major: Psychology
School: The Cathedral & John Connon School, Mumbai, India
Hometown: Mumbai, India

'*No, no, no. You must have something to drink!*'

My piano instructor, Ms Norma Gasper, is, as of this writing, lying in a coma at a nearby hospital.

I first met Ms Gasper eight years back, when the music bug bit me. I had been searching for a piano instructor for weeks, and she had a stellar reputation, naturally leading me to her doorstep, 1 Cambridge Court, Peddar Road.

Yes, as the name might suggest, Ms Gasper was as British as you can get. A wonderful relic of the British colonial rule in India, she was born in the 1920s, amidst the then typical colonial wealth the British families possessed. She has lived her life through thick and thin, witnessing the demise of her parents, siblings and friends. She has made Bombay her home, forging her own life, through her love for the piano. Through all my acquaintance with her, she only ever interacted with her students.

It is with this pristine British accent and memorable degree of polish that she said these words to me, frequently repeated and certain to be perpetually remembered. I walked in amidst a particularly warm streak of afternoon weather, but still politely declined the water she offered me.

In a surprisingly vehement voice, she herself got up—and it must be remembered that she was seventy-six back then—and got me a large glass of orange juice, saying, in that ever so quivery British voice, 'No, no, no. You must have something to drink!'

I always associate the sentence with her. She has imparted a lifetime of experience to me and truly made me love music. We would sit together twice a week, as she taught me, by first demonstrating herself, and then pushing me to attempt the toughest of pieces. From Bach to Beethoven, Ms Gasper is my guiding light.

When I was accepted into the church choir, she was overjoyed. And this was not the fake happiness a teacher may seem compelled to have when a student brings good news. It was the same when I was appointed music secretary for the school. Her own smile made me feel better, it was so warming.

Ms Gasper taught me the hymns I now play daily in the morning assembly. One December, she also taught me Christmas carols with a startling degree of enthusiasm, as if the holiday season had engulfed her too. She always cared for me, and I felt a genuine love, as if from a grandmother.

And now, as her life hangs in the balance, the doctors do not say pleasant things. But I will always remember her love and care, embodied in her never leaving me thirsty.

No, no, no. You must have something to drink!

OUR THOUGHTS ON DHAWAL'S ESSAY

Dhawal starts with one of the best 'hook' strategies to get us interested—a short, sharp, exclaimed sentence. *'No, no, no. You must have something to drink!'* gets all the 'Wh' questions popping up—Why? Who? What? Clearly a polite host or hostess. Then in harsh contrast, we hear about Ms Gasper 'lying in a coma'! We guess she is the person who has had a significant influence on Dhawal. He goes on with his story about her, setting the context of his search for a reputed piano instructor.

Dhawal's description of Ms Gasper, also sets the ambience—the 'wonderful relic of the British colonial rule in India... born in the 1920s, amidst... typical colonial wealth', the 'pristine British accent and memorable degree of polish'.

The 'surprisingly vehement voice' at seventy-six, 'imparted a lifetime of experience to me and truly made me love music', 'pushing me to attempt the toughest of pieces. From Bach to Beethoven, Ms Gasper is my guiding light.' Dhawal's wonderfully simple and gentle description reminds us what 'influence' really means. Her actions resulted in an effect on his actions, and achievements—'accepted into the church choir' and 'appointed [school] music secretary', 'the hymns I now play daily in the morning assembly' and the 'Christmas carols [she also taught] with a startling degree of enthusiasm'.

Dhawal does not try to explain too much or impress us by using glowing terms. Instead, he uses vocabulary to create a sensory and emotional ambience—'a particularly warm streak of afternoon weather', 'Her own smile made me feel better, it was so warming', 'always cared for me...I felt a genuine love, as if from a grandmother'.

We can assume Dhawal's own character was strengthened by Ms Gasper's nurturing influence, which he 'will always remember'—so much 'love and care, embodied in her [really simple, small action of] never leaving me thirsty'. All of this making him a more empathetic and caring individual, which shows in his concern for her critical health condition.

Dhawal's essay stands out because he has written a unique and evocative essay that no other student could have written—by describing in specific detail, something small, almost intangible, only he and no other applicant could have experienced.

DHRUV KHARABANDA

Brown, Class of 2021

Major: Computer Science and Economics
School: The Doon School, Dehradun, India
Hometown: Jalandhar, India

Flipping through the postcards I made on Jalandhar brought back memories of a chance encounter with Ajay, a boy who lived in the cluster of broken houses surrounding the 800-year-old mosque of Imam Nasir in the old town of Jalandhar. Ignorant of its history, his knowledge of surroundings was limited to the famous kulfi (Indian ice-cream) shop adjacent to the monument. His free time was spent assisting his parents to stitch footballs.

Next in the pack was the postcard of the Tomb of Nakodar. Driving through the maize fields one enters the semi-urban sprawl adjacent to the tomb. This stellar work of Mughal architecture is a must for visitors to Jalandhar. Its grandeur starkly contrasts the mud-brick huts abutting the fields, one of them home to a young bright-eyed boy Reyhman. His family migrated from Pakistan during the Partition of 1947. He stitched footballs to supplement his family's income. He began working as a toddler and remained unschooled till he was twelve.

I wondered at their lives, many had lost years of their childhood, victims to poverty. Questioning my parents, I heard some sobering truths on child labor. Wanting to use my skills to help these beleaguered children, I leveraged my talent in photography and clicked several historical monuments around our city, which I then transformed into sepia-tinted postcards. Approaching shopkeepers and explaining my initiative, they readily agreed to displaying them in their shops. The proceeds, I decided, would be utilized for child education. Extending this, I volunteered at two schools to educate children in local history and teach them the requisite protocol and etiquette for tour guides. I then met their families.

Convincing the children's parents was challenging. The prospect of losing a crucial income generator to schooling was unpalatable. My exhortations that with the education there would be an opportunity to earn supplemental income was the game-changer. Tellingly though, the children were determined to learn and when this tour guide program was introduced in school, most volunteered unprompted. Through the training manual I created, they were taught about the city, its history, culture and heritage and how to handle Q&A with tourists. Now at legal working ages, they learn at school, articulate well and double as tour guides, something never predicated by their family backgrounds. Ajay and Reyhman are amongst the very few lucky ones.

Ajay, now trained as a historical guide, often guides tourists for a tour of the mosque and an ice-cream thereafter. His family, initially reluctant to enroll him in school, feels optimistic about his future as in the evenings, post school, he works to augment the family income. Rehyman was perforce put into a school by an NGO that was alerted by me on his circumstances. He had an aptitude for learning and soon absorbed the minutiae of local history. Today he guides tourists, explaining the significance and history of the monument. He too is one of the success stories of my project.

But these are just two stories in a society rife with poverty, illiteracy, and the scourge of child labor. Spread across India there are many workplaces, houses and warehouses employing children in flagrant contravention of labor laws, denying them access to education. All cities like Jalandhar, my hometown, are culpable.

I was born into an affluent business family that never has and never will propagate child labor. But I am alive to the surrounding reality. The postcards and promoting learning are my ways of attempting to solve a problem endemic to several developing economies. I am working hard to sell these postcards across Jalandhar; the proceeds of which go towards the cause of educating the children. The sports industry—my family business—may successfully eradicate child labor but the problem still exists elsewhere. I hope to use the SGFI model and work towards the eradication of child labor by empowering through education.

OUR THOUGHTS ON DHRUV'S ESSAY

This is a layered piece with two compelling narratives—one that feels like a drive through the Indian city of Jalandhar, and the other—a literacy development project with the children of daily-wage earners. Both show the writer as a compassionate, motivated individual, aware of his privilege and proud of his city's architectural heritage.

Dhruv's descriptions of Jalandhar's Islamic architecture are not space-fillers, they frame his context, his home. A home that he freezes in postcards and then effectively weaves into possible career options for underprivileged boys. Much of this essay is spent describing how Dhruv went about speaking with shopkeepers, the boys' parents, and the impact his literacy project had on the two boys mentioned in the essay. All these conversations add color to Dhruv's context, inform his worldview, and juxtapose his life with the lives of others in the city—much like the architecture does.

Critically, Dhruv describes his persuasion of the children's parents to allow their kids to study—this underscores both the abysmal poverty in India that forces parents to make their children earn a livelihood; and his recognition of how this must change. That the postcards of Jalandhar's monuments suggested the way forward for his kids in a possible career path is an interesting revelation of how life plays itself out.

While this essay could have easily fallen into the trap of the savior complex, it does not. The last two paragraphs of his essay adeptly summarize what we, by this point, already know: he was born into privilege, and in a small way attempted to grapple with a pressing global issue with no easy solutions. His intention to continue empowering communities through education is a compelling, pointed finale to a robust piece.

10

THE EXPLORERS

'All that is gold does not glitter,
Not all those who wander are lost.'

—J.R.R. Tolkien

We end our list of themes with the explorers. The essayists whose curiosity is their compass and life-source wrapped into one. The writings in this section are structured by questions, existential ruminations and self-aware, self-referential commentary that runs parallel to discovery.

Multi-faceted renaissance people, the narrators of these expositions provide invaluable snapshots into their patterns of thinking and the values that guide them even as they wander through multiple interests, balancing their inquiring minds in a world that likes simple, single answers.

Emblematic of the spirit of exploration encoded into the liberal arts, these students are skilled improvizers, responding to every opportunity with a resounding yes.

GAYATRIDEVI TARCAR

Stanford, Class of 2024

Major: Economics and Public Policy
School: Sharada Mandir School, Goa, India
Hometown: Panaji, India

YOU HAVE MY WORD

When Lucy Pevensie was eight years old, she stumbled into Narnia. When I was eight and read *The Chronicles of Narnia*, I too wished to find new worlds through cupboards and have unforgettable adventures, not knowing that I had already discovered a world so vast that even Aslan's country could not compete. This world could take me down rabbit holes and through the winding corridors of Hogwarts; it could transport me anywhere from Styles to Middle Earth. But, most importantly, words helped me travel inward, to find myself.

Some words have helped me connect with my '*bhutkaal*', my past. They carry me through space and time to 1950s Goa. After four centuries of colonization, the 'Goenkars', indigenous Goans, were finding their voice. Not just their voice, but their language. For too long the Portuguese '*por favor*' had wantonly subjugated local Konkani '*upkaar karoo*' in the lexicon of power. My grandfather fought and struggled to reclaim both our territory and our identity. From a young age, listening to stories from his youth as a Patrol during the liberation war, translating Portuguese secrets for the Indian government or after, when he fought to conserve Konkani in the Devanagari script, I understood that languages can be used to subjugate, but they can also be used to liberate. His example inspires me to stand up for what I believe in.

Some words have helped me sculpt my *'astitva'*, my presence. In school, everyone calls me the *'loquaciousgirlwiththelongwords'*. Few things excite me more than a new expression that is more complicated to whip up in conversation than it is to bake a Croquembouche. Locutions like *honorificabilitudinitatibus* burst through the quotidian. Each syllable urges me to look for more: to explore new things. Whether it's the syntax of debate, Shakespeare's Victorian couplets, or BTS's Korean pop songs—I stretch across the pages of time and place, of discipline and genre, to voraciously expand my vocabulary. Often, people dismiss this habit of mine as *floccinaucinihilipilification*; but how can it be worthless if it is part of my very essence? It is by using words that I've won debates; it is by using words that I grant cachet.

Some words, well, there are some—no, so many—that I am yet to encounter. Perhaps I will find a few wandering the streets of Fountainhas, Goa, in search of the perfect *pao* (bread). And a few more, as I try to capture the legato, moving seamlessly from note to note, while playing *Claire de Lune*. And still more, hidden between the lines when I research the intricacies of public policy or report on statecraft. While I don't know what these words are yet, I know I will use them to string together stories; to write climate fiction where the Ganges river is my heroine and autobiographical accounts of a teenage existentialist. And, I will use the power of my diction to advocate: to critically analyze the inequity of public systems—in healthcare and education, to address the preservation of language and traditions and to vociferously demand representation for women in all functions of the state

That is not to say that I do not value the silence, the punctuation and spaces between words. Every now and then, I'm overwhelmed by my travels to unearth words that fit me; like the Japanese *'nito-onna'*, which means 'a woman who is so dedicated to her work that she has no time to iron blouses, so she dresses only in knitted tops', or the

German *'Dreikäsehoch'* that implies 'one is only as tall as three wheels of cheese placed on top of each other'. It is in those moments that I enjoy the feeling of warm comfort that no words can contain: the afternoon breeze at the hillock of Altinho, my mother's genteel crooning and the aroma of my grandmother's lusciously sweet *Bhooktaanladdoos*.

OUR THOUGHTS ON GAYATRIDEVI'S ESSAY

'You have my word'—Gayatridevi begins with an enigmatic, yet strategically effective title sentence for a Common App essay, which, in itself, packs a massive punch on so many levels!

She seems to address the admissions commissioners' plight of having to plough through hundreds of essays per day, saying: Here's something short and sharp to pique your interest, not one more long-drawn-out introduction to decipher or pick apart. She very artfully hooks the readers' attention with a powerful albeit simple four-word story, not just her own, but also theirs, with what initially seems to be an oath or promise—perhaps to respect their intelligence, their time, the purpose of the Common App... connecting to whatever they are thinking about that instant. It speaks volumes, and yet... has them wanting to read ahead for more! 'You have my word' for what? They are intrigued and involved!

Right from the very beginning, Gayatridevi uses the power of her talent with words to meaningfully draw in and lead readers through her pursuits, identity and beliefs. She masterfully interlaces the familiarity of popular fantasy stories to invite, then lead the readers into her inner world, giving them permission and free rein to use their imagination, to explore the gallery of her prolific mind, her thoughts, desires, undiscovered realizations.

As they stroll through, Gayatridevi provides descriptive glimpses into stories from her past to establish a solid historical background and context even as she skillfully weaves intimate connections to her grandfather—his story, his principles, the amazing significance of his momentous actions. And so we learn of the inspirations and role models that have shaped her beliefs and personality.

She introduces light, melodious, multilingual notes—warmly familiar to the accustomed ear, exotic to foreign. And then this profound power punch: '...languages can be used to subjugate, but they can also be used to liberate.' What a life-changing 'Aha!' revelation for all—herself and readers—such simple, insightful words illuminating monumental deeds.

From here on her title sentence gains yet more traction. Readers realize Gayatridevi is referring to her gift with language, and her exploration of it, to communicate in a singularly effective and engaging manner—using the essay itself as clear proof, while defining herself, conveying her own essence, self-knowledge and academic prowess. She ends by celebrating the pauses and silence, expressing a charming susceptible curiosity for the unknown, while confessing to sometimes seeking comfort in the familial and familiar.

BURJIS GODREJ

Stanford, Class of 2014

Major: Earth Systems
School: The Cathedral & John Connon School, Mumbai, India
Hometown: Mumbai, India

The procession followed the young boy around the temple. The boy's entire family followed, filled with pride. The boy was about to be invested with a special title. This title was to endow the boy with great responsibilities. I was that boy.

Shortly after my 14th birthday, I underwent a sacred Zoroastrian rite, the Navar, to become a priest. This ritual gave me the right to perform marriages, death ceremonies and initiation ceremonies. The thought of three arduous weeks of harsh conditions in the temple was daunting. But it was exciting to be a part of this tradition which has survived for over a thousand years.

When I was young, religion was a mere habit. I learnt prayers by rote and lit candles in the dark corners of the temple. The secular part of me had always been attracted to the core values of my religion—an environmental conscience, the importance of joy and fun, and an unflinching belief in being righteous. After my ceremony, I began to realize that there was also value in our spiritual teachings. I used to find rituals senseless, a relic of ancient irrelevant symbolism. But now I'm different. I believe rituals can be meaningful. Careful study of them leads to a greater historical understanding of our ancestors' thoughts and beliefs.

Those three weeks of strict concentration on mental discipline, study and prayer in the temple taught me to think more deeply when I make a moral decision. It inspired me to read many books on theology and philosophy.

I am interested in both religion and science. I don't think that they are incompatible. I am puzzled about prevalent attitudes. Why does religion not accept established scientific facts? Why is science so hostile to religion? Perhaps what taught me to consider both religion and science as integral components of an overall philosophy is that Zoroastrianism has no such inherent conflict. Why can't there be more constructive dialogue instead of prejudice?

Both ritual and science must be examined. Zoroastrianism claims to be the first proponent of ecology. We revere the natural elements—fire, water, air. Our rituals, however, always call for a fire to be burning. High quality sandalwood is now being used as fuel. Unfortunately, the trees which produce sandalwood are getting depleted fast. If we could use another more abundant type of wood or develop a method of apportioning sandalwood use, we would truly be an environmental faith. Rituals should not be followed blindly. What counts is the meaning behind the ritual. On the other hand, I also believe that the ethics of religion can prevent scientists from letting intellectual curiosity be their only guide.

The basic Zoroastrian guideline 'Humata, Hukhta, Hvarshta'—Good thoughts, good words and good deeds –are words which took on a new meaning through the explanations of the priests. The Navar ceremony is a commitment to service. Though I am proud of my family's tradition of philanthropy, I can't take credit for the contributions they have made in the last 112 years. We have been fortunate enough to be able to make contributions to the welfare of thousands of Indians of all faiths. My family has endowed schools, hospitals and affordable housing schemes but I still feel that I must find my own way to contribute. My dream is to ensure that the vast tracts of mangrove wetlands we administer survive intact throughout my lifetime and beyond. That would be my legacy.

Now, after my Navar ceremony, what matters to me most is to reach my potential both academically and personally so that I can continue to build on what my family has done and find my own way to make it a better society.

At university, I would love to have an opportunity to critically examine various religious theories. I have seen animosity and violence in India arising from religious differences. I have seen much good done in the name of religion. I can understand that religion is considered both a cause of and a solution to global problems. While religion is infamous for breeding fanaticism, I firmly believe that faith has the power and potential to create a more peaceful and united world.

OUR THOUGHTS ON BURJIS'S ESSAY

Burjis starts his essay with a 'young boy', a 'special title' that carries 'great responsibility', and 'The boy's entire family [following], filled with pride'—all in simple, solemn tones. We read in anticipation until we realize this is Burjis's story.

Setting the context for a genuinely meaningful and clearly unique experience, linguistic simplicity allows our imagination to conjure our own versions of temple and religion-related images. The 'movement' in the introduction has us joining 'The procession [that] followed the young boy around the temple.' With each reader, a different temple might spring to mind.

We cannot emphasize strongly enough how critical the 'set-up' or 'hook' is. An essay title and/or introduction that fully engages admissions commissioners within seconds, tells them a lot about the candidate—because an admission committee's time is valued. A concerted effort made to ensure reading the essay is worth their while would only increase their positive regard for the applicant. Next, Burjis...

a) details his beliefs and attitudes prior to this life experience of undergoing an over one-thousand-year-old tradition—'a sacred Zoroastrian rite... to become a priest...';
b) describes his inner journey through 'three weeks of strict concentration on mental discipline, study and prayer';
c) and finally, through deep reflection, ties it all together, showing us how he synthesizes his new beliefs, personality facets and his significant experiences. We see clearly the person that he has now become—the maturation of identity.

His introspection pinpoints transformation, demonstrating his personal growth: 'Rituals should not be followed blindly. What counts is the meaning behind the ritual. ...[but] also... the ethics of religion can prevent scientists from letting intellectual curiosity be their only guide', and 'Though I am proud of my family's tradition of philanthropy,... I must find my own way to contribute.'

And then, Burjis is curious about entrenched attitudes—'Why can't there be more constructive dialogue instead of prejudice?' It reveals his thoughtfulness about the world around him. He challenges certain traditional Zoroastrian religious practices, that contradict their claim 'to be the first proponent of ecology'.

Burjis does not pretend to have all the answers, therefore values opportunities to critically examine various religious theories. This he will take forward, at university, we are decisively told. Through his concluding remarks, he exhibits a strong sense of purpose beyond his own needs, and an openness to examine, understand and validate his new-found but firm belief 'that faith has the power and potential to create a more peaceful and united world.'

MALLIKA JHAMB

Stanford, Class of 2021

Major: Management Science and Engineering
School: Marymount International School, London, UK
Hometown: London, UK

Perched atop the table, I impersonate Macbeth and belligerently emote: 'Avaunt, and quit my sight! Let the earth hide thee!' I project to the chimera before me, summoning emotions of guilt and anger. The audience, spellbound, awaits Macbeth's next move as the culpability of regicide stokes the fury of ambitions denied. To simultaneously emote conflicting emotions of guilt and fury, I was deploying the Brechtian techniques that inspired my ENERGISE campaign.

I discovered Epic theater in England, reading *Burning Bird*, the play we'd later enact, with classmates. Its wit and pathos flew off the page, but Brecht's pragmatic techniques truly animated during our adaptation. Actors summarily broke from dialogue, directly addressed the audience with placards, prop movements and song, conveying potent messages. Playing an Off-license shop owner (during the London riots), I was inspired—a clothes hanger encrusted with packets of crisps portrayed the shop which I moved without blackout, in stark white lighting. Objects and feelings were placards that, equally starkly, stated 'car' and 'I am worried'. Be informed, *this is a play*, I projected. Brechtian theater starkly reminds audiences of their own reality, distinct from the play's fictional reality. My drama teacher, recalling the London riots, said my acting represented the troubled times.

Insidiously, almost, I started viewing theater as a clarion call for action. Brechtian techniques comprehensively shaped my ENERGISE campaign.

At the genetics lab at Cambridge, peering through the microscope, establishing if the cells I'd split were free before starting my immune fluorescence experiment's primary antibody incubation, I set the timer for an hour, and contemplated the lab's skewed demographics—thirteen men and six women. My Biology teacher had earlier opined that most girls bypass the sciences in high school as they perceived few career options. Appalled, I determined to showcase the limitless opportunities following immersion in our physical and natural worlds. Could I teach girls to grasp life's absolute moments using Brechtian techniques?

My ENERGISE campaign—an acronym for Empower, iNspire and EncouRage Girls InSciencE flowed from this as did the Science Olympiads I initiated in school. Entering the wrought-iron gates one morning, I approached Julieta, Seoyeon and Mira, 8th graders, and expressed my passion prudently—the Brechtian way, critical to eliciting a response. I played diverse roles—as I had in *The Grimm Tales*. As their senior, seeing interest, I invited participation, then deftly assuming a mentor's persona, nudged them onwards. My approach was vindicated. Seventeen middle- and high-school girls participated in the Olympiads, fifteen winning bronze, silver, or gold medals. Motivated to initiate change outside school, I became an intermediary, interviewing successful women in diverse professions who had studied STEM, requesting them to elucidate to girls the vast opportunities a STEM education births. And I wasn't acting! Encouraging girls to shed preconceived notions and enter the STEM arena is what I reflected on while playing Macbeth.

I had to be Macbeth, not act him.

Back onstage, I have successfully broken the Fourth Wall—the barrier between audience and actor. Their sharp breaths tell me Macbeth's overpowering guilt over regicide is viscerally felt. I recall the sparkle in Mira's eyes last week, when informed a mentor could guide her while studying cosmic rays' effects on vulnerable instrumentation and astronauts in space. Descending from the table I'd collapsed on; I fixate the audience with my eyes. 'Can such things be, And overcome us like a summer's cloud, Without our special wonder?' says Macbeth. The audience's eyes reiterate that they are indeed watching Macbeth's ambition animate the stage. Like Mira's, my eyes too sparkle, and I exit the stage comfortable in the knowledge that tomorrow, I will ignite passion in schoolgirls through a panel discussion with accomplished STEM women on ENERGISE Day, just as today, I mobilized the audience to feel Macbeth's callousness.

And now, I prime for another stage in my life—Brecht has prepared me well!

OUR THOUGHTS ON MALLIKA'S ESSAY

This essay makes apparent that Mallika has a spectrum of diverse interests—theater, the biological sciences and encouraging women to study and pursue careers in science. While theater and science seem unrelated, they relate to her. She weaves them together seamlessly to introduce these two particularly important life facets to her readers. Along the way, she presents a compelling vision of who she is.

Making Macbeth a thematic constant in this essay was a risky move—he is a complex personality, has questionable ethics, and is not always sympathetic. Also, the Brechtian techniques may have been perplexing for the uninitiated but are clearly foundational for her. With that said, this essay embraces the intricacies and opposing forces inherent in real life and describes experiences as calls to action.

Mallika's essay opens with that acceptance of complexity—guilt and anger. Macbeth (the character, not the play) is both a foil unto himself and, for Mallika, a springboard for greater things. In this case, an agent of change. There is passion here, plainly apparent in the problem that is presented through empirical observation—less than a third of Mallika's colleagues in the Cambridge lab were women, and women do not see science as viable careers. And then, there is the difference between 'acting' and 'being'. Mallika acts, seizing the moment evident in the approach taken to solve the problem.

The passion with which Mallika essays a believable Macbeth is tempered by empathy, an approach she espouses while mentoring younger female students as they explore their interests in science. And we see results in stark numbers—women participating in and winning awards in Science Olympiads. We then see an intention to broaden impact by learning from the experiences of women who have succeeded in STEM fields. She starts small, and then expands her stage of impact.

In explaining what she did, and elucidating her thought process, Mallika reveals herself to be a number of things: multifaceted (interests in theater and biology), empathetic (how else does one convincingly play Macbeth?), a leader (encouraging legions of girls to explore their scientific interests), and highly motivated (looking beyond her high school gates to understand how women make careers in STEM). We are left knowing that Mallika will always be looking beyond—beyond the high gates of the institution she belongs to, raising the bar, and creating impact.

UTSAV JALAN

Dartmouth, Class of 2021

Major: Economics
School: Modern School Vasant Vihar, New Delhi, India
Hometown: New Delhi, India

'*What does that mean?*' Rohan whispered as I enthusiastically outlined ways of preserving monuments. My outing for twenty-five children of Ishwar, a Delhi NGO, to heritage sites specifically, the Baolis, to showcase heritage degradation was disaster-bound. They were totally uninterested. Recently, I had developed a comprehensive program aimed at spreading awareness of heritage and culture—initially amongst underprivileged kids from an NGO, taking them on a tour which I expected they would enjoy as a break from routine. *I was wrong.*

So, I stood inside a monument, a national treasure, appalled on seeing the historic edifice crumbling into extinction. The Baolis, or step-wells, once 15th-century social hotspots, were now littered, their intricately carved brick walls blanketed in moss, mute victims to apathy and neglect. Yet, this monument was located in a busy thoroughfare of New Delhi.

Hoping to improve matters, I began illustrating my talk with my freshman year documentary on Baolis on my tablet. Their ennui gave away to fascination as they crowded around me, manipulating the touchscreen interface. Returning home, gazing ruefully at my tablet's fingerprint-smudged screen, I considered their fascination for technology.

I continued my initiative, taking them to sites such as Qutab Minar and Humayun's Tomb as a new idea germinated. Although continuing with my original intent, I devised a program that would facilitate their access to computers. However, obstacles loomed. The required capital investment was prohibitive for poorly funded non-profit schools. I approached Firm ABC, a financial institution I had interned with, and XYZ. Firm ABC donated its spare computers to XYZ, as part of its corporate social responsibility compliance.

This enabled over fifty children to receive hands-on experience of operating the machines post their installation, affording them a computer education. However, soon enough, all 200 plus children in the NGO were eager to learn and the computers fell short.

Impelled to think divergently, I contemplated deploying Thin Client Servers: using several monitors connected to a single CPU. I had bypassed fiscal issues by creatively applying my knowledge of computers. This, incidentally, led to some unintended peripheral benefits: the electricity and maintenance expenses of the NGO plummeted!

Conventional wisdom posits that every cause has a predictable effect, every problem a solution. As a Science student, I blindly believed in Newton's third law—an action will have an equal and opposite reaction. However, the 'best laid schemes o'mice an' men' often change—so true. The pathway to a goal can meander, each turn revealing another opportunity. Rather than dogmatically travelling a preconceived route, fortuitously, I took the longer path with its twists and turns to my intended destination. Knowledge comes from unexpected places: in this case, a heritage-awareness initiative led to the establishment of a computer center.

During this journey, perceiving a problem, I had convinced institutions, raised funds, driven donations, dynamically adapted to changing circumstances, transited theory to practice and engineered creative solutions, leveraging my knowledge of economics (cost minimization through efficiency maximization), computer science and Indian history! I also realized that success often necessitates taking a path tangential to the original intent and executing peripheral actions first, actions that might be germane to central goals.

At the Ishwar NGO, the faint clicking of keyboards now underscores the sound bytes of heritage documentaries. I see children discover the intricacies of technology as I had once discovered the Baoli. I smile hearing the chatter about the monuments they had visited earlier, with a newfound respect.

OUR THOUGHTS ON UTSAV'S ESSAY

Utsav's essay is powerful because it shows the reader how he addresses adversity. Simultaneously, it highlights Utsav's interest in preserving historical relics. This essay is less about achievement than it is about process, and the insights that derive from perceived failure. Overall, it shows Utsav to be adept at navigating uncertainty and thinking laterally.

We like that this essay begins *in media res*—not at the beginning, but in the moment Utsav realizes that his plan to preserve New Delhi's crumbling monuments may be coming apart at the seams. Without explicit background narrative, Utsav shows us what his project is about through storytelling. This is an important literary device to keep the reader engaged. Remember, admissions officers read thousands of essays, so being able to avoid boring narratives while still being compelling can only work to a student's advantage.

Utsav's pivot from wanting to teach street children history to teaching them how to work on computers eventually allows him to do both things. He realized that technology is more interesting to them than old buildings because he engaged with his audience with an open mind. Instead of being rigid in his initial plans, Utsav opts to innovate and put together a project that allowed him to achieve both his and the children's goals. His insight that the pathway to a specific goal can change is an important one—it shows flexibility and a comfort with uncertainty. In this specific instance, it appears that Utsav focused on the factors he could control—access to computers through a network and his knowledge of how they work. He also took a risk by changing his approach—one that worked to both his and the NGO Ishwar's advantage. He recognizes that the proverbial fork in the road, or a hurdle, can lead down a longer untrodden route, one that is not planned for, with the silver lining of unpredictable, exciting outcomes. That heritage conservation would lead to computer literacy was not, at the outset, preordained.

The essay highlights other positive qualities along the way, including Utsav's ability to communicate with students and organizations, his commitment to service and a love for conservation. However, being open to change while accepting and learning from failure are both hallmarks of this essay and markedly important lessons for life in college and beyond—learnings that Utsav clearly demonstrates.

SHYAMOLI SANGHI

Stanford, Class of 2021

Major: Mathematics and Philosophy
School: The Cathedral & John Connon School, Mumbai, India
Hometown: Mumbai, India

Toyota Corolla MH 9823. M+H=8+13=21 and 4+4+6+5=19. Simple addition's not working. Perhaps, 9* 3–8+2+5=21?
Bingo!
Next car…
I was subconsciously using mathematical formulae on the digits such that they would equal the sum of the numerical values of the letters swiftly; the speed of my thoughts competing with the speed of the number plates whizzing past. I am the girl who loves finding patterns in random numbers.

In a Statistics class, we were asked to test a hypothesis. With the test method formulated, everybody used calculators to find the 'p-value', mirroring the teacher's expectation in this complex calculation. However, I exulted in finding patterns of root 2 and 3 in the numerator and denominator; and cancelled them to obtain the answer, first! I am the girl who enjoys computations so much that she shuns the calculator.

Monday morning, Physics. Mr Mehra on electricity: 'The formula for Electric Potential at the end-on point (axial point) from a dipole is $1/4\pi e_0{}^*p/4 \wedge 2$, where p is the dipole moment, r is the distance from the dipole and e_0 is the permittivity of free space. And at the broad side point (on the perpendicular bisector) of the dipole, the electric potential is 0'. This got me seeking a formula to calculate the potential at any point from a dipole. I saw the pattern: at an angle of 90° between the point and the dipole, the potential was zero. And at 0°, the potential was the non-zero magnitude. I concluded that they must be related to cosine of angle theta. Just as I mentally completed that formulation, Mr Mehra announced the same answer. I am the girl who finds patterns in scientific data points.

Federer vs Djokovic. Wimbledon Final, Centre Court. 5th set. On serve. Federer to serve. The third game starts ... and the TV screen blacks out! All I hear is the sound of tennis balls. I subconsciously start calculating the number of shots till the 17th, after which I hear the audience applaud. I hear the ball hitting the sweet spot on the last shot, and since 17 is an odd number, I figure Federer has won the rally, even before the commentator makes the announcement (as a Federer fan, I knew that the shot was in). I'm the girl who loves Federer and enjoys finding patterns even in tennis matches.

My penchant for finding patterns stems from my first brush with Indian classical music at age 6. I was exposed to '*ragas*', a group of five-9 notes used for constructing a melody. I also learnt complex compositions, which required a deeper understanding of notes and rhythm, especially since Indian classical music lays emphasis on improvisation within the *raga's* parameters.

My training involved identifying *ragas* by listening to snippets; I relied on melodic patterns that the *raga* evoked. Given the number of *ragas* I'd learnt, each uniquely differentiated, identification was challenging. Training in tabla, an Indian percussion instrument, I learnt '*taal*' (a rhythmic pattern), followed by its systematic variations. The piano, with its scales and arpeggios, was similarly defining.

I took this learning to municipal school children, teaching them Indian classical music from a studio, using a real-time satellite link that beamed simultaneously to 480 schools. While introducing a *raga* to them, I would simplify it by interpreting its '*pakkad*' (characteristic note pattern) through popular film songs that they loved; such as the song *'Tum hi ho'*, based on *'raga yaman'*. This elegantly highlighted how two unlike melodies—one classical, the other popular, had the same characteristic pattern of notes. Their eyes gleamed with this new knowledge; mine at the realization that I had discovered a method of generating an appreciation for Indian classical music with pattern-recognition.

Deciphering and discovering patterns gives me an ineffable thrill—it has honed creativity, sharpened my reasoning abilities, and made me a lot more intuitive and discerning; taking me strides closer to being a sounder, more empathetic scientist.

OUR THOUGHTS ON SHYAMOLI'S ESSAY

We like Shyamoli's essay because of its effervescent deep dive into a personality quirk. We go down the rabbit hole with her, and en route, understand the curious, playful joy she derives from playing with numbers and patterns. This play thematically binds this essay together. It invites us to observe snippets of her life and understand how she approaches the world.

We like that the essay begins with a view into Shyamoli's life in a moment of stasis, describing how she bides time when no one is watching. It is a profound view of her in life's 'in between' phase, on the road to somewhere, neither at the beginning or the destination. What we do in these supposedly empty moments says a lot about us. In this case, it tells us that Shyamoli finds the sublime in the everyday and enjoys the mental gymnastics of finding patterns in random alpha-numeric combinations. We see a similar drive in her rejection of the calculator, and in independently determining how potential varies around a dipole.

We learn that Shyamoli is a Roger Federer/tennis fan, and even in the absence of a working TV will use her love of patterns and numbers to predict the outcome of a game. This penchant for patterns derives from an early exposure to Indian classical music and its instruments, and she takes its lessons to the field, to municipal schools, which typically provide education to underprivileged students. Bridging the gap between the girl that she is and the scientist she hopes to be, the essay's penultimate paragraph adds an audience to Shyamoli's largely private pattern-finding. Her teaching of ragas through popular music is an innovative and dynamic way of sharing knowledge, setting Shyamoli up as an 'empathetic musician and scientist'.

This essay's power lies in its depiction of a life, a habit of mind, a passion, and sharing that passion. Shyamoli's exhilaration for observing the world and its patterns is palpable. It is a great example of an essay in which the student does not just speak of accolades, but instead focuses on personal attributes. Often, these essays are the most compelling.

PRADHI AGGARWAL

Yale, Class of 2021

Major: Applied Mathematics
School: Singapore International School, Mumbai, India
Hometown: Mumbai, India

I stared in dismay at the wobbly lump of flour and sugar in front of my eyes. It held its shape for all of thirty seconds before collapsing into an amorphous mess. My brownies were a disaster, and I had nothing to sell for the annual charity fair at school. As I averted my eyes from the disappointing result, my inner physicist desperately tried to pinpoint the source of the problem. Had I baked it for too little time? Or maybe I had forgotten an ingredient. I ran through the various possibilities in my head, until I finally decided I should try again. I could not show up empty-handed at the fair.

With only a few hours to go for the fair, I baked again, double-checking everything. Thankfully, the resulting product both looked and tasted like a brownie, and I found myself standing in the kitchen covered in chocolate stains, beaming proudly at the 300 neatly packed brownies. It struck me that the key was in the ingredients. Each ingredient played a role—the sugar lent its sweetness, the flour helped the cake rise, and the butter added moisture. But simply adding these ingredients together wasn't enough—it was just as crucial to mix them in the right amounts. Only by finding the balance between the right components would I be able to achieve the desired result. Over the years, as my fascination with baking evolved into a passion, I noticed that I could extrapolate this notion to my life at large, and my culinary endeavors pushed me to view the world with a perspective previously unknown.

Each one of my pursuits, whether it is a subject in school or something beyond the scope of my academics, is a new ingredient in my journey. As I venture into undiscovered realms in Mathematics, question the laws of Physics, grapple with Plato's hypotheses in *Theory of Knowledge*, or explore Haydn's *Rondos* on the piano, I am constantly looking for the ingredients that fit me and flavor my endeavors. Will three cups of Trigonometry, two cups of Shakespeare, and five tablespoons of Microeconomics result in the perfect intellectual experience? I am not content with restricting myself to one area; the synergy between my love for piano, my aptitude for Mathematics, and my passion for creative writing is what defines me. As I strive to find links between my various pursuits, I find myself pondering the activation energy needed to bake a cake, or the monopolistic competition between the brands I purchase ingredients from. If I move from the disorder of random ingredients to the order of a perfectly baked cookie, am I defying the second law of Thermodynamics? My insatiable curiosity and welcoming attitude towards the unknown serve as the whisk to whip all these experiences into a decadent amalgamation.

From homely chocolate chip cookies to cheesecakes with popcorn crusts, I have eagerly tried my hand at any recipe I could find, although admittedly, it did occasionally end with the resulting product looking quite different from the glossy picture in the cookbook. Along with experiments inside the kitchen, I also fuel my desire to try out new things outside the kitchen, from undersea walking to learning French to dyeing my hair blue. This has pushed me to strive for a balance between a wide range of pursuits, from engaging conversation with neuroscientist Shubha Tole to goofy storytelling sessions with cancer patients.

Baking has nurtured my unbridled desire to try the things that excite me and pursue the things I love. As I experience the world with the excitement of a child and the patience of a baker, I realize that I will sometimes burn my fingers. But I also know that someday I will emerge a masterpiece, one that is a product of many years of education and exploration, representative of my ability to combine various ingredients in the perfect manner.

OUR THOUGHTS ON PRADHI'S ESSAY

Pradhi adroitly whisks us (no pun intended) through her sojourn in baking. This culinary art, as she tells it, gives her the language and lens to ruminate on her interests and discuss her motivations and her goals. By focusing on the measuring, mixing, blending, and experimentation with diverse ingredients—she creates metaphors for herself. Peer into her mixing bowl and you can see Pradhi's textured life—the activation energy required to bake a cake, the monopolistic competition between the brands she purchases. Not to mention, Thermodynamics. And yes, she makes a compelling case for being open to every shade of opportunity (and hair color!).

Her choiceful decision to start with an incident where her creative endeavors, quite literally blew up in her face, is canny. We see her now as an advocate for failure, a theme that runs through her essay. Implicit in her emphasis on the positive impact of baking on her worldview, are the 'what-if' scenarios wherein she had not failed at first, or perhaps had not persevered. By including the collapse of her first batch of brownies (despite adhering to prescribed protocols), Pradhi reflects on the process that made the product more than the sum of its parts. Clearly, baking 'unbridles her'. Yet, balance is key, to making a good cake. And a good, value-filled life. Her life.

As the essay transitions into Pradhi's varied interests, we have an appreciation for the journey she is on. As she describes her thoughts and interests, flitting between the amount of sugar in a cake to the physics behind its use and the nature of its sale, there is notable clarity. In this context, her wandering, questioning, and curious mind come through as her greatest assets. Pradhi is not torn between her many pursuits and curiosities; she is empowered and energized by them. She is willing to put in the time and effort it takes to settle into herself, and that's what defines her. As she puts it, 'I am not content with restricting myself to one area.'

The image of Pradhi that emerges from this essay is one who not only has the intellectual knowledge and creative energy to succeed in a rigorous academic community, but the openness and patience to make her efforts count.

SANA CHAWLA

Cornell, Class of 2025

Major: Computer Science
School: The Cathedral & John Connon School, Mumbai, India
Hometown: Mumbai, India

'But it is not everything in life that has its ticket, so much. There are things that are not for sale.'

Like Agatha Christie's persistent Hercule Poirot, I like to dive head-first into mystery, gathering clues and questioning everything and everyone around me until I am satisfied. Unfortunately, this means that I am not the best travel companion on a family outing.

Boating on the Chilika Lake in Odisha (a state in Eastern India) four years ago under a smooth-as-silk summer sky, the dolphins were taken for granted as part of the perfect picture.

I had to spoil it.

Why were the dolphins swifter than our speed boat? Why did the dolphins come here every summer? How were they so good at identifying schools of fish to prey on? The tour guide wiped his brow. He did not know.

Curiosity can make me a tedious companion, so I always rely on private investigations to find answers. In this case, I learnt from Google that the speed of the dolphins comes from their soft skin which reduces the friction and pressure of water against their bodies. Scientists believe that the dolphins from rivers in the north are attracted to the warmer waters in the south and therefore travel southwards when the water temperature drops. Dolphins use echolocation, a technique based on the Physics principle of echo, to gauge the location of large schools of fish in their path. Still waters do run deep.

I have developed the habit, or perhaps skill, of looking for connections between invisibly and intangibly connected aspects of my life around me. I learnt about Optimal Stopping—a Computer Science theory that can help one choose where to park their car. Broadly, this principle says that choosing the best option after reviewing some pre-defined percentage of the available options results in maximum benefit and minimum cost. When it comes to parking a car, this percentage depends on the number of spots that are already occupied, the occupancy rate. An occupancy rate of eighty-five percent is statistically most beneficial to the driver and fuel-efficient by reducing time spent looking for a spot.

As our family often travels to explore the rich culture and heritage of India, food, an important affair, becomes a subject of interrogation. How does the eggplant make it to dishes of almost every state? In the north it is stuffed and smoked, in the east it is fried and in the south, it is steamed. When I asked the chefs, they told me about recipes that are century-old family legacies—magic spells that once originated in the kitchens of maharajas and merchants. This led me to greedily devour information on British and Mughal influences on so-called Indian cuisine. I still need to know how eggplant is cooked in western India, and that is an investigation in progress.

Over the years, I have adopted similar investigations in my academic endeavors. When I began searching for connections between Computer Science and the other sciences, the 2020 Chemistry Nobel Prize winning CRISPR technology developed by J. Doudna and E. Charpentier grabbed my attention. How fascinating—a tool that can cut and edit genes, an amalgamation of Biology, Chemistry and Computer Science principles! I read about Artificial Intelligence devices that are being developed to perform complex surgical procedures and computer stimulations being used to study chemical reactions difficult to perform in labs.

I believe that my ability to look for a mystery in every aspect of the world around me is my greatest skill. Moments of investigation and discovery also become my refuge from a socially demanding world and Google is a close friend. The universe holds within it, billions of years of secrets and mystery, a fraction of which I at least hope to solve. My unfettered curiosity shows me connections between worlds that I could not even imagine existed.

OUR THOUGHTS ON SANA'S ESSAY

Speaking of things that are 'not for sale', the courage that springs from Sana's all-encompassing, unabashed curiosity instantly comes to the fore, illuminating the silhouette of her thoughts which emerge from this essay. Standing the test of time, steadfast in the face of disapproval and exasperation, her questioning spirit and unquenched thirst for knowledge come through as sheer life force; this motivates and empowers her actions.

Sana starts by being flippant about the inconvenient (if you ask others) times at which her curiosity pops up, situation, mood and audience notwithstanding. She goes on to admit that she is often considered a less-than-ideal travel companion, and, unbothered by the somewhat unflattering designation, she deems herself to be akin to a Hercule Poirot, Agatha Christie's iconic, erudite (and annoying) Belgian detective. These observations and musings are cross-stitched over eclectic and delightful troves of information that Sana collects in her curiosity-driven questioning. Nothing is too odd, too complex, or too trivial: from echolocation in marine dolphins to the diverse preparations of eggplant across India, to the applications of statistical stopping theories as relevant to parking.

There isn't any specific kind of information that Sana focuses on, it's all grist for the mill ergo fair game. Even as an essay, the chunks of space she devotes to pockets of information she has collected show that she is a master of her own mind. The questions she poses and the answers she sources are a snapshot of the method to her willfulness, revealing her to be a lot more intentional and structured than randomly inquisitive. For a generation growing up in a paradigm shift of information availability and accessibility, asking the right questions, the way Sana does, is paramount. Additionally, the essay underlines both, Sana's thought process and her commitment to seeing each line of questioning the whole way through, forming a veritable Museum of the Mind.

We can thus see Sana in an academic environment, thriving in a rich diversity of subjects, courses, clubs, and peers. Learning. Growing. Discovering. Unleashing her curiosity and seeing it lead the way.

SIDHARTH SANKHE

UPenn, Class of 2022

Major: Computer Science and Finance
School: Dhirubhai Ambani International School, Mumbai, India
Hometown: Mumbai, India

'To draw a square, click and drag until the dimensions are approximate.'

My first tutorial in drawing shapes, and I was clueless, surrounded by strange faces, in an alien place.

The PhD computational facility at the Institute of Chemical Technology (ICT) is embedded in a wooded area in Central Mumbai. Within, I struggled to learn Ansys 16.0, a complex software that simulates turbulent fluid flows through a constructed geometry.

I've always revered those who dig deep to unearth things hitherto unseen—that embodied the research culture at ICT. I came in anticipating enlightening conversations with campus denizens, and was met by... grunts, their principal mode of communication.

Intimidated by their intellectual aura, I felt isolated. On being quizzed on my work, I'd stammer 'cavitation' and turn away. I would lunch alone in the cafeteria, rendered shy and quiet, wishing for the comfort of the swimming pool!

However, science prevailed. Cavitation fascinated me: the high-pressure collapse of bubbles in liquid; to disinfect water in hand pumps and eliminate water-borne diseases. When I asked Ketan, my mentor, for direction, he responded laconically, 'Read Shirish's PhD thesis and we'll work together next week.' They were all friendly but too busy to teach me anything from scratch. Desperately wanting to contribute, I decided to teach myself.

I was ready to dive in, ready for the race ahead. I tried reading papers on cavitation independently, but couldn't comprehend. Logging onto Coursera, I painstakingly scoured it for a course on cavitation, flows, anything! No results. The next day I tried again, and found a course at the University of Minnesota on the fundamentals of Fluid Power. First tiny victory! It took eight weeks to finish, but I garnered a solid base understanding of how... water flows!

The race had just begun. I wanted to design the bottom of the hand pump to facilitate the maximum intensity of cavitation. But to do that, I needed to learn how to operate Ansys.

So back to the square.

And... I finally got it! Second tiny victory!

I luxuriated in my tiny victories, as major ones were so few, so elusive. I became more confident, nagging PhD students with the same determination that I nag my little sister. I got tutorials for Ansys, to learn building entire 3D assemblies. I learned to mesh each one of these structures to ensure accurate calculation. And a month later, I ran my first simulation.

It was a failure. The pressure of the bubbles when they collapsed was not high enough. Some bubbles remained stubbornly 'solid'.

For three months, every simulation I ran failed. Even as I began to master the software, improving the detailing in geometry construction and meshing, high-pressure collapses still proved elusive.

At that point I really wanted to emulate the recalcitrant bubbles, and just collapse in on myself.

Suddenly, it struck me to contact Shirish (author of the original PhD thesis) who emailed me a tip to hand-solve the data obtained from the simulations, rather than rely on a computer code. Runge-Kutta-4, he said. So, I began trying to learn Runge-Kutta-4, a strange word for approximating differential equations. After four days of incessant

YouTube videos and lengthy PDFs, I solved it and finally got my first high-pressure collapse!

Euphoria. I pumped my fist in the air. I ran home and told my dad, 'It worked!'

There has been no looking back since. I optimized the geometry and took my results for field trials. Standing in the green, serene village of Bhadas, placing a design that we'd worked so hard on into a hand pump, I look back and it's almost surreal. Just six months ago, I was this wannabe, with no knowledge of fluid dynamics, and unable to create even squares on Ansys.

I am so grateful to everyone for not spoon-feeding me, because they gave me a peek into the real world of research.

OUR THOUGHTS ON SIDHARTH'S ESSAY

In this involved account, Sidharth fills the gaps between his expectations of an active research community at ICT and the tepid reality that confronted him, with a fruitful pursuit of his passion for Science. Drawing from his hard-earned feeling of accomplishment, the essay succeeds in contextualizing Sidharth's exploration with the environment that fostered it.

Sidharth's use of pace is masterful. Despite beginning the essay without a prelude to his joining ICT, he is able to infuse his expectations from the course effectively. As readers, we can understand how the unintentional, but apparent indifference of his colleagues might have dampened his initial excitement over joining the institute. Reflected in the slower pace of the first half of the essay, his isolation and confusion over the way ahead is palpable. However, as he takes to independent study like a fish to water, his excitement bleeds into a well-paced second half. The essay is then able to symbolize Sidharth's changing mindset and acceptance in the community. This is especially useful in a college application for Ivy League schools, where a student's ability to motivate themselves internally is considered essential to their success.

The fulcrum in Sidharth's journey is his passion for Science, which drives him. His sheer need to contribute and make a difference in his field powers him, and he clears the marsh of confusion and indecision to take his first, sure steps as a researcher. Highlighting this in the essay ('Desperately wanting to contribute, I decided to teach myself'), he builds anticipation for what comes next. As he collects small victories, building from the basics and teaching himself using the resources at his disposal, our investment in Sidharth's growth increases. His curiosity-powered exploration matters because of the lesson he learns through it and that is his impact.

There is no defined end to Sidharth's essay; instead, he closes with possibility. Yes, he's learnt specifics about fluid dynamics and learnt to navigate Ansys systems, but the lasting impression he leaves is that of a researcher and a doer, ready for his next challenge.

ARYAMAN MAHANT

Cornell, Class of 2024

Major: Economics
School: Modern School Barakhamba Road, New Delhi, India
Hometown: New Delhi, India

'Swing with such nonchalance that the club becomes an extension of your arm, no pressure,' says my coach and mentor Nonita Quereshi, swinging her arm alongside mine, creating every golfer's dream arc. Eyes closed, breathing deep, I visualize quadrilaterals in circles, recalling my Math teacher, Mr Subramaniam's lecture. As my physical movement traces the mental arc, I swing, repeating the movement.

Red-brick monuments. Lush-green fairways. The insouciance of a visiting peacock. My caddy 'Ganesh'. Ever-constant chicken sandwiches. Trailing my sister, mimicking her swing. Then, international circuits. It all began at Delhi Golf Course.

Golf helped me through tough decision-making and emotional extremes from my first, unforgettable tournament! Teeing off, my ball nestled behind a hundred-year-old oak tree. I looked around wildly for my sister, my coach, my caddy... anybody? 'Men at such times are masters of their fate.' Shakespeare. True! I made my first solo decision.

Fortunately, *Golf is not a Game of Perfect* by Bob Rotella brought deliverance. After much deliberation I settled upon curving the ball at a 60-degrees tangent around the tree. It paid off. The ball took flight and dropped... six feet from the flag! That day, the curving ball sparked a learning curve—of the value of imagination, decision-making, and informed risk-taking.

I saw my two favorite worlds, golf and math, intertwine at the USGA qualifier in New Hartford, a tournament I'd dedicatedly prepared for.

The weather gods were in full spate; the flag fluttered furiously, driving rain blinded me and the icy wind pierced my bones. I had to calculate distances, account for wind, and estimate slope angles in a fleeting forty-five seconds. Tough, right? Not for me—I soon discovered that math analogized golf. Gradually, math became my indispensable ally in my ongoing golf journey. Solving reams of complex trigonometric and calculus problems seemed fun and more relevant now.

Most significant of the learning opportunities golf afforded me, was on the final day of the Hudson Invitational, Ohio. On the fifteenth tee, the tension in the match play was palpable as my opponent, Sean Minor, and I were tied for the lead. I drove... watched the ball soar... and land plumb fairway center. Sensing commotion, I noticed Sean rummage frantically through his bag, to discover he had run out of balls! I could have won the tournament right then, by default; yet, something deep within prompted me to offer him one. I lost the match, but won a lifelong friend; and I had the satisfaction of giving away something important to me spontaneously, in the true spirit of sportsmanship.

Beyond this, there are the life lessons learned. 'Golf is a game of inches. The most important are the six inches between your ears,' said Arnold Palmer. He was right. I'd grown eight inches taller in seven months; my swing went awry, and my ball consistently sought water bodies and petunia beds. My ranking and confidence nose-dived, and I lamented the truancy of both my golf sticks and my now stork-like legs. On the cusp of quitting, I met Dennis Walters, a professional golfer paralyzed waist down in an accident at nineteen. At seventy, he performed golfing trick-shots as a show-artist. His mindful perseverance inspired me. Understanding how my relationship with golf was pivotal in developing self-awareness, I upped my mental strength quotient.

Golf taught other life lessons in adjusting and adapting! I'm adept at packing my life (neatly) into a suitcase for tournament travels, finding the 'sweet spot' on pillows across geographies; waking only to caravan across the US and choking down waffles for breakfast—again! Craving spicy fare and parathas, I've foregone birthday parties and family vacations to train, train and train!

Golf and math dominate my every hour, even night, when I drift off pondering an existential dilemma:

'Will I be a Hawking, Aryabhata or Newton? Or a Palmer, Nicklaus or Tiger Woods?'

Perhaps… all?

I smile. And dream on.

OUR THOUGHTS ON ARYAMAN'S ESSAY

Aryaman's essay explores his sense of self and identity. Self-assured, determined, active and creative, he draws his narrative voice from his conviction that his two all-absorbing worlds of golf and math seamlessly work together to make him who he is.

The mathematical universe is notably alive in Aryaman's writing. The calm greens of the golf course are animated by vivid visual imagery of arcs, angles and aggregations, and provide telling insights into how Aryaman experiences a game. This is made all the more riveting by his astute application of self-effacing dry wit and situations all can identify with ('my ball consistently sought water bodies and petunia beds'; 'choking down waffles for breakfast—again'). Descriptions of shots and games are also peppered with numerical details ('six feet from the flag', '60-degrees tangent', 'fleeting forty-five seconds') that complement the sense of physicality and movement—a constant in the essay: movement on the golf course, movement through the golfing circuit and the passage of Aryaman's evolution as a golfer. Quantifying and grounding the essay through these numerical estimates, he makes his story engaging and accessible while ensuring that it remains a unique exploration of identity. *His* identity. Aryaman is *himself* when on the golf course, a place where he learns, applies what he learns and grows.

The essay succeeds because Aryaman does not limit his lessons to golf and math although they do provide the tools and avenues for his adventures and achievements. His commitment to fair play and sportsmanship, exemplified by him forgoing a victory to help his competitor at the Hudson Invitational speak for him as a person and not just a sportsman. His adjustment to a game-altering change in height demonstrates his ability to overcome the odds with focus and determination. There is also an acknowledgement of the memories, connections and comforts he has actively sacrificed to train and hone his skill, quantified albeit briefly when lamenting deprivation of 'spicy fare'.

Overall, Aryaman writes this essay as a tribute to golf and math, and all that he has gained from these worlds—life-lessons, values and a sense of self. As he dreams of what lies ahead, the reader recognizes that the essay, is, in fact, a celebration of the explorer that he will be.

RAJ BHUVA

UPenn, Class of 2020

Major: Chemical and Biomolecular Engineering
School: Dhirubhai Ambani International School, Mumbai, India
Hometown: Mumbai, India

THE BARD AND CHEMISTRY— THE TWAIN CAN MEET

Could Macbeth care less about citric acid's radical scavenging property?

Then why was I worried? Wrapped in a sinister black shawl, I tried clearing my head before stepping into the arena theater (actually, the rough circle created by a score of my drowsy friends). It was show time at the DAIS IB Literature Festival.

The audience observed the troubled Macbeth in me as I paced with constrained steps and anxious countenance. For twenty minutes that 10x10, drab top-floor classroom transformed into a dim, grey-stone Scottish castle in Glamis, a cauldron of murderous conspiracy. There was passion in my hands yet apprehension in my eyes as I tried to create an atmosphere of foreboding. The key was to emote the tension and ambition that was gnawing Macbeth from the inside, fiercely denying his conscience.

'Is this a dagger which I see before me?' I murmured.

Vacant faces lit up with undiluted fascination as Macbeth played out his emotional and ethical dilemma, fluctuating between states of mind.

His glaring hunger for kingship did not mitigate those clear moments of hesitation, evidence of his surviving conscience, as he hallucinated in such perplexing and emotionally disturbing circumstances that it was almost inconceivable how the actor playing him could emote this in a single expression of confusion.

I was really just thinking about citric acid.

How could those tiny organic molecules delay oxidation yet facilitate oxygen-based hydrogen peroxide in bleaching stains? How could they fend off an army of $O^{\bullet}$ radicals but still make peace with them? The chemical conundrum paralleled Macbeth's dilemma and all that thinking about it did was give me a most perplexed expression...

That I was something of a chemical oxymoron was established.

Comfortable in this knowledge, I recall tilting my head 90 degrees, waiting interminably for that final drop of liquid to descend. All was tense near the third bench of the DAIS Chemistry Laboratory—an otherwise unremarkable place. The drop that would transform the blood-red solution in the beaker into a colorless clarity (like Macbeth's irresolution would into regicidal intent? Yes!). Just another drop of the thiosulphate and I would have significant bleaching capacity for my concocted toilet cleaner, taking my Extended Essay research to fruition. The pungent iodine vapors that tickled my nostrils were no longer an irritation as I entered my billionth trial but, hey, if I were to go by Edison's maxim, I had found 999999999 ways that wouldn't work. Surveying the empty lab, I sighed: from the first attempt, the citric acid seemed incompatible with the peroxide. It was weirdly as though Lady Macbeth's shrewd superiority was crushing her lord's self-esteem (or in this case his oxidizing capacity). Surely highlighting the dominant character would only augment the other's suppression. Then again, it was Lady Macbeth's overbearing malice that produced a colder, stronger Macbeth by the end of the play. Could it work on this stage of science? Could a surfeit of the citric acid's intimidation work to goad my oxidant to retain greater bleaching power instead of surrendering to fear? A single drop splashed into the blood-red solution.

'Out, damn'd spot!' The blood wash'd off the Macbeths.

So was I being a method actor that day on stage, drawing inspiration from invisible atoms? Or was I disrespecting scientific thought by connecting it to a classic Shakespearean tragedy? I do believe I was simply at the intersection of Chemistry and Theater, attempting to connect the dots.

It's like a compound. Take A + B and you'll end up with Z. And perhaps that's the beauty of linking two passions—they reveal a side of you that you've never met, a side yet unknown. A side of an innovative thinker who dares to see the 'bonding' of different disciplines and uses them to transform the way he works.

So, are the laws of Thermodynamics related to inflation rates? You bet I'll find out some day!

OUR THOUGHTS ON RAJ'S ESSAY

This essay is a masterstroke. Raj invites us to listen in on his internal monologue and reveals himself as a ponderer of the way seemingly disparate things can have an uncanny, almost organic connection. Connecting Macbeth's ethical dilemma with citric acid's effects on hydrogen peroxide is far-fetched, but Raj does it effectively, unpretentiously, and with a dash of humor.

While this essay deals with two of Raj's key interests—Theater and Chemistry—its impact lies more in *how* he thinks about these things and draws compelling parallels, not what they are. Articulating his thought process allows Raj to showcase that he is a thoughtful, critical thinker, capable of grappling with the connections between his academic interests and blurring their borders. This is most apparent in his description of his attempt to evoke Macbeth's moral dilemma—to project Macbeth's struggle, he draws on his struggles with citric acid.

He elevates the elemental challenges of Organic Chemistry to the level of high art. Both things are sublime, and both hold his interest in equal measure.

Citric acid is a conduit of Raj's human and academic experience—like Lady Macbeth, it can stonewall his plans. But also, like Lady Macbeth, it pushes him to work harder, and think more critically about how to get his bleach to work. Here, he cleverly works in Lady Macbeth's attempt at removing the blood stains from her hands—unlike her, he is redeemed by Chemistry.

Raj closes the essay by making clear why he values his ability to see connections between disparate things—they make him work better by providing new perspectives. We like how the last sentence links to the first, in a clever nod that connects Raj's past to his future.

11

MIRROR, MIRROR...

'Mirror, mirror on the wall,
Who is the...?'

Interesting question. In all fairness, it wouldn't be a stretch to say that were it possible to view someone multidimensionally 'Through the Looking Glass', one would find that the persons and personas under scrutiny reflect, and are products of their milieu and environment. As you will find reading the eight essays that follow, each is a chronicle of triumphs, compromises, sometimes setbacks, and the environments that influenced the essayists' perspectives and life trajectories.

More insightfully, we will understand, while reading these, the many ways the protagonists' environments, be they school, family or social, factored their growth. You will read how the narrators did not allow their environment or circumstances to disadvantage them; of how they struggled, then triumphed. You will empathize with them as they navigate teenage angst and challenge the status quo, maybe, even identify with them. You'll viscerally feel their emotions, and draw inspiration. And perhaps, mirrored in their stories, you'll find yours.

Pulitzer awardee Frank McCourt said, 'Everyone has a story to tell. All you have to do is write it.' That's just what they've done.

So think of the environment you inhabit—because that's what you reflect, and have the power to embrace, reject or change—as some of these essayists have done.

AANYA PARIKH

Brown, Class of 2021

Major: Economics and International Relations
School: Bombay International School, Mumbai, India
Hometown: Mumbai, India

Me: Anam, I feel sorry you have to spend your life behind this dark veil; isn't it suffocating?
Anam: Suffocating? That's your assumption. Would I choose to wear it if it really was?
Me: You mean you wear it out of choice?
Anam: The veil is a symbol of who I am. Not suppression and regression as the world finds it convenient to believe. If the Christian veil is a symbol of virtue, why can't you accept the *burkha*?

'Why can't you accept the burkha?'

These words spoken straight from the heart have defined the way I think about Islam. It took me back to the time I heard the words '*Allah-o-Akbar*!' for the first time at the Haji Ali Mosque, which stands in the middle of the Arabian Sea, just off the coast of Mumbai where I live. I was scared – of the sea of white skullcaps and black burkhas, of the Islamic chants blaring over the speakers, and of the eyes that, I sensed, were watching me.

Growing up Hindu in a community that harbors religious stereotypes, I was fed nationalistic propaganda. Hindus and Muslims were on the opposite ends of a spectrum. Hindus made peace while Muslims waged war. Hindus liberated while Muslims oppressed. Hindus understood, while Muslims condemned. So, when I visited the mosque at the tender age of fourteen, I carried these bigoted notions with me.

This deep-rooted bigotry was challenged at the Seeds of Peace Camp in Maine, which is where I met Anam, my Pakistani friend. To say that Seeds is a non-profit, non-political body and a network between thousands of people from various conflict zones would be far too technical and impersonal for something that has had such a profound impact on my life. Seeds was much more.

It was there that I understood Islamic culture through unique and heart-opening ways. We were given five cards labelled education, family, religion, security and wealth. We were asked to retain the card that best symbolized the most important aspect of our life, the card that defined us the most. The Pakistanis and Afghans without exception chose one card – religion. Immediately, labels such as fanatics, myopic, extremist and hard-liners began doing the rounds amongst the Indian contingent. My thoughts instantly jumped to my conversations with Anam – clothes, music, Bollywood, family stories, religious beliefs. We were amazed to see how much we had in common. I knew she was neither a fanatic nor an extremist. While many thought Anam was the exception, I believed she was the rule.

It wasn't just me. I saw the transformation happening all across the camp, one delegate at a time. While we were at Seeds, the Israeli bombing of Palestine shook everyone, especially the Palestinians who were fraught with worry for their families, unable to handle the uncertainty. It was the Israeli delegation that spent the whole night awake with them, bringing them comfort food and coffee and giving up their phone privileges so that the Palestinians could speak for longer to their families. Stereotypes were being debunked across the board.

Seeds wasn't just a camp, it was a journey; one in which I sat and watched a sunset with a Pakistani girl who is one of my closest friends today; in which I helped an Afghan wear one of my *saris* and ultimately one in which my beliefs were challenged and my foundation of knowledge shattered.

This journey continues every August 14th and 15th, when the Facebook pages of my Indian and Pakistani Seeds friends are filled with Independence Day greetings to each other. However, for me, real independence arrived when I was unshackled from my narrow-minded thoughts, from my misconceptions and assumptions.

I had occasion to re-visit the Haji Ali mosque again. All I saw this time was symmetry in the skullcaps, the wind teasing the burkhas, Quranic verses profound in their meaning, lilting like music over the ocean.

OUR THOUGHTS ON AANYA'S ESSAY

Aanya immediately compels by opening with a dialogue that touches upon a globally contentious topic. Arguing her viewpoint with another, she faces uncomfortable questions that start her questioning her entrenched conceptions – '*Why can't you accept the burkha?*' Interestingly, this perhaps challenges several readers' beliefs, and nudges them to revisit their own perspectives. This opening effectively piques their curiosity about how Aanya's journey of personal development progresses.

This 'hook' establishes Aanya's ability to introspect on deep-rooted misconceptions, which she thereafter elaborates with vulnerability. Here, she revisits her past to investigate when and how her unconscious 'bigoted notions' were formed, sans excuses; vividly describing her memories, she subtly invites readers to delve into theirs for similar early life experiences.

Having sketched out this backdrop, she details her encounter at events that sparked this self-enquiry – making friends with Anam, a Pakistani girl, at the Seeds of Peace Camp in Maine. She demonstrates her openness to reviewing her past understanding, factoring in learnings from her interactions with others' perspectives to determine her own values. She saw how quickly prejudices could be formed, and conversely, saw the humanity that contradicted these blinding 'labels'. 'We were amazed to see how much we had in common.' She takes pains to recount how through the camps activities, she 'saw the transformation happening all across the camp, one delegate at a time.'

Then, the unthinkable happens while yet at camp. Aanya cogently narrates how the students' reacted when the horrifying 'Israeli bombing of Palestine shook everyone', and how superficial 'Stereotypes were being debunked across the board' as the Israeli delegation openly empathized with 'the Palestinians [students] who were fraught with worry', 'giving up their phone privileges so that the Palestinians could speak for longer to their families.'

These intense personal experiences made Seeds not 'just a camp' but 'a journey' for Aanya, giving readers emotionally loaded insights into her 'rite of passage' that transitioned what she unforgivingly calls her original, albeit unintentional, 'deep-rooted bigotry' to open-hearted acceptance of diversity, and heart-warming relationships. The sequence of her experiences and related responses suggests immense potential for growth – personal and interpersonal.

She brilliantly connects Indian independence day to her own independence of thought, 'when I was unshackled from my narrow-minded thoughts, from my misconceptions and assumptions' – giving the latter heightened 'transferred' significance, accented with the warmth of camaraderie across cultures. The conclusion brings this narrative full-circle, to how her internal reformation altered her perceptions of 'the Haji-Ali Mosque', with the now breathtakingly described 'symmetry in the skullcaps, the wind teasing the *burkhas*, Quranic verses profound in their meaning, lilting like music over the ocean' – impactfully strengthening Aanya's change of heart, and her essay.

ANANYA BANSAL

Cornell, Class of 2027

Major: Chemical Engineering
School: The Shri Ram School Aravalli, Gurgaon, India
Hometown: New Delhi, India

A 'spirit chemical'? Ever heard of one? Neither had I – until I met Miss C6H6.

As my chemistry teacher screen-shared a hexagonal diagram of Benzene (C6H6), I started to imagine the six carbon atoms reaching out to each other as an aerial view of my six pillars of support: my friends who have stayed bonded through boiling and freezing points. We have propelled each other towards our endeavors – they've assisted me to qualify as the Head of the Innovation Society, by helping me articulate answers, taking mock interviews, and ensuring I felt confident through the process. Meanwhile, I noticed one of my friends develop erratic eating habits to lose weight. By reassuring her to believe more in herself and follow healthier habits, we supported her to overcome this. Our collective empathy motivates us to grow together, through proactive encouragement and direction.

Unraveling benzene's properties, I realized that this molecule mirrored my personality – I had found my 'spirit chemical'. The deeper I looked, the more I identified with it.

When combined with potent electrophiles, the usually stable benzene responds strongly, much like the way I thrive when the bounds of my creativity are tested. My love for art led me to discover Andy Warhol's pop art and Yayoi Kusama's Flower Obsession and mirrored infinity rooms. This beckoned me to blend their art styles with my interests: leading me to paint four zebras, representing my love for animals, in Warhol's signature style. Pop art's bright colors and satirical elements inspired me to explore caricature as a medium of self-expression. This enabled me to capture complex themes like gender equality and diversity and change perspectives through a single picture during the Counter Speech Fellowship, providing purpose to my art. Sketching caricatures for dog adoption followed, inspiring me to fight for causes close to my heart.

Benzene's combustion transforms it to products with entirely different structures and properties. Similarly, I adapt and enhance my skill set to different avenues, such as using my passion for art in new ways. Applying mehendi (traditional henna tattoos) for my mother on Karva Chauth, or making rangolis (decorative patterns with colored sand) on Diwali, festivals become artistic opportunities. Replacing mehendi cones with fabric paint cones enabled me to conceive personalized dog collar tags to raise funds for homeless dogs. By designing the right shape of the template, experimenting with paints to ensure longevity, ideating attractive packages, and seeking feedback from neighbors for sample tags, I sought to make saleable merchandise, thereby initiating 'Paws for Dogs', a social entrepreneurial venture. Looking to maximize funds, I also promoted the dog accessories by putting up posters at vet clinics and dog spas besides Instagram and word of mouth publicity. It empowered me to be able to combine my skills to make a difference.

'Why do I resonate with Benzene, though?' you may wonder.

The answer is simple. Benzene's ever-shifting bonds ensure its stability, as contradictory as it may appear. Likewise, I have learned to bring opposing concepts in tandem. As a founding member of the Spa Green Soldiers, a junior environmental group, my suggestion of washing kitchen bins instead of using plastic liners was met with resistance by people, 'they're a pain to wash daily'. A middle ground was required, and the significance of 'sustainable sustainability' dawned on me when the team made a compromise of proposing newspaper bin liners instead of no liners. Till date, I carry this balanced mindset in all my endeavors, viewing situations through diverse lenses.

All these reflections lead up to my recent birthday, when my family made a fond gesture of preparing a cake shaped like a benzene ring. As I smiled at the sugar-laced carbon atoms, they seemed to form a portal, enticing me to jump into what lay on the other side – a lifetime of discovering new fascinations.

OUR THOUGHTS ON ANANYA'S ESSAY

Really? Ananya is akin to a… chemical? And that too, benzene?

To say Ananya Bansal's essay is 'spirited', would be, to say the least, understating its bubbly effervescence. In this exceptional piece of writing, Ananya takes the art of analogizing to stratospheric levels.

She adroitly aligns benzene's qualities with her own life, the synergies she uncovers both highlighting her immersions and passions. This, while underscoring her inherent affinity and 'bonding' for chemistry, where the characteristics she has grown to love about benzene both awe her and permeate her persona.

Benzene is a bold, audacious choice. If we were to hear it from Ananya, it fosters cohesiveness, is stable (most times), and is always up to being 'tested'. To Ananya it narrates the story of her life: her unbridled creativity in art, her social impact and her environmental empathy. Much like benzene, Ananya thrives in milieus that offer fodder for growth. In her exploration of various art forms from caricature to mehndi and fabric painting, she showcases her versatility, adaptability, and resourcefulness. Like her 'spirit chemical'.Ananya starts at a place closest to her heart – her friend group, her support system. Like benzene, her circle of friends, her carbon atoms, have nourished her in her endeavors. Through this unconventional analogy, we discern how the relationships she has forged have become her bulwark, not unlike the atoms of the chemical that adhere to create the molecule. They make her more empathetic, stronger, and reliable. They forge her into that special molecule. They make her, well, *her.*

So too, her symbiotic bond with benzene speaks volumes of her inquisitive and exploratory nature, as she probes every nook and cranny of the chemical to know its essence, and its likeness to her. Through this, the admissions officer understands that Ananya will leave no stone unturned and go the distance – whether navigating troubled waters with equanimity, or considering opposing concepts in tandem to see the bigger picture. She has subtly yet cogently given notice that she'll employ her balanced mindset in all her future ventures.

You might start off with incredulity, but you conclude the essay satisfied that her exploration of the self is a work-in-progress and will remain so for the foreseeable future, as a lifetime of new experiences and fascinations await her discovery.

AYUSHI CHANDARIA

Stanford, Class of 2020

Major: Computer Science and Product Design
School: Tanglin Trust School, Singapore
Hometown: Singapore

The ride to Nairobi's notorious Kibera slums was nerve-wracking. Sitting with Triza, a disabled swimmer, I clung to the seat of the Matatu, a form of public transportation. Many windows were broken, and I remembered hearing that thieves could reach inside to steal purses. My family had tried to insist that I take a private car to visit Triza, and as we drove further into the filthy slum roads, I wondered if I should have listened.

After volunteering weekly for years to help paraplegic swimmers in Singapore, I had decided to undertake a similar role in my home country, Kenya. Unfortunately, despite the need for paraplegic swim training, no program existed. With support from local philanthropists and foundations, I managed to arrange a modest program, hiring a coach and signing up swimmers. When I entered Kasarani Swimming Stadium that Tuesday morning at 10 a.m., I was met with silence. No swimmers, no coach, nothing. In Singapore, when we arrive to teach, we are greeted with dozens of smiles. Some even arrive early because of excitement. Yet in Nairobi, there was still no one at 10.45 a.m. Frustration swept through me. How could no one show up after I had worked so hard to provide this opportunity?

Then I heard voices, and slowly, swimmers began limping in. It turned out that given transportation constraints, it took them over an hour to reach, after which they had to walk an entire kilometer on their prostheses and/or crutches. As they greeted me 'Jambo' and thanked me 'Asante Sana' repeatedly, I felt badly for my earlier annoyance. By the time all the swimmers had arrived, however, the heavens opened up and cold rains poured down – winter weather in Nairobi. There was no way we could swim now. I went inside for an umbrella and returned to regretfully inform them that swimming would be canceled. However, I was amazed to see the swimmers sliding into the cold water! Without proper swimming gear, they began swimming, painfully, but with smiles on their faces. They were exhausted after the first length but continued to swim in the freezing water. I taught them various drills to improve their stroke and balance better in the water. By the end, they were tired, hungry, and shivering, having neither towels nor warm clothes to change into. Despite all this, they asked me eagerly when the next session was.

As a national Kenyan swimmer myself, my motivation comes from representing my country at international competitions, winning medals, and breaking national records. My swimming equipment fills up multiple cupboards, from basic goggles to technical racing swimsuits. I feel I am dedicated because I train up to fifty kilometers a week. Yet, these paraplegic swimmers, who haven't had a proper meal for days, were showing up to swim in the rain when every step they take is a struggle.

I had asked one of the swimmers, Triza, if I could go home with her one day. I wanted to understand where her motivation came from. Sitting there with Triza, in the tin shack that served as both kitchen and sleeping area, I asked her why she loved to swim. 'I want swimming to be my livelihood. I want to earn money for my family so that my sister can go to school,' she told me in Kiswahili. Knowing that her mom sold vegetables on the road to support the family, I realized the depth of Triza's hope, and how powerful a motivation that was.

Today when I wake up at 5.10 a.m. and arrive at the pool for practice, I feel sleepy but don't say it, feel tired but push myself further, and do my best to channel Triza's mindset and motivation. I'm not always successful, but when I am I feel overwhelming gratitude. Swimmers like Triza have redefined my idea of success, and motivated me in a way that no medal or national record ever could.

OUR THOUGHTS ON AYUSHI'S ESSAY

Ayushi's essay reads like a short story: there is a plot, there are characters, each with a context, and there is tension between those contexts. Ayushi examines that tension through her narrative, and in doing so, reveals to the reader so much about who she is, and how her world view was challenged, without stating it explicitly. This essay flows effortlessly, and is deeply authentic – it is underwritten with passion.

We learn that Ayushi lives between places – Nairobi and Singapore – physically and culturally worlds apart. We learn that she is an accomplished national-level swimmer, and perhaps unsurprisingly (or perhaps because of this), she is gritty—taking public transport through Nairobi's slums, despite her family's entreaties. And it's here, on the rickety Matatu, we see her humanity. There is fear: should she have taken a private car? The unwritten answer is *no*. As the essay progresses, we understand why: there is compassion, fueling a drive to understand the circumstances her Kenyan charges occupy, for she cannot teach without a deeper knowing of their motivations and contexts.

The logistical dissonance between Nairobi and Singapore widens, which is a vehicle for Ayushi's developing awe at the Kenyan children's resilience. The transportation is inadequate, even more so when one is disabled. Singaporean punctuality is absent, and it cannot be expected. When she understands why, she revises her biases: 'I felt badly for my earlier annoyance.'

And then, despite the pouring rain, the children hit the water. Interestingly, Ayushi spends little space in this essay describing what she actually taught the children. The essay is more focused on what the children taught her. They redefined what it meant to be committed: not closets of swimming paraphernalia, but the ability and willingness to train in a cold pool, in the rain, with limited physical ability and resources.

Ayushi holds a critical mirror to herself: 'I wake up at 5.10 a.m. and arrive at the pool for practice, I feel sleepy but don't say it', because she is aware of her privilege. She's also aware that she's imperfect (aren't we all?): she acknowledges her opportunities with gratitude, but also admits that sometimes the motivation does not come easy. And finally, there is realization: that sometimes the goal is the grind itself, and not so much the medals.

FALAK PABARI
Brown, Class of 2026

Major: Computer Science and Design Engineering
School: FIITJEE Vadodara, Gujarat, India
Hometown: Jamnagar, India

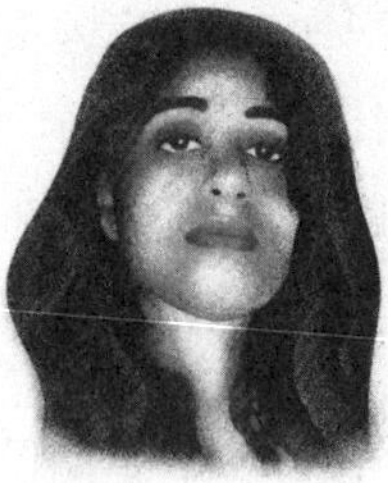

RENAISSANCE

Blank. My mind froze.

The wooden cut-outs in my storeroom contradicted the original dimensions I'd established for my project. Growing increasingly frustrated, I second-guessed my decision to do this without help from seasoned CNC machine aficionados. The CorelDRAW document lay before me, mocking, daring me to give up.

I was at the M.D. Mehta Science Centre, Dhrol's lead volunteer, inspiring students and their families in 100+ encircling villages to appreciate Science. Impassioned about design, I was readying to donate an LIPT (life-sized interactive periodic table), displaying examples and vital information for each element on a large screen. Three years of volunteering had shown me their needs. My project had to be worthy of both present student expectations, and future generations.

The design and engineering included setting up the electric circuit, already six months in the making. What remained was to populate it with objects representing each element, write codes to make the components work in tandem, and ensure the parts worked harmoniously.

The loud doorbell shook me from my stupor, announcing Rajat, my cheerful weekly Amazon-parcels-delivery man and the arrival of another parcel.

The vacuum tubes I'd ordered, to represent thorium oxide's presence in tungsten wires, lay before me. Despite product details being double-checked, they didn't nearly fit my element box's dimensions. My heart sank. Shipped from China with a no return policy – another order was impossible! I was no closer to a prototype than six months ago, and my notepad still had a three-page-long tasks list yet to complete.

- *complete wooden cut-outs*
- *schedule carpenter visit for assembly*
- *design matrix circuit to connect 118 switches to screen*
- *use raspberry pie 28 gpio output pins*
- *list on-screen element information display button press*
- *start writing corresponding code*
- *make all element information slides*
- *research real-life uses items of last 30 elements*
- *choose acrylic sheet thickness + quality*

I now added two more.

- *tweak design dimensions!*
- *re-engineer necessary parts!*

This would set me back by months! Feeling momentarily smothered by these obstacles, I fought hard against the little voice urging me to quit.

The next day, I made my way to the M.D. Mehta Science Centre, with a heavy heart, to teach my weekly science lesson.

While mulling over my slow progress, I was approached by a group of brightly loquacious students who had, on my suggestion, studiously recreated the 'lemon-juice-hot-iron' invisible ink experiment at home.

Despite not owning an iron, Dinesh had persevered, holding the paper above a lit candle until the transparent ink-marks became visible. His eyes glowed as he regaled me with his success story.

Scarce resources... inappropriate lab equipment... nothing deterred my students! They would never relinquish their knowledge quest!

I chided myself for even considering giving up, and left the Science Centre feeling resolute. Once home, I recalculated the dimensions and set to work again. Several unsuccessful attempts later, I achieved perfect wooden cut-outs. Enlisting the help of my chemistry teacher, I scoured local pawn shops, to source vacuum tubes.

Three months on, I stood before the fruits of my labour – my life-sized interactive Periodic Table, proudly displayed at the M.D. Mehta Science Centre – shining under the warmth of 118 lights, and the calculating gaze of countless young scientists. Their eagerness to explore different elements was palpable, and the accompanying treasure of information showcased on the giant screen, enthusing.

The air in the room was electrified with excitement. Fascinated students keenly scanned the glass boxes and the elements they contained, frequently inquiring about unique items. Pointing out the vacuum tube, Dinesh asked me about the lightbulb I'd set up inside the Thorium box. Delighted by his curiosity, I explained its role in improving Tungsten's resistance to heat. Later, hearing Dinesh enthusiastically tell his friends about the Thorium box, my heart soared.

Even if the cost of human upliftment runs into countless failed attempts, I am ready to pay that price again...

And again.

OUR THOUGHTS ON FALAK'S ESSAY

Having a title for your essay is optional, but if you do plan to use one, it is critical to get it right. The title 'Renaissance' instantly captures our complete attention, optimizing opportunities to: 1. set the theme of the essay; 2. provide a fascinating clue to the essay's main idea; and 3. create interest. Following which the 'hook' or the first couple of lines, brilliantly draw us in by switching from initial interest to the immediate sharp intrigue of crisis – 'Blank. My mind froze.' Straight to the point, this no fuss or frills 'hook' sets the stage – and now, we are players in the dramatic journey that ensues through this commonly experienced state of mind!

Next, the technical details of the dilemma – and we are well and truly welded to the challenge as Falak is. We identify! It is ours, and hers, to solve.

In these few paragraphs we encounter Falak as a passionate engineer, a reflective thinker, a caring and responsible mentor – all spiced with a dash of self-deprecating humor with which she imagines her handiwork 'mocking, daring me to give up!'

The 'loud doorbell' and 'Rajat, my cheerful weekly Amazon-parcels-delivery man' are welcome light distractions, like 'brain-breaks' from the intensity of the earlier brooding – just as we are often advised to get up and move when stuck. It lifts the ambience, refocuses us to the present – 'the arrival of another parcel', and the renewed hope for a solution. But no, it's the wrong solution! This see-saw contrast of ups and downs effectively builds in a high-tension pivot point into the narrative, while providing deeper detail of her endeavor.

The use of the task checklist is an underused approach for 'show not tell'. It brilliantly establishes the enormity of the task before Falak, like a looming mountain, and further hints at her diligent and methodical thought process. This allows the reader to suspect that she may have what it takes to 'fight' her way to the top somehow, despite feeling 'momentarily smothered by these obstacles' and the 'little voice urging me to quit.'

The elements of questioning oneself, admitting to anxious emotions, and the 'heavy heart', color in her personality with humanity and allude to her passionate concern for her community and especially for the children. The very relatable and endearing anecdote that follows takes readers through the humbling, hope-giving interaction with some of her 'brightly loquacious students'. When we see, through her, their determination to 'never relinquish their knowledge quest', we know that she, too, 'never will'. And just like that, we are 'three months on', to the glowingly described finished LIPT (life-sized interactive periodic table). We feel the students' reaction, 'electrified with excitement'. We feel delight with Falak at their curiosity and enthusiastic recounting of their new knowledge and experience. 'My heart soared', she says, and ours too, soars.

Her concluding sentence ('And again.') neatly encases her overarching values of patience and indefatigable perseverance!

NIHAL MAMMEN MATHEW

Columbia, Class of 2026

Major: Economics
School: Pallikoodam, Kerala, India
Hometown: Kottayam, India

THE CURRY-PATTA EFFECT

What makes a sandwich perfect?

This was the question that the 'Bon Appetit' magazine, resting idly on my couch, sought to answer. As a consummate consumer, I usually leave the art of cooking to those better suited for the task. However, pure reflex had me reaching for the magazine.

To my surprise, sandwiches, much like a Kubrick movie, were riddled with challenges and intricate complexities that one can only hope to master by taking certain calculated, artistic risks. The science of the perfect sandwich varied from source to sauce, with Gastronomica advocating the use of lightly toasted bread, and *Epicurious.com* insisting that one layer of sauce worked best.

Like Lewis and Clark, I set sail on the internet's wide seas, guided by my worthy Sacagawea (Google), to discover the snack's secrets. Sifting through videos with conflicting opinions, I concluded that a verdict could only be reached after copious experimentation. So, I got to work in my lab (kitchen), beginning with whole-wheat toasted bread, sesame-encrusted bagels, bacon, pepperoni, caramelized onions, lettuce, and an assortment of sauces. Despite weeks of sustained trial and error, the mystery of the perfect sandwich kept slipping through my fingers, much like Tantalus's fruits.

After much deliberation, I concluded that my main problem was the sauce – the unsung hero, which effortlessly brings various flavors to life. My struggle for culinary perfection, however, was eclipsed by another struggle – one for thespian brilliance, as I was chosen to play the lead in my school's production of 'Joseph and the Amazing Technicolour Dreamcoat'.

Awkward in the limelight and crippled by stage fright, I struggled to slip into the role. To exacerbate matters, I was racked with a heavy cold, which precluded me from hitting the high notes. Each time I sang, my voice tremulously broke much like an inadequately toasted or overly sauced sandwich. A particularly challenging scene was the one in which my character had just been thrown into prison. This scene also marked my first solo as a grieving and broken man. As hard as I tried, on those final lyrics, 'Close every door to me', the scene remained elusive, with every door and pathway seeming to close.

Terrified that I'd be replaced or demoted, I scrambled to locate that missing ingredient, that sauce for my performance. An in-depth character study on YouTube ensued, revealing Joseph in every avatar, from young, naive boy to powerful leader helming a nation. After months of training, my voice carried, reaching those inaccessible high notes. Finally, with scant warning, opening day arrived. Although jittery with nerves, I wouldn't let my anxieties get in the way of my performance. And so, channelling Daniel Day-Lewis, I delivered the show of a lifetime.

Unfortunately, months after I attained brilliance as a thespian, the sandwich saga had still not reached a delectable conclusion. That was, until I fell headfirst into a bed of curry patta (leaves) – a herb native to India, and therefore ignored by websites. Epiphany struck and I could now clearly see the recipe for the extraordinary sauce I would make – a blend of curry leaves, kasundi mustard, mayonnaise, and 'kandhari' chilli.

I knew instinctively that this was the ingredient missing from the precise science of western sandwiches. So, I rushed to my trusty lab, where I chopped, sliced, and blended ingredients, finally and hopefully assembling the perfect sandwich. Sweat beaded my brow as I brought it to my mouth. A single bite transported me to the seventh dimension. Like Archimedes in his bathtub, I realized that I had 'found it' – the curry-patta effect!

Having perfected the science of the sandwich, the quest to match the curry-patta effect propels me onwards. I now know that a flavorful ally – that pungent leaf, or Daniel Day-Lewis – is what will carry me through life's highest waves and gravest challenges. Without that special curry-leaf effect, it's still work-in-progress!

OUR THOUGHTS ON NIHAL'S ESSAY

Nihal immediately rivets by opening with a question that compels as many answers as there are sandwich makers—or eaters. For few among us would not have an immediate answer or be driven by culinary curiosity to read through till the end. This essay does not disappoint. It is crisp, clean and clever – a difficult task given how subjective, even esoteric, the topic is. On the one hand, Nihal's pursuit of the 'perfect' sandwich seems, prima facie, a facetious endeavor. A light-hearted distraction from life, perhaps, or a way to enhance life through a humble bread-and-filling construction. But the sandwich is a window into his curiosity – the research, the experiments, the perusal of culinary magazines that meld gastronomy with philosophy. On the other hand, he has a more daunting task: to do justice to his role as Joseph and achieve those elusive high notes. He links the two with a clever play on the word 'sauce' – both condiment and secret ingredient. This is a risky choice, because the connection is subtle, but it works.

As much as this essay is about the work and growth that comes with chasing high standards, it is also revealing of Nihal's personality. His whimsical analogizing through the sandwich tells us that he is a foodie, but does not take himself too seriously. He thinks out of the box – and this is revealed in tiers (not unlike the delectable layering of the sandwich!): First, in finding common ground between a snack and theater, and the second in demonstrating that both need a 'sauce' – a secret ingredient, a *je ne sais quoi* to tie it together. Then in his appropriation of the curry leaf as a sauce component in an otherwise arguably western dish, hitherto hiding from plain sight due to its ubiquity in Indian cooking. Lastly, in his peppering the essay with film and philosophical references: *Lewis & Clark*, Daniel Day-Lewis and Archimedes.

In all, Nihal projects an easy-going, creative, incisive, thoughtful, and hard-working personality. A great set of character traits for college, and for life.

NIKHIL KAMAT

Harvard, Class of 2025

Major: Concentration in Applied Math in Economics and a Secondary in Theater, Dance and Media
School: American School of Bombay, Mumbai, India
Hometown: Mumbai, India

Nothing is more electrifying than standing in Times Square looking at all the brilliant neon Broadway signs lit up and stare down on you. Nothing is more surreal than a 'flashmob' on a major city highway in *La La Land*. Or more powerful than the entire kingdom arriving for the birth of Simba in *The Lion King*. Or in my case, lighting the Christmas tree in elementary school!

I really, really wanted to push that button to light it up for the school Christmas concert. I badgered my school principal every day leading up to the event, until I got to light the tree! It was a moment topped only by the excitement of being cast in a professional production of *The Sound of Music*, in ninth grade. I realized just how much I wanted to pursue musical theater. All those 'relatives' chuckling about the younger me performing to Shakira at family Christmas parties and holidays, finally stopped.

The production taught me a lot! I had to learn to balance my passion with academics, and that was a challenge. Why? My imagination moves like that Honda Accord car parts commercial, telling its story through a Rube Goldberg Machine sequence, and fast. I have to rein it in. I have to channel every ounce of my energy into constant little victories over this unstoppable chain reaction of fantastical thoughts, with mindful balance and persistence – a rhythm I have worked hard to achieve.

When learning Pascal's Triangle, a triangular array of the binomial coefficients, my left hemisphere was present and focused on learning about the binomial theorem; my feet were tapping out time steps under my desk. Moving from single time steps to quadruple to sextuple, my brain recalled the rows of Pascal's Triangle without writing them down: third row... a 1,4,6,4,1 pattern. I tapped out in a short routine of corresponding timed steps: 1 – 1234 – 123456 – 1234 – 1.

Tap dancing helps me maintain rhythm, order and precision; to ensure the perfect sound, you hit the floor at the perfect angle. *Shuffle. Hop. Shuffle. Drop. Brush. Step. Step.*

Just like William Barfée, uses his dance-like 'magic foot' to spell out words in the 25th Annual Putnam County Spelling Bee, I recall trigonometric equation signs by swapping the lyrics of 'If you're happy and you know it...' with the order and signs of the trigonometric double-angle identities, such as sin(2x) or cos(2x).

'Child, why are you always singing?' Quizzical judgement oozed from neighbourhood Academic Aunty's face. When first asked, I had stuttered. Little did either of us know then, how much discipline, focus, and knowledge vocal training requires.

The performing arts and academia persist in living together in my system. Having to choose between Math Club and the Musical, felt like I was going to lose a part of myself. I was consumed with regret before I even made the decision. After working all my life to find a balance, I felt like I was separated into two different people. I realized then that I needed more than just balance. I needed to build a bridge. And I am my own architect.

I've always loved strategies that involve me in channelling visions and imagination into STEM related projects using complex functions and equations. The delight is to have the opportunity to pass on these blueprints: to students who have an interest in both STEM and the ARTS and want to bridge them in some way; and to younger kids, more specifically boys, in India who have the desire and the drive for the performing arts, and want to explore them in ways deemed appropriate by convention-ridden Indian society.

I belt out the lyrics of 'Seize the Day' at my school musical, almost jubilant about my future. I walk the talk, I...

'Stare down the odds
and seize the day
minute by minute
that's how *I* win it.
I will find a way.'

OUR THOUGHTS ON NIKHIL'S ESSAY

Nikhil's opening paragraph does two things: it tells us he has an affinity for the dramatic, and an ability to see the magic in the mundane, so clear in his excitement to light his school's Christmas tree. Both these flow seamlessly into the rest of the essay about his love for theater, and his confronting the tensions that came with it. Through the essay, we see glimpses of the world he inhabits: the silencing of (perhaps conservative?) relatives and neighbors snickering at his Shakira performances once he was cast in *The Sound of Music*. Theater is a notoriously difficult career and passion – so parts won, and critics silenced, are celebrated.

We especially appreciate how he explores balancing his theatrical side – wild, unbridled, mile-a-minute musicality with academic interests. Though it is challenging to do, music and math, he demonstrates, are not so different. Both are patterned, both rhythmic, and both lend themselves to recall through pneumonic devices. He takes care to demonstrate this, tell us how he 'recall(s) trigonometric equation signs by swapping the lyrics of "If you're happy and you know it..."

with the order and signs of the trigonometric double-angle identities, such as sin(2x) or cos(2x).' Which lyrics he replaces, and with what, aren't immediately clear, but it doesn't matter – because the clever use of the numbers, rhythm patterns and lyrics, peppered with a bit of 'Academic Aunty' humor helps us briefly step into his shoes, with the takeaway that he makes it work, as he marches to the beat of his own drum and tempo.

Nikhil found a way to effectively engage with both – his passion for mathematics and for theater, and it would have been unthinkable for his essay to not reflect this. He also seized opportunities to share his insights with others, especially boys, acknowledging the cultural tendency to think of the Arts as a primarily female inclination.

Overarchingly, Nikhil found a way to engage with and entertain us through his passions, his essay, and also his unique quirky personality – dramatic, creative, thoughtful, a recognizer of patterns, and generous with his knowledge.

PARITOSH KANORIA

Stanford, Class of 2019

Major: Art History
School: Bombay International School, Mumbai, India
Hometown: Mumbai, India

Clanging metals and vibrating chords resonate as I scrabble through the empty vessels. I fiddle with the grunting eggbeater and am taken back to my childhood, when as a toddler, my trips to the kitchen were mainly to derive pleasure from this amusing ruckus, which I now enjoy in the form of Vocals and Piano. Little did I know that this place would soon come to mean so much more. Smiling, I pull out all the crockery, and intuitively buy ingredients that I need, and arrange them in the order that I will use them.

As I start the pastry, I dwell upon how it is a reflection of me. I see my emotional side, the side that appreciates the aesthetics of life, in the softness of the butter. I see my rationality in the flour that effectively holds the butter together. But I also see the tangerine zest, a perfect encapsulation of my personality – zingy. These ingredients, mixed, kneaded and rolled out, form a base, which has a thirst to hold layers of flavors, ideas and experiences.

Enveloped in the bubbling pops of the lemon curd, and the musical ticking of the oven, I feel comfortable. As I whip the egg-whites, they elevate from flat transparency into frothy whiteness. I wonder why it is here that I somehow feel elevated as well! Is it because my creative self, otherwise hidden behind the academic drape of school assignments, emerges?

Perhaps it is only here that I can really try, without calculating, without walking so cautiously on eggshells, terrified to fail. This is the place where I can experiment with my intuition, learn through experience, and make mistakes without regretting them.

After the exhausting, yet fulfilling hours of cooking, I push myself to create balance: adjusting flavors, contrasting textures, and harmonizing temperatures. My Lemon Meringue Pie represents equilibrium, and somewhere is a reflection of me – someone who believes in holism, progress, and experience of all spheres of life.

I learn about flavor, texture, culture, and their relationships. My interests in world, and historic cultures stem from here too, and have led me to strive to spread such awareness by initiating and organizing events such as 'La Fiesta Hispana', that spread understanding of Hispanic Culture to the entire BIS family. As I learn, I begin to wish to share these experiences and knowledge with others around me as well – which ultimately led me to design and conduct my own baking classes for children.

Following recipes is a sin to me; like serving someone else's creation. Any dish that I recreate, I make differently each time – else the element of fun dissipates, the thrill of experimentation dies. In fact, the entire purpose of cooking is lost. I always make it my own, a skill I developed through countless books, shows, and my internship at the Hyatt Regency Hotel, where I was guided by the Italian head chef himself.

My food isn't delicate; it is earthy, hearty, and most importantly bold and expressive. Creative expression is something that means the world to me, and I have expressed myself such through art, food and even chemistry through my video – 'Flaming Green' – about global warming.

The quick, yellow sparks that erupt into ferocious, golden fires; the applauding sizzles that overpower surrounding sounds; the loading clouds of aromas that diffuse all over. This dramatic performance drives me forward, forward like a fuel that keeps me going, but more importantly keeps me inspired. The thrills I get from speaking at a national debate, acting for the finales of Founders' Day shows, or singing in front of examiners are unmatchable. I feed off from them.

The food world is where I feel most independent. What I create, how I can make it my own, how I present it – it is all my decision. I am the leader, and the follower of the one person who I completely trust – myself.

OUR THOUGHTS ON PARITOSH'S ESSAY

A Buddhist sage once said that the environment is a faithful mirror, a reflection of who we are and what we do. Many of our students recognize this, but perhaps none as brightly and reflectively as Paritosh does. And what a brilliant mirror it is!

Paritosh muses on perhaps the favorite place in his home from the very start! The idea of 'empty vessels' allures. What will he fill these with, we wonder? With all manner of things! But not before we realize that the clanging of vessels, the 'amusing ruckus' is a deliberate evocation of his love for music. But then he begins to use these very vessels to gather, assemble, knead, blend, and we see him come alive: there is aestheticism, in both him, and the pastry. Also, rationality and logicality – after all the flour holds the butter – and rolled out, is a base for the fruit of knowledge, for 'flavors, ideas and experiences'.

And don't forget the zing of 'tangerine zest' elevating the mundanity of pastry flour, elevating *him*. We marvel at his brilliance of the dramatic transmutation of egg whites from translucence to snow-peak frothiness, a reflection of his creative self, hidden behind the garb of schoolwork, waiting to peak. Yes, Paritosh writes with all his senses, so we virtually inhale who he is. The kitchen is his place of comfort, it has molded him into that person who does not shy away from walking on eggshells, that person who is unterrified of failing, that person who works on both intuition and calculation.

What does he do for balance, after hours of cooking/assignments? Why, make lemon merengue pie, of course. We discern in this pie, his sense of fun, balance, adventure (following recipes is a 'sin'). And now, it suddenly becomes credible that he would spur events like 'La Fiesta Hispana', that spread understanding of Hispanic Culture amongst his school community; and twice learn, as he extends his skill in baking to teaching young children. Or marshals his creativity in a video on global warming.

Finally, in learning about his kitchen endeavors, through 'the ferocious, golden fires' and the 'applauding sizzles' we learn about him beyond the kitchen as a fiery debater, an actor, an environmentalist. The deterministic powerful last line, of what he creates and how he creates it being a reflection of who he is, is the final, validating and irresistible offering to the admissions committee.

SHEEN GUPTA

UPenn, Class of 2027

Major: Business Economics and Public Policy, Finance (Wharton)
School: Indus International School, Hyderabad, India
Hometown: Hyderabad, India

The moving finger writes; and having writ, moves on.

– Omar Khayyam

Cobwebs clear, and I focus my pen's dance across the page, completing the image of a forest brimming with life; each movement knitting together the blank spaces of a story waiting to unfold.

Opening my sketchbook at random, I gaze at the page in front of me – every nook and cranny packed with scribbled words, reminiscent of a typical issue of *The Eagles' Bulletin*, the school newspaper I founded to give the student body a voice. I remember our very first issue, the first time I worked with the writers, editors, and designers I now call friends – the people that taught me so much in such little time. Over the past three years, *The Eagles' Bulletin* became a platform for social commentary, reminding the school that the duty to heal the world lay within each of us – something I'd realized while doodling blueprints for the first issue. Pleased, I flip the page.

Dha dhin dhin dha, the four beats that will forever resonate within me are scribbled in five different fonts. An artform that has allowed me to tell innumerable stories over the years; from my juvenile performance depicting Mother Nature as a six-year-old, to a more mature 'thumri' embodying the unbreakable bond between Radha and Krishna in my adult years, Kathak mirrors my doodles, helping me embrace my identity.

I turn to another tale, marveling at the thicket of scribbles that transports me to the heartland of India – its forests and the women within – a setting I became deeply acquainted with through my work in the Indian Forest Economy Project. While my initial sketches portray the typical fauna and flora of the forest, the next few drawings depict the Dabur Amla hair oil I use twice a week, the jar of Nutella made with cocoa and hazelnuts – products reaped from the arduous toil of tribal women to supply the modern world with things we consider indispensable – a realization that fuels my work towards economic, social, and environmental sustainability.

Doodling takes me on various scenic routes, emulating pathways in the international trade networks I analyzed in my research paper as part of the 'Computational Economics and Social Science: Networks and Modeling of the Real World' course. I examine the complex lines in my sketchbook, observing their similarities with trade networks – weighted graphs showing links between the world's nations. Finally understanding the networks between my imaginativeness and my passion for Economics, I question how I can use my creativity to portray Economics as an amalgamation of human behavior and data analysis resulting in pertinent policies.

Turning to my latest doodle, I'm greeted by streets of square boxes, reflecting my initial disappointment in failing to acquire an internship with the National Institute of Rural Development on the grounds that they only accepted graduate students. Looking at the constrictive boxes, I realized that I didn't need to fit within their confines. I needed to think beyond. Reapproaching the institute, I advocated for my desire to do good, presenting a portfolio of success stories that demonstrated my aptitude, which subsequently landed me the position. I recognized then, that patience and persistence are integral in pushing boundaries.

The resemblance of design thinking – a tool collected from an Innovation Council project – to doodling allures me: both processes being non-linear and interactive. They help me understand people, challenge stereotypes, redefine problems, and innovate solutions. Ultimately, this is what I aspire to accomplish in all my endeavors.

Over the years, my doodles have contained both exultations and pitfalls – never quite perfect, yet perfectly balanced in their variety – like me. This brings me to my current sketch. Despite having spent days working on it, it remains unfinished. Incomplete. Perhaps it should be. I have miles to go, with ample time for the in-progress doodle to gain new angles, explore new shapes, imbibe new perspectives; as I will.

OUR THOUGHTS ON SHEEN'S ESSAY

The Common Application's prompt asks students to discuss their backgrounds, interests, identities or talents. This essay does all the above, taking us through Sheen's life and interests via her doodling. It is clear that she processes her experiences through drawings – pictorial journaling, if you will – and in transporting her reader on a visual ride through some of her most meaningful sketches, she tells us who she is, what she has accomplished, and what is most important to her. Critically, through her spontaneous doodles and drawings, this essay shows us Sheen's multiple facets and passions.

The doodling fuels realizations and we learn of her passion for social and economic justice, first revealed through *The Eagle's Bulletin* – 'the duty to heal the world lay within each of us'. The tempo changes, and you can visualize the arabesques and sweeping arcs wrought by her pen as you jump with her, onstage, to witness her performing Kathak. Dance, like drawing, is expressive: sometimes free form, sometimes premeditated, but always edifying. Ordinarily, this might have been too abrupt a switch, but we love how this essay's narrative continues to be seamlessly driven by pages in Sheen's sketchbook, opened at random.

And then we're back to social justice, and the crux of Sheen's academic motivations: economics, the environment, sustainability. The pen stops, mid-air. We learn of Sheen's (perhaps first) brush with rejection, and her lessons in the power of persistence, being prepared, and advocating for oneself. All insights that will forge her character, and age well, through college and beyond.

The thrill, as they say, is in the unexpected twists and turns of the journey; and here, we are left with a sense of how the 'non-linear and interactive' aspects of doodling will continue to be analogous to a life rich in exploration and learning. We especially liked the way the essay concluded, in that there was no conclusion, but an open door with the cautious execution of the 'in-progress doodle to gain new angles, explore new shapes, imbibe new perspectives'. It leaves space for evolution, change, and challenge. This last doodle in question, much like her life, is unfinished, there's no knowing where it might go, and that's okay, even thrilling. Sheen's essay embodies this viewpoint perfectly.

12

METAMORPHOSIS

metamorphosis (n.)
'change of form or structure, action or process of changing in form,'
'a transforming, a transformation,'
'to transform, to be transfigured,' from meta, here indicating 'change'

The cliché of a reticent, shy child emboldened to take on the world begs the existential question: Does anyone really change, metamorphose? Wasn't the Ugly Duckling always a swan albeit a swan-in-waiting? Or the caterpillar a butterfly awaiting wings? Yes, though their metamorphoses were foregone conclusions, none would have metamorphosed without catalyzing factors such as (in these cases), time and seasons. The writers of the eight essays that follow have narrated their journey of transformation and growth in response to the factors that catalyzed them, while still retaining their core individuality, and identity.

Their metamorphosis or transformation required more than external factors as fuel – it required an inner will or yearning, a commitment to excavate their very best, change, and thrive.

The transformation is not pat, these are not superficial changes responding to an abracadabra moment. Instead, we have a ringside view as they, under varied, sometimes extenuating circumstances, evolve and grow. You'll learn of the catalysts that triggered transformations – these catalysts are of their choosing. They seized opportunities, tweaked and often overhauled their perspectives, and were unafraid of changing trajectories.

Hopefully their stories will inspire you to revisit how you've evolved, and reflect on the events, circumstances or changes in perception that triggered your transformation.

ASHMIT SINGH

Harvard, Class of 2027

Major: Economics and Psychology
School: Modern School Barakhamba Road, New Delhi, India
Hometown: New Delhi, India

The lights dimmed out. Silence enveloped the cavernous interiors. A blinding spotlight aimed at the rear of the school's main auditorium: a cortège began walking down the central aisle, its members, all clad in white, chanting in unison at the top of their voices, 'All hail Mangal Pandey!'

While the other actors revised their lines for the school's premier theatrical production, staged on the occasion of India's 72nd Independence Day, I looked down at the procession hailing a casket on their shoulders and felt my knees weaken. Was it nervousness? No. It was fear. The incessant chanting of the name of the martyred 'sepoy' sent me back in time by a decade, where I once stood facing a bronze statue in my mother's ancestral home. The statue covered in garlands, with a beautifully sculpted military hat and uniform, was of my maternal uncle or mamu, a braveheart who had sacrificed himself for our nation at the young age of twenty-one. The echoing chants evoked my most vulnerable fear, one I had been suppressing for what felt like eternity: the fear for my father's life.

Jammu and Kashmir, the home of my forefathers, had been stripped of its special status only a week before the performance. A fear of increased insurgency and riots had sent the entire region into a state of lockdown and media blackout, with both internet and communication lines having been suspended indefinitely. No one knew what was transpiring there, and at the center of this situation was my father, an officer posted in one of the most tumultuous parts of Kashmir.

As a feeling of dread surged through my veins, the chants gradually subsided. This was my cue, and I realized that much like my dad and mamu, I had a duty to fulfil. I felt submerged by the weakness in my gut, but drawing strength from the trust placed in me as the youngest actor of the cast playing a major role, I leaped into character. For a good hour, then, I forgot myself and my trepidations. The next thing I knew, everyone in the audience was up on their feet, clapping and hooting deafeningly.

It was not the first time I had felt afraid and I was sure it wouldn't be the last, but I had learned that even in the most treacherous and overwhelming situations, one ought to perform one's duty. The duty to our nation, our family, our school, their team or in my case, my fellow cast members and audience.

Standing on the stage, feeling overwhelmed by the applause, I scanned the audience, unable to catch a glimpse of my father. Before the agitation could, once again, entrap me, I locked eyes with the group cheering the loudest: my second family, my fellow boarders.

In the twelve years before moving to the boarding house, I had lived in six different cities, and as soon as I would begin to feel at home, my father would be posted elsewhere. With time, these different cities and their different people blended into each other, leaving me with a pernicious sense of indifference towards them. In those years, I frequently chose to seek solace in a book instead of a conversation, creating a myriad of ideas in my mind—ideas I had no outlet to express, to voice. Finally, when that reclusive and naive boy was forced into a bustling atmosphere teeming with boisterous children, commotion, and a certain sense of camaraderie, the aloofness gradually faded.

Instead of receding into my shell, I finally felt free to converse about the numerous thoughts and ideas in my mind, and learnt to express myself with newfound coherence and liberty. Whether the discussions were with children from the slums of Tilak Nagar or the brave war widows from Kargil Colony, the teams I debated against or even in the articles I authored, I had developed a unique voice.

OUR THOUGHTS ON ASHMIT'S ESSAY

Ashmit introduces the essay's premise at the beginning, transporting us to his world of theater, of contrasts and conflicts – the cortège before him urging him to explore his inner life, an adventure that builds through his essay.

Theater coaxes him to connect aspects of his life: his persistent fear about the safety of his father, a police officer in rife-torn Jammu and Kashmir, and his reflections on two martyred soldiers – Mangal Pandey, a preeminent freedom fighter in India, and his maternal uncle, martyred at twenty-one. He makes clear that he has dealt with fear and anxiety before – it marked the life of his ancestors, marked his childhood, marked also, his days as a student in six cities, where books became his mooring. In theater, the territory is often familiar.

On stage his mind ricochets to the media blackouts in Kashmir. These remind him that no matter how strong we are, there are things out of our control that can overturn our perceptions of the world, and our belief systems, in a heartbeat. Being part of the system does not protect one from being affected by it – as someone hailing from a family of police personnel, he bravely exemplifies this.

Like his father, and other family members, duty drives Ashmit. Despite his anxiety about the unfurling situation in Kashmir, he perseveres, navigating conflicting emotions to ably play his role in the Independence Day performance. 'It was not the first time I had felt afraid, and I was sure it wouldn't be the last, but I had learned that even in the most treacherous and overwhelming situations, one ought to perform one's duty.' In enacting a role, his sense of responsibility amplifies – to the school, the audience, to himself. He expertly draws on his father and maternal uncle's duty-infused lives to give a masterful performance worthy of a standing ovation.

The essay also touches on his ventures across geographies, reflecting the tapestry of his life. As the son of a police officer in the Jammu and Kashmir Police, Ashmit drew lessons from the places he's lived in. These built him, brick by brick, even as his courage burgeoned. It takes strength to survive each day not knowing whether your loved ones are safe. This is the strength he will carry to his life in university, even as he rises to acclimate and surmount other challenges, drawing inspiration from his role models – his uncle and father. After all, those forged in fire will not wilt in mere sunlight.

KARAN SINGH MADIA

Cornell, Class of 2029

Major: Computer Science
School: Singapore American School, Singapore
Hometown: Singapore

Eighteen months into the pandemic and I hadn't stepped out of Singapore. Family vacations and time with cousins in India were nostalgic memories. I even craved the once-despised airline provender!

One day, my weekend chess session with Grandad was interrupted when Christy, our live-in Filipino helper, entered the room disturbed. 'My life is unbearable… I have not seen my son and husband for two years and can't even meet friends here. There are many from my hometown in Singapore, but I don't know who or where they are.'

A chord struck, and seeing her sadness, I was ashamed of my trivial yearnings. It was a rude awakening that had me reflect on our contrasting worlds. I was moved by her plight and felt I had to do something, for her, and for her fraternity.

Coding enraptures me: it makes me feel that nothing is too far-fetched, that all things are attainable. I helped build a platform to track flights, created a web-app to reduce wind turbine emissions, and devised a solution for remotely accessing medical services. What seemed like a ticket to creating startups had now found its true calling.

Since most helpers had smartphones, a mobile app seemed a viable solution for their challenges.

I knew little about apps then, but how hard could it be? When only a clunky prototype emerged after sixty days of hard toil, the answer became obvious. Each time I tackled an issue, another materialized. But I was unstoppable: I had the opportunity to enhance actual lives and was determined to give it my all.

This entailed self-learning several skills such as front-end designing, database linking, and API creation. Along the way, I searched online for a mentor and stumbled upon Harshaan Nihal, a software engineer at BigBinary. Though busy with his day job, he too was captivated by the cause.

With Harshaan's invaluable advice, creating the app seemed attainable. Meanwhile, I settled on the title 'Mary Amma' as a tribute to my retired doting nanny.

Finally, the day dawned bright and sunny and voilà, the app was ready. I downloaded it for Christy and illustrated how she could find helpers in Singapore from her hometown Iloilo. In another tab she found helpers who lived in our neighborhood! Other features: anonymity for registering abuse, access to helplines and mental health resources, and in-built messaging. Her instant smile and the spring in her step buoyed me, showed the reach of technology, and justified months of effort.

To take the app to every helper in Singapore, I sought support from the Ministry of Manpower (MOM), the Indian High Commission, and NGOs associated with domestic workers.

Stepping out of my comfort zone, I connected with complete strangers: shared the app with groups of helpers in the morning, presented to NGOs in the afternoon, and to the MOM in the evening. Naturally reticent, I now exult in conveying my passion and communicating the significance of the app.

Rejections were aplenty. However, so were triumphs! I had never imagined receiving an invitation from the Singapore Government to support their upcoming technology initiatives for helpers. The Crest Gold Award from the British Science Association was similarly uplifting.

The app was only made possible by the guidance I had received from those who had traversed the path before. The journey taught me that teamwork and common purpose are potent force multipliers. To support others looking to similarly impact, including those with limited language skills, I made twenty-eight YouTube programming tutorials in English and Hindi.

Mary Amma is just a beginning. My mind travels from Singapore to Dubai and beyond, the places where foreign domestic workers yearn to but cannot connect with each another. I will leave no stone unturned to help them link, knowing that in connecting they will thrive. Over a year and a half, my life's mission has been repurposed to innovate for the greatest good and the greatest numbers!

OUR THOUGHTS ON KARAN'S ESSAY

Karan opens with a comment about his quotidian existence during the pandemic, a truth that would have been bizarre at any other time in history, except perhaps during the Spanish Flu of 1918. He then validates it with a glimpse of his life at that time: chess with his grandfather, presumably a way for them both to pass time and keep their minds alert. In sweeps the helper, who shares Karan's space, but whose life and pandemic experience is vastly different from his own, shattering his musings: she is isolated in the truest sense – sequestered with strangers, and unable to meet or even contact those in her fraternity. Here we see Karan's compassion and empathetic side well.

He then shifts gear to show us his brainy side: It becomes clear that he is both enraptured by and a star at coding, which beams to him that all things are attainable. Philosophically, and practically, the sky is the limit. He has the motivation, and practically, is driven to connect the multitudes of domestic workers with shared origins in Singapore. We love how Karan walks the reader through his process while developing the app, and the snippets of his internal monologue: How hard can it be? Will it succeed? We can feel the breathy excitement of starting something new, something with the potential to change the world, one life at a time. But enthusiasm and excitement notwithstanding, gravity reigns supreme, and the 'clunky prototype' brings him crashing down to earth. Now, he shows us grit and frustration, solving one issue while another insidiously makes appearance. He realizes at some point that he needs help and seeks out a mentor. This, to us, speaks of his humility and foresight: we rarely have all the answers, and admitting and resolving for this fact is smart.

Karan's app's success arrives eventually (reflected in the tropical sun – bright and sunny), and we appreciate that he stressed on the travails faced in its development as much as the accolades he received afterwards. Importantly, he makes it abundantly clear that he garnered lessons from the experience: connecting with strangers despite being shy, creating tutorials for others in similar situations, seeking to create impact at scale, and the realization that 'teamwork and common purpose are potent force multipliers'. The essay ends with the same headiness of novelty, creation, and innovation – but we sense he is a little older, a little wiser, a little more deliberate. The universe, for him, where he can innovate and catalyze change, is indeed, infinite.

MANAS SANKAR

UPenn, Class of 2026

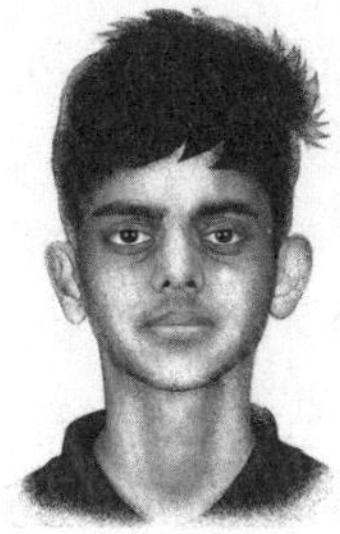

Major: Chemical and Biomolecular Engineering
School: Vidya Mandir Senior Secondary School, Chennai, India
Hometown: Chennai, India

The lessons we take from obstacles we encounter can be fundamental to later success. Recount a time when you faced a challenge, setback, or failure. How did it affect you, and what did you learn from the experience?

'May I now call "*The Voice*" of the camp, Manas Sankar, to the podium?'

'The Voice' – that was the nickname my mentor conferred on me during the two-week Aspen Leadership camp I attended during the summer of 2019. I cannot forget the joy this name brought to me. After all, it was a welcome change from my identity as the tongue-tied boy of my class.

Throughout middle school, crowds intimidated me as they brought out the worst of my fears, namely, conversations with unfamiliar people. The words would get jumbled up, and my voice would fade away mid-sentence. Consequently, I refused to join the clubs and activities my school offered out of fear of being judged and ridiculed. I found solace in sports, a space where I didn't need to utter a word to anyone.

On a dare from my school friends, I applied to the Aspen Leadership Camp (an intensive camp focused on building communication and team-building skills). I remember my mouth drying up when I received my acceptance letter. Two weeks away from home, amidst the beautiful foothills of the Himalayas, might seem exciting to others but not to me. I couldn't sleep all night, sweating profusely at the thought of interacting with seventy-two unfamiliar people. However, the thought of being trolled by my friends for backing down scared me more. Summoning up the courage, I decided to attend the camp, and in hindsight, it was the best decision I've ever made.

One of the early workshops for self-expression at the camp was theater. My mentor called upon me to deliver short dialogues and read from a script without using a microphone. Hearing my voice bounce around the hall helped me loosen up. Theater taught me how to effectively use my voice and body, and I began to shed the meek and shy layers I hid behind. Soon, my nickname was 'The Voice', and at the end of the two-week camp, I addressed an audience of over 300 people without a microphone.

This transformative experience served as positive reinforcement and was my first step towards facing my fears. I realized that my voice was powerful and clear, and using my body to emote calmed my nerves. My apprehensions about striking conversations with strangers and public speaking did not vanish immediately, but I no longer stopped trying.

Back at school, I surprised everyone when I signed up to represent my school at debates and the Model United Nations (MUN) competitions. Instead of dwelling on my insecurities, I focused my energies on developing the skills needed to win. I worked hard at maintaining eye contact and appropriating easy body language. Gaining confidence with every new competition and my newfound 'voice', I contributed to my school's success at inter-school events. I was thrilled to be elected the Secretary-General of my school MUN. Stepping outside my self-imposed box gave me the tools to emote, express, analyze, and, more importantly, learn through questioning.

A few months ago, I struck up a conversation with Veeramma, who helps my mother with household chores. She mentioned how her husband was unable to secure a good job due to his weak communication skills. Personally identifying with his insecurity, I reflected on my difficult middle school years. With the support from my family and friends, I created a platform to augment the communication skills of people like Veeramma's husband. The platform helps people cope with communication challenges (specifically in English), schoolwork and even prepare for job interviews.

A simple reassurance from my mentor gave me the courage to take that first step. I am by no means perfect, but I use my voice now with more confidence. Just as I found mine, I hope to positively impact my community by helping others find their 'voice'.

OUR THOUGHTS ON MANAS'S ESSAY

As Manas begins his essay, he invites the reader into a single, charged moment—readying to face a crowd as 'The Voice', compelling us to explore what Manas is about to do, and importantly, how he has reached this precipice. He then transports himself, and us, back in time to set the stage for the development arc that has led him to this point: standing in the wings, ready to face a crowd.

The elucidation of this moment—as Manas takes the stage at a two-week summer camp in the Himalayas—does not begin with the logistics of applying and being accepted into this prestigious camp, but rather with his long-term anxieties about public speaking, reiterating that it is his personal journey and growth that he is celebrating in this essay, and not primarily earning a coveted spot at this leadership camp.

As Manas gains confidence through his learnings at the camp, he transposes these into exploring new opportunities—and the reader celebrates him as he challenges himself, and then excels. He uses simple but descriptive language conveying palpable sensations that allow the reader to feel the anxious emotional tension – 'words would get jumbled up', 'voice would fade away mid-sentence', 'my mouth drying up'. We are with Manas in these moments, subconsciously accessing such experiences we have all had, as we relate and empathize.

We are on the ride with Manas, exploring his learnings during a transformative, shining journey that shapes him into a reflective and confident young individual. Importantly, he understands that success must be shared, as he takes these learnings to later undertakings, further illustrating his own personal development, especially with the endearing anecdote of how he was inspired to help others 'find their voice', just as he found his own.

Coming through strongly in this personal story is Manas's 'genuineness', his humility and warmth, and his gratitude for the 'simple reassurance' and 'the courage to take that first step' that his mentor gave him, interspersed with subtle highlights of his recognition of his own strengths and subsequent achievements. The experiences he has chosen to recount are strong, and the straightforward language structure used make them very relatable. By the end, the reader shares the feeling of satisfaction of a challenge well-overcome, and a wonderfully defined personal profile.

SAANVI CHAWLA

Stanford, Class of 2026

Major: Computer Science
School: Navrachana International School Vadodara, Gujarat, India
Hometown: Vadodara, India

'Thank you for pushing my wheelchair at school today.'
'Thank you for battling my demons with me.'
'Thank you for believing in my worth, when I didn't believe it myself.'
Ding!

Another message from The Gracias Initiative lit up my phone, but its radiance travelled far beyond the pixels on my screen. The string of characters ignited smiles, rekindled relationships and strengthened bonds. The Gracias Initiative is a platform that allows people to express gratitude. Through it, I let people send notes of appreciation to anyone that has touched their lives.

And me? I am the dutiful messenger, a mailman who comes home with a heart full of joy and a rucksack worn from carrying letters of gratitude. Every day, I go to bed content with the knowledge that I delivered several parcels of joy, undoubtedly making someone's day. The initiative that gives to so many, gave to me a sense of purpose.

Gratitude has been somewhat of a guardian angel for me, keeping me humble and shaping me into the young, compassionate woman I am today. *Gracias* is the Spanish word for *thank you*, and there is truly so much I'm grateful for.

'To my guitar journey –

Thank you for teaching me that giving up is never an option.'

I clutch at my bleeding fingers, scarred by the sharp metal strings of my guitar. They beg me for respite, but unrelenting, I place my fingers on the fretboard with newfound fervor, eager to conquer the dreaded barre chord. As the pick strums my strings, I am rewarded with a vibrant harmony, each note ringing clear, emitting the perfect F chord – a satisfying culmination of the ruthless practice I had subjected myself to over the past six months.

The following eight years are filled with blissful melodies emanating from my guitar – an instrument I now equated with solace and joy. Feelings I wanted to share. And so, on the Christmas of 2016, I found myself at the WonderKids orphanage, performing carols and sharing in the holiday cheer with the children. That was the first of many instances of shared joy, followed by evenings at Swarg Old Age Home, performances at Disha Autism Centre, and melodies for recovering COVID patients. These make up the garland of memories adorning my life.

'To my little sister Siya – thank you for inspiring my dreams.'

Excitedly greeting me with an assortment of damaged mechanical toys, remote controls, alarm clocks, and even a Barbie dollhouse, Siya animatedly explains, *'I told my friends that my sister can fix anything, so they brought their broken things to school today.'* Determined to mend them all, I grabbed my pink toolbox and set to work in our spare room. After hours of poring over manuals, and various creative combinations guided by mere intuition, I somehow managed to get it all working. Today, that spare room serves as my personal workshop, with new tools, wires, and bits and bobs sent for restoration from anyone who knows my family, littering the floor.

'To those who tried to show me that I wasn't enough –

Thank you for teaching me to face obstacles headfirst.'

A frail girl of ten, I stand meekly as a pack of flawless, self-assured girls encircle me. My intellect the only weapon in my arsenal, now theirs to wield. Mocked for being a 'know-it-all', ridiculed for the way I spoke, and scorned for the pimples blooming on my face.

As time ran its course, my once-tormentors came to be my closest friends, their characters aging like fine wine. Six years later, with steady legs and an unshakeable voice, I delivered a speech as Head Girl. Then, the girls who once embodied my greatest fears, made up various parts of my support system.

Ding!

Another message glides into my inbox, but this one's different.

'To The Gracias Initiative –

Thank you for helping me express the emotions I didn't realize I felt.'

OUR THOUGHTS ON SAANVI'S ESSAY

This essay is unexpected and powerful. Gratitude is an ineffable thing – both ubiquitous and therefore mundane, but also transformative. Saanvi wields it with power as a defining principle of her life and a window to her world. With gratitude as a prism, we see Saanvi's quirkiness, perseverance, ability to reflect, and growth.

We especially like the mix of anecdotes she has chosen to elucidate her identity – collectively, they give the reader a glimpse of how Saanvi defines herself. Compassionate musician, fixer of broken things, big sister, self-starter, forgiver, friend and, most of all, thankful. In giving thanks to her guitar, she shows us her determination to master the instrument through bleeding fingers, through pain, and proactively share her love for music with others. Her sister, she says, inspired her dreams while getting her to mend broken toys and electronics. What these dreams are is unclear and that is fine, as there are spaces elsewhere in the application to address that. However, while reading this exceptionally wrought piece of writing we can guess at what these might be from the 'new tools, wires, and bits and bobs sent for restoration from anyone who knows my family, littering the floor'.

And then we see this engineer-in-the-making in a make-or-break situation, in a moment of difficult vulnerability – she was bullied, but was open to that great restorer, time, to heal and mend fences. However, though clarity on what facing 'obstacles headfirst' meant for Saanvi is not there, given the limitations of space, we know from her catapult into captaincy, that the hurdles in her path would have been surmounted with grace and fortitude.

In summary, this is a compelling, heartfelt essay that tells the reader what they need to know, without laboring on the anecdotes she touches upon. It is noteworthy to mention here that the common application essay is read alongside other aspects of the application including the activity list and resume.

SOURAV ROY

Yale, Class of 2025

Major: Molecular, Cellular and Developmental Biology
School: Dubai College, Dubai, UAE
Hometown: Dubai, UAE

Sitting tall before the black concert grand piano in Sofitel's gargantuan ballroom, I take a deep breath to calm myself. I am performing at the finals of the prestigious 'Young Musicians of the Gulf 2020' competition in Bahrain. I have just finished playing Jeux d'eau by Ravel, the first of my two pieces, and an ominous feeling of trepidation is enveloping my mind.

Since the age of four, the piano has been omnipresent in my life. I have played many pieces over the years but Rachmaninoff's Prelude in D flat major opus 32 no. 13 stands out. My first performance of this piece at my school's music competition was a flop. I opened with what the judges deemed an 'unengaging set of chords with little weight'. A memory lapse towards the end, covered up with atonal improvisation, underlined a shaky beginning that undermined my confidence as a musician and raised significant self-doubt.

The applause for my first piece has subsided. I can feel my nerves take over before I play Rachmaninoff. As my overactive mind escalates this sudden onset of stage fright, thoughts of my journey with this prelude flash by.

My second experience with the Rachmaninoff Prelude, after a month of practice and listening to Vladimir Ashkenazy's recordings, was a more polished performance at the Fujairah International Piano Competition. The opening bore more direction, and the ending felt grander. One of the judges, who had seen my earlier school performance, complimented me on the improvement but advised me to get the 'sound' right.

Seconds pass but the apprehension persists: have I come far enough for a flawless execution of this pièce de résistance of my performance?

Just one week earlier, a masterclass at the Dubai Opera with the great pianist Alexander Ghindin jolted my confidence as I learned that my delivery of this piece was wrong. The opening still lacked power, even though I could not hit the keys any harder. I was at a complete loss until Ghindin directed me to the fundamental feature of Rachmaninoff's life and artistic soundscape: the sound of church bells. The secret to the sound rested with the composer all this time.

My mind is calmer and I begin to play my final piece. I put more weight into the opening – as if I am ringing those heavy bells – and the sound emanating from the Yamaha 'tolls' in a steady tempo just like the church bells. I play the bass in the meno mosso section as quietly as I can. The piu vivo section ensues with cleaner voicing, building tension till tempo primo, where the crashing chords use all of my energy. I use my entire body to power through the ending, letting the sound ring to the back of the auditorium. My performance ends with a long, escalating wall of applause. Shortly, the results are announced, and I am placed in first place overall. I receive the heavy YMOG lifetime trophy, the Stella Taylor shield, and the coveted title of 'Young Musician of the Gulf 2020'.

All my life, music has defined me. It has reinforced discipline and focus. Solo and ensemble performances have further imbibed me with confidence and collaborative skills which help me in debating and Head Boy duties. However, more importantly, music has revealed to me the value of empathy. From Rachmaninoff's Prelude, I learnt of the true nature and purpose of classical music: to form a connection with the composer and ascertain their deepest motivations. In music lies a valuable link to the thought process of a completely different human being and the key to understanding those around you.

It is a surreal feeling. Surrounded by great musicians, the final moments of the evening are sinking in. My future is unknown except for one fundamental fact: I will always pursue a life filled with music.

OUR THOUGHTS ON SOURAV'S ESSAY

The clear physical tension and familiar 'deep breath' right at the start of the essay draws the reader into Sourav's state of mind – his nervousness at the end of his piano performance piece in a very important competition and his need to collect himself before he starts the next one. We soon find out that the applause after his first piano piece does little to calm him, for the real challenge he has taken on is the piece by Rachmaninoff. The tension mounts.

Short flashbacks woven between his music recital color in a parallel background story about where he started and where his journey playing the piano has taken him. These reminiscences add depth to the challenge presented by the ivory keys before him. They also help to demonstrate his determination to continually work hard at conquering the uphill battle that is 'getting the sound right' for one of the most difficult pieces of music written by Rachmaninoff, a world-famous piano virtuoso whose piano repertoire is considered overwhelming even in the 'difficult' category. This knowledge somehow brilliantly transfers to the gravity of the task ahead of Sourav, and reveals the strengths in his personality that help him navigate through it.

Powerful moments of self-reflection, vulnerability, resolve and persistence come through... and he seems to be playing his emotions on his piano, fast, slow, pensive, jubilant, humble. And thus, his personality profile is composed and assembled for the target reader – in this case the admissions commissioners. What is astonishing is that at no point does he mention academics, and yet we know exactly what kind of student and lifelong learner he would be. He concludes his musical journey with a huge victory, and yet, more important to him is the empathy he learnt, which allowed him to discover the composer's secret. He sees his musical rite of passage, especially this particularly poignant one, as a life-lesson, 'a valuable link to the thought process of a completely different human being, and the key to understanding those around you'.

SERENA MALIK

Dartmouth, Class of 2026

Major: Biology/Psychology on the pre-health track
School: Jamnabai Narsee International School, Mumbai, India
Hometown: Mumbai, India

Cenchrus Macrourus wrapped around my ankles; I was caught in the weeds, grappling with the taxonomy of my being. It felt like the only way to find the sunlight was to resort to floral mimicry: 'I have to—I should, I absolutely need to be like them.'

June 2018; my first day of high school, that bastion of adulthood. As I walked through the hallowed gate for the very first time, I felt so grown-up; far more self-assuredly than when I'd worn my mother's saree and pretended to do the taxes. This was my moment to shine: to (finally) get access to the biology lab, to join the school newspaper, to command/lead dining-hall conversations about our school garden's population of gastropods. So many fascinating things to explore.

But, wait a second, had I got it all wrong? A cold shiver crept up my spine.

My jewel-studded backpack floundered in a sea of muted designer bags, my denim-blue Converse sneakers stuck out sorely amongst strappy sandals. Had something changed over the summer? Had I been too buried in the *Diary of a Wimpy Kid* to notice? Is this what Darwin would call evolution?

Yes, yes, I had. And it was survival of the coolest, wasn't it? So, I observed, and I noted, and I Googled what 'it-girls' did with microscopic attention. And, on a few weeks, I had enough field data to cover my room in Post-Its that I could piece together, square-by-square, to make it to the Jamnabai International inner circle.

The Dionaea Muscipula drew me in; in trying to find the sun, I'd let the stimulus of my tropism alter. I was no longer searching for my light; I was over-exposed by someone else's. Is this what speciation feels like?

Did I just say, 'YAS, that party was high key-snatched?' Check. Did I apply a nauseating amount of Chanel No.5? Check. Did I achieve my goal? Also, check. It was easier than I thought to be an 'it-girl'.

However, as I began pretending to murmur lyrics to songs I didn't like, I began to realize I was living in a material world, but, I wasn't a material, a material girl. Perhaps I had dug myself out of one social grave, but I had pushed my self, my true self, into another one. Is this what adulthood had in store for me? I knew you were supposed to 'bloom', but a gnawing feeling in my gut told me that I was actually wilting.

Passiflora incarnata, that's what I really wanted to be; a vine perennially reaching to pursue my passions, vibrant in color and spirit. I knew I had to plant my own garden, with my own ideas, true to my own identity.

A dozen 'Be yourself' Buzzfeed quizzes and hours of contemplation later, I realized that the only way out of the claustrophobic labyrinth of social expectations was to, unabashedly, be myself. And once again, it was easier than I'd imagined. I exhumed my *Big Bang Theory* sweatshirt indifferent to the fact that it would catapult me into social oblivion. I replaced spending Sunday mornings aimlessly scrolling through H&M's website with choosing the right words for essays on identity and philosophy. I watched *Monsters Inside Me*, a show about fascinatingly gross intestinal parasites instead of shows about their more social incarnations. Fundamentally, I traded inauthenticity for fulfillment – social and intellectual.

Passiflora is the larval host plant for butterflies. It reminds me that transitionary states are a part of life, that they exist so you can mature before breaking out of your chrysalis with outstretched wings. When I look back on my misadventures with popularity, I'm not necessarily proud, but I am grateful. Because now, I know, that I'm most comfortable in my own skin; that being grown-up has nothing to do with fitting in, it's about carving space for yourself whenever you get caught in the weeds.

Being almost famous as somebody else showed me that I can't wait to be famous as myself: as a writer, a woman in science, a passionflower, and so many other identities I'm yet to discover.

OUR THOUGHTS ON SERENA'S ESSAY

Serena's essay opens with an impassioned declaration to 'absolutely (need to) be like them'—setting the stage for her personal journey through high school and battle between conformity and authenticity.

Beginning high school, Serena has her hopes of an academically and socially fulfilling year dashed when she realizes that her expectations are unrealistic, largely because she does not seem to belong to the crowds of effortlessly 'cool' girls overrunning the school, a situation that she immediately aims to rectify—inviting the reader to accompany her on the journey.

While Serena takes us on her quest for popularity, her much-loved scientific approach remains true: she molds herself into an admired 'it girl', but through classic methods of research, trial and error, absorbing popular jargon through late-night reading and checklists and observing her peers like samples in the lab. Broadly, her transformation is relayed through the lens of her scientific experiments—moving from the lab to the 'Jamnabai inner circle', thereby relinquishing 'inauthenticity for fulfillment – social and intellectual'.

Her movement from the larger, universal setting of the natural world to a specific, striated section of society introduces the reader to how she views the world, and then focuses that lens on the hypothetical Petri dish of her high school.

Her constant return to scientific language—viewing herself as perhaps another data point, another sample in her biological musings—anchors the essay and reminds the reader of her true passions, even as she flounders in the shifting social tides of her high school, trying to find joy in her newly realized popularity.

As Serena journeys through seeming unpopularity, a quest for approval, and the inevitable realization that abandoning one's true self at the altar of social acceptance is eventually unfulfilling, she tells her story with charming self-deprecation and humour, as she continues to monitor herself much like one of her biological samples. The movement between scientific jargon and her personal angst, flipping between clinical detachment and immediacy creates interest and depth, as she creates a new version of herself and then steps back to observe how successful she's been. We are invited to accompany her on this scientific experiment, empathizing with her, but also viewing this shift from both within and without.

The juxtaposition between Latin taxonomy and popular material culture of BuzzFeed quizzes to excavate her true self—as she walks through the hallowed halls of social laudation and wafting clouds of Chanel No. 5—creates a complex, interesting tableau. So, while she opens the essay caught in the weeds—her self-assessment of her social positioning, she concludes with a declared desire to be a 'Passiflora incarnata'—recognizing that the journey to authenticity or commitment to one's true self is not a race with a finish line, but a work in progress—constant, and evolving—striving to climb higher and higher to revel in the sunshine.

TRISHLA GUPTA

Columbia, Class of 2025

Major: Industrial Engineering and Operations
Research: Engineering Management Systems
School: The Shri Ram School, Moulsari, India
Hometown: New Delhi, India

I could feel the prickly goosebumps pop all over my skin. These were, I knew, precipitated by the smell of the refrigerated anesthesia, the chilled air-conditioning and the fear of the impending treatment.

I was here because of the blue-black blemishes spread across my arms, neck and back. I had insisted that my parents take me to a dermatologist. I didn't want to be an outlier anymore.

'What happened to your neck?'

My friends huddled around me, pointing fingers. I felt like an installation on display, only no one seemed to appreciate what they saw. Teary-eyed, I trudged to the nearest shower stall, shuffling into my uniform and fixing a towel around my neck. At home, I applied layers of sunscreen, desperate to block out the sun. I even started 'forgetting' my swimsuit at home.

I was tired of the scrutiny by my peers every time I emerged from the pool after swimming.

Thus began my weekly hangouts at Dr Kiran's clinic. 'Will the laser make any visible changes?' I questioned every week, prompting her to specify the intensity of the laser and how deeply it would penetrate my skin. Sensing my agitation, she patiently explained how the patches resulted from my amniotic sac being temporarily detached from my mother's placenta. She said this made me unique. For me, however, the uneven pigmentation on my skin represented my fear of being different, of being left out.

It was then that my mother handed me an illustrated account of *Lord Krishna*, the blue-skinned Indian God beloved by so many.

I was riveted by how Krishna's dark blue skin tone was a mystical representation of cosmic grace and heroic bravery. The color symbolized all-inclusiveness; a powerful metaphor for the vast expanse of the ocean and ideas stretching beyond human perception.

Increasingly fascinated by this mythological God, I was drawn to reading verses from his discourse. Krishna had discussions for everything through his seven-hundred verse ancient Hindu scripture, *The Bhagavad Gita.*

After the fifteenth sitting, the treatment made little difference. It was supposed to be okay someday, but nobody knew when. Sensing my disappointment, my mother tried to comfort me. She pointed me to an underlined Sanskrit quote in the book.

uddhared ātmanātmānaā nātmānam avasādayet
ātmaiva hyātmano bandhur ātmaiva ripur ātmanaā

'Elevate yourself through the power of your mind, and do not degrade yourself, for the mind can be the friend and also the enemy of the self.'
(Chapter 6, Verse 5)

Krishna is portrayed in Hindu mythology as blue-skinned, yet He never perceived this as an obstacle on His path. Just as I had been conditioned to be fearful, I had to train myself to be free.

I had been viewing myself through the perspectives of others, not realizing that true beauty emanates from within. I once again visualized myself in the pool, fluttering my limbs like a butterfly's wings. It was time for me to break out of my cocoon, uplift myself, and soar over the seas, or rather in them.

I ceased treatment and took to swimming once again. 15, 30, 45, and finally 60 minutes. I built my confidence, step by step. Three months later, I returned to the pool at school. This time without a towel wrapped around my neck. When someone taunted me about the blemishes, I did not flinch. I stood my ground and told them that it was something that happened during my birth. I had learned from Krishna to be strong. I discovered that if I did not focus on my blemishes, neither did my friends.

I went on to become a PADI-certified diver. The now tattered book accompanies me on each of my SCUBA diving adventures – from the Maldives to Oman to the Andamans. Krishna's legend and the swirling shoals of fish remind me to embrace my imperfections and appreciate the beauty of diversity around me.

OUR THOUGHTS ON TRISHLA'S ESSAY

Trishla immediately hooks us with her descriptive narration of the doctor's clinic that hints at the dread within. We can feel her fear, even before she subtly expresses her teenage angst occasioned by an extended blue-black birthmark, which she views as a blemish, that she believes makes her an outlier.

It particularly resonates, as, given the unrealistic conceptions of 'perfection' as dictated by social media, few are entirely secure about their body images. Trishla talks frankly about her travails and peer ridicule; what particularly impresses is that at no time is she maudlin or self-pitying, but rather, matter-of-fact, almost dispassionate. In applying sunscreen to 'block out the sun', we read that she is 'blocking out' unwanted glares and scrutiny. This sets the trajectory for the rest of the essay, where, rather than dwelling on the birthmark, she focuses on her efforts to draw inspiration from it. In this she is helped, as one often is, by a family member, in her case her mother.

Yet, even as she seeks resolve in a doctor's clinic, we sense her resentment at being arbitrarily judged as she questions the treatment, and know viscerally that rebellion is nigh. The doctor finding her 'unique' due to the exceptional medical circumstances of her birth is the start of Trishla's growing awareness to use her situation, blemishes et al., and evolve from it.

So, several treatments in, as she faces her existential dilemma, she finds resolve in the millennia-old epic *The Bhagavad Gita*, wherein Lord Krishna, the blue-hued God (he is famously unhindered by his novel blue coloration) informs that 'the mind can be the friend and also the enemy of the self'. His wisdom is revelatory and cathartic – her blemish is what she chooses it to be – so, she consciously decides that it distinguishes her from the stereotypical, as it did Lord Krishna. The liberation is slow: she ceases the treatment, returns to swim training, travels the world as a scuba diver and wears her mark with pride, sans neck-hugging towel or scarf, comforted in the strength of her knowledge that she is so much more than the blemish. She has set the stage, and we know, that there is more to come, more oceans that she will courageously traverse.

VAISHNAV GARODIA

Stanford, Class of 2026

Major: Undecided
School: Delhi Public School, Ranchi, India
Hometown: Ranchi, India

'What? You're from Pakistan!' the surprised faces on the train exclaimed. Their excitement was justified: for Indians to see Pakistanis is as rare as spotting UFOs. But all the amusement quickly faded when I explained that they had misheard, and I am from 'Ranchi', a small town in India, not 'Karachi', the largest city in Pakistan.

We have electricity (ignoring the gazillion power cuts), we have four lanes (ignoring the moon-like craters), we have even had working wi-fi for the last couple of years. What bothers me (other than the absence of McDonald's) is the apparent non-existence of my city. Even my school is ridiculously named Delhi Public School, even though Delhi is light-years away, and decades ahead.

In ninth grade, my school hosted a Model United Nations conference. Almost everyone was new to it, and I enjoyed the concept of imitating diplomats. After just one more event weeks later, the city's MUN circuit went completely silent. I kept preparing and waited eagerly for more events but to no avail. Maybe it was time to break up with my city:

Dear Ranchi,

All these years, we have enjoyed exciting times together, but sadly, things have changed. I think now it's time for me to move on. I hate saying this but it's not me, it's you. Once, we were perfect for each other, but I have evolved while you have not. I need to go somewhere else, to a bigger school in a bigger city with greater opportunities so that I can continue growing.

Love,
Vaishnav

After grinding away through grade ten, I succeeded in gaining admission to Delhi Public School RK Puram as a boarding student—a real 'Delhi' Public School this time, located in the heart of New Delhi. Unfortunately, this was the exact time that the pandemic struck, making it extremely risky to enroll at a boarding school. But I took a chance, and luckily, a wonderful year followed: meeting people from different places, participating in a myriad of clubs and competitions, and being exposed to many new ideas.

Next year, in an unexpected turn of events, the deadly second wave of the pandemic hit India. I did not want to spend my senior year living with the persistent uncertainty of being enrolled in a boarding school during lockdown. Suddenly, returning to Ranchi seemed the best option. But would my school take me back? How would the students and teachers react? Would I still fit in? Would I survive without McDonald's?

Fortunately, my honest break-up letter made things much easier. DPS Ranchi understandingly took me back. The perks of being in a school with 6,000 students? Some didn't care I was back, some didn't even notice I had gone, and the rest were welcoming. I fitted back in perfectly.

Then came my Eureka moment—the realization that Delhi has many competitions and events, partly because they are student-run. I was eager to introduce this culture to Ranchi. I was aware of similar big-city culture adaptation attempts failing before, like Starbucks: Ranchi locals are too smart to pay 5 bucks for a miniature paper cup with incorrect spelling. Was the city ready for the change I wished to bring?

I decided to implement a long-time idea I had: an inter-school quizzing tournament, with league stage quizzes, leaderboard rankings, and a grand finale. My only new condition: everything must be student-led. Starting alone, my team of first-timers grew in size and experience with time, and we organized trailblazing events. All participating schools appreciated that students were taking the lead.

Ranchi is absorbing the new culture; the prize I sought is won. The Karachi misnomer doesn't bother me anymore. As for McDonald's, I guess we'll just wait for UberEats to start airplane deliveries.

OUR THOUGHTS ON VAISHNAV'S ESSAY

Opening with a whimsical anecdote, about a casually mistaken geographic location, creates a lightly amusing 'hook' for the reader, which always makes a refreshing start amongst the hundreds of typically fairly serious common application essays. It also suggests the essay's underlying theme 'the apparent non-existence' of Ranchi, Vaishnav's home city. Reading a bit further, we understand the reason for this dark sarcasm. 'Even my school is ridiculously named Delhi Public School, even though Delhi is light-years away, and decades ahead.'

Then, before the reader can mull sadly over the only highlight event of Vaishnav's secondary school life, 'the city's MUN circuit', going 'completely silent', he delivers another volley of unique humor – a hilarious 'Dear John' '*...it's not me, it's you*' letter to Ranchi, having decided 'Maybe it was time to break up with my city'. This is such a clever means of conveying that he had outgrown his little, limiting city. We discern how he feels the need for a more progressive environment with '*greater opportunities*'.

The use of humor invariably alludes to an author's sense of self-confidence, and an ability to see the lighter side of what might have come across as complaining. Instead, it becomes a matter of evolving beyond available prospects, or the lack thereof – '(other than the absence of McDonald's)'.

Vaishnav next goes on to talk about the 'grind' through tenth grade which enables him to successfully join 'a real "Delhi" Public School this time, located in the heart of New Delhi'. His risky decision to continue boarding there despite the pandemic paid off, giving him room and occasion to grow. While appreciative of what he has gained, he considers returning to Ranchi during the pandemic's deadly second wave, which brought uncertainty and fear. Here is a clear-thinking, decisive young man, who introspects, reflects and makes well-considered choices for himself. He is not afraid to let his vulnerability show, lightly garnishing his humility with humor yet again – 'Would I survive without McDonald's?'

Grateful for being 'taken back', and finding that he 'fitted back in perfectly', he has his really insightful 'Eureka moment'. Realising that 'Delhi has many competitions and events, partly because they are student-run', Vaishnav decides to take positive action to create the progressive environment he longs for, through leadership prospects on the march forward, not just for himself, but for all students in his city's schools.

Despite his initial doubts, his openness and wit persist. It becomes clear that behind the wry smile readers can now visualise, lies an active, forward-thinking, constructive and creative personality. His ability to adapt and independently implement in his little-known city what he learnt from his sojourn in India's big capital speaks volumes about Vaishnav's progression as a leader and as an active contributor to his home community's development.

This essay's easy narrative and appealing humor – down to the last hopeful line of UberEats starting airplane deliveries – succeed in presenting Vaishnav's positive personality traits, including his strengths, skills and achievements.

SO, WHAT NEXT?

We like to tell students there are no conclusions, only new beginnings.

You have now traced many journeys of reflection. Perhaps taken delight in the big and small ideas the students have explored – external and internal. And you may have realized that every idea is authentic and significant!

Even though we have clubbed the essays in thematic sections, they are diametrically different. Inarguably, there could be many more sections and themes and narratives, not yet written… as many as the millions of students who apply for admissions each year to their dream colleges.

Yet, each of these essays show dramatic growth and transformation… and realizations, even epiphanies, which have fueled further growth. In the telling of their journeys, students have taken ownership – of their lives, their failures, and their victories. Every essay gives readers a sense that the best is yet to come!

Remember, you are the first specialist of your life – and there is a bounty within that you can dig into without any formal research. So,

Be prepared to be inventive, brave, reflective, and above all, authentic.

Be prepared to enthral, intrigue and interest your reader from, and then past, the very first sentence!

Be prepared to show them, not just tell them about, anecdotes from all your life experiences.

So be brave! Pull out all the stops. Deeply excavate your rich life, and write about your experience-filled journey so far… foretelling your very best. Get ready to pen your own admissions adventure!

ACKNOWLEDGEMENTS

We have seen over the years, that in writing books, the process, in its many dimensions and facets, equally pervades not just our lives, but those of our families, immediate and extended. They, willingly or not, live through the journey with us. We gratefully acknowledge the invaluable contributions of these stoic beings:

Sucheta, Viral's wife, for being a patient traveling companion, a willing and supportive sounding board, and a ready listener to the analyses as they evolved. His son, Sudeep, and daughter-in-law, Gitanjali, for their invaluable inputs. Viral's brother, Mihir, and sister-in-law, Amishi, for the stream of suggestions and ideas.

Mridula's husband, Nandan, her daughter, Avanti, and son-in-law, Sachit, whose love, suggestions and support buoyed us. Sunil and Neena, for their encouragement and levity through the journey. Avanti and Tehnaz, who continued to assist us with the analyses of this new addition, giving us trenchant insights, shaping the book in novel, unanticipated and remarkable ways. And to our editorial team, Pradeep, Arti and Anna, whose unflagging enthusiasm, no matter the hour, never fails to astound us. Anna, Tehnaz and Nikita, additionally, are shaping the book's incandescent presence on social media, for which we thank them.

Shannon, from Viral's office, who was integral to this journey; her Teutonic precision, record-keeping and cataloguing skills are the stuff of legends. And thank you, Joanna, Salma and Syanne, for supporting her so adeptly in sourcing student details, documentation, and updates.

AND, of course we thank our literary agents, Jayapriya and Smita, for their initial reach-out to initiate the project. They placed their faith in us, and guided us through the process. And then, challenged us with the idea, of another, expanded, revised edition.

Special gratitude to Rashmi Menon, our managing editor, and senior editor Bidisha Srivastava, for being our indefatigable cheerleaders at Amaryllis! Nor can we forget the scintillating contributions of the core team: Vikas Rakheja, Manoj Kulkarni, Sunil Vohra, Ankita Menghwani, Ritu Rajdev, and Kriti Chauhan Srivastava for ensuring the books reach in every corner of the world. And, of course, the contribution of Bhavi Mehta, our cover designer, for rising to the challenge of a captivating new design, in entrancing colours, which responded to our appeal for a cover that is 'the same, though different'.

And, if you spend time admiring the illustrations contained in the pages, you have designer Wasim Helal to thank, as do we!

Lastly, and unmissably, we thank our now 101 students – the protagonists and true authors of this book! This would not have been possible without them.

ABOUT VIRAL DOSHI AND MRIDULA MALUSTE

Viral Doshi has been helping young people around the world discover and fulfil their passions for almost four decades. As the founder of Viral Doshi Associates, he provides a holistic set of services to his clients, ranging from psychometric testing and mentoring to career and college planning. His work has taken him around the world, shuttling between his Mumbai and New York offices while frequently visiting Singapore, Dubai, and London. His mostly high-school aged students are from countries as far afield as Peru, Nigeria, Switzerland, Sri Lanka, Lebanon, and Japan.

'Advise as a parent, and not as a counselor' is the pervasive and longstanding mantra that Viral has used to guide hundreds of students (and their families) and to help them gain admission into their dream colleges, including the eight Ivy League universities and other flagship institutions such as MIT, Caltech, Stanford, Oxford, and Cambridge.

Viral writes prolifically on careers and education for magazines, newspapers, and online portals, serves as an advisor and board member of several educational institutes in India and overseas, and is a frequent speaker and workshop facilitator at schools, colleges, and leadership associations across India. In his (limited) spare time, you will see him spending time with his family (especially his two grandchildren) or catching a late-night movie at INOX in Mumbai, where he will inevitably run into several students that he knows and several others who he is about to know!

Viral did his schooling from The Cathedral & John Connon School, his A levels in the UK, and graduated in engineering from Cornell. His quest is ultimately about helping his students discover the joy of pursuing something that they are truly suited for and excited about, regardless of external expectations or pressures. And that is the story of his own life—he converted a calling into a hobby and eventually into a profession. And that's what he wants to pass on.

Mridula Maluste runs a writing and editorial consultancy. She has conducted critical reading, thinking and writing workshops for executives as well as undergraduates, advised university application essays for well over a decade, and is also an author, specializing in boutique editorial projects. She co-authored *Dhurrie* with Meera and Shyam Ahuja, on the dhurrie weavers of UP and Rajasthan. Along with Viral Doshi, Mridula co-authored *An Undefiled Heritage,* a book that chronicles the centuries-old history of their alma mater, The Cathedral & John Connon School. The book is on the 'must-have' list of Cathedral alumni worldwide.

Mridula's experiences at a unique Harvard publishing program and while visiting the world's top universities that her family and friends attended, provide her with rare insight and access. Along with her early career as a journalist, this helped her further develop a keen understanding of the language and vocabulary of the admissions process.

Her passion for serving students, draws from Mridula's own background as a lifelong learner from her days studying Economics at Mumbai University, conceiving book series and editing books, transiting to magazine and newspaper journalism, and later to scripting TV shows and corporate documentaries. The breadth of this journey gives her the exceptional ability to connect with and elicit self-discovery from the most diverse students. Her instincts are student-centered and creative, while keeping a keen eye on university expectations. Mridula is attuned to helping students excavate their most unique and authentic experiences, advising them in framing these into compelling stories, thereby connecting aspiring candidates and the exacting standards of their dream colleges. Her process is highly customized to suit each individual's special needs.

When not sitting at a laptop screen, discussing essays with students and talking them through their anxiety and writer's blocks, Mridula spends time with husband Nandan, her daughter Avanti, son-in-law, Sachit, and their two rescues – Prince and Laddoo, a street cat and an Indie canine. She loves to travel, jumping through lives and history through her favorite historical fiction, and explore the world (especially its museums and cafes).

Her favorite places include Greece, where the interplay between mortals and gods is alive in the people, architecture, and ever-present stories; and the farm near Mumbai that she and Nandan have rewilded – in the hope of drawing birds, butterflies, dragonflies and fireflies. They have not been disappointed.

To know more about Mridula, visit www.mridulamaluste.com

INDEX